Recent
Archaeology
in the
Land of
Israel

RECENT ARCHAEOLOGY IN THE LAND OF ISRAEL

Edited by
Hershel Shanks
English Edition
and
Benjamin Mazar
Hebrew Edition

Translated by
Aryeh Finklestein

Biblical Archaeology Society
Washington, D.C.
Israel Exploration Society
Jerusalem

Second Printing, 1985

Dedicated to

Joseph Aviram

*for his extraordinary
contributions
to Israeli archaeology*

Joseph Aviram

Contents

I Excavations and Discoveries

II "Break Forth Together Into Singing, You Waste Places of Jerusalem"

III Israel Through the Ages

To Joseph Aviram

This book is dedicated to Joseph Aviram in recognition of his 40 years of devoted service to the Israel Exploration Society. From his initial position as Secretary of the Society, until his appointment as Director of the Institute of Archaeology of the Hebrew University, Joseph Aviram has given indefatigable dedication, extraordinary initiative, and great organizational skill to almost every aspect of Israel's archaeological endeavor. Throughout this period, his colleagues have also been privileged to call him their friend.

Since his first involvement in the Society's activities and his participation in the Beth She'arim excavations in the 1930s, Joseph Aviram has been one of that small group that has shaped the Society and given it direction, so that today it leads the way in archaeological research of the Land of Israel. The many archaeological expeditions sponsored by the Society (most of which are conducted jointly with Hebrew University's Institute of Archaeology, and sometimes in cooperation with the Department of Antiquities and Museums and other institutions), as well as the annual conferences held under its auspices, have contributed greatly to the popular dissemination of the latest data that have been uncovered. Joseph Aviram played a special role in much of this activity—especially in major archaeological expeditions in the Judean Desert and on the western shores of the Dead Sea, and at Masada, and at Ein-Gedi, and, since 1968, in Jerusalem.

His contribution has been crucial in the preparation for publication of many seminal scientific works on the archaeology of Israel, in both Hebrew and English. Many of these the Society published in cooperation with the Institute of Archaeology, the Bialik Foundation, and the "Masada" and "Carta" publishing companies as well as other institutions.

Joseph Aviram has also been responsible for the appearance of many well-known journals and monographs that have been universally praised for their consistently high quality, not only as to content but also as to editing and style.

As is well-known, Joseph Aviram has often been the sole instigator and driving force behind a number of the Society's publications, which he saw through the various phases of the publication process.

On the occasion of his 50th birthday, in 1967, the 31st volume of the *Israel Exploration Journal* was dedicated to him. Since the publication of that volume, containing articles by many of his colleagues and friends, the activities of the Society have happily continued to diversify and expand. Joseph Aviram has been the acknowledged guiding light in all these new endeavors. His critical role in assisting both older and younger scholars to realize important archaeological goals (some of which are very ambitious indeed!) has become increasingly evident in recent years. Indeed, his helping hand is ubiquitous in the world of Israeli archaeology.

It is thus with great gratitude and high esteem that the entire scholarly community engaged in researching Israel's ancient past dedicates this book to Joseph Aviram in recognition of his many praiseworthy efforts and achievements. The contributors to this volume wish thereby to express their appreciation to and love for a colleague who has labored so hard in their behalf during the last 40 years. We wish him continued success in his important undertakings.

Benjamin Mazar

Jerusalem

English Editor's Foreword

It is a welcome privilege for the **Biblical Archaeology Society** to join hands with the **Israel Exploration Society** in bringing out the English edition of this important book. It is a great personal pleasure to participate in its dedication to that multi-talented colossus of Israeli archaeology, Joseph Aviram.

The Hebrew edition of this book, first published in 1981, consisted of papers delivered at the 35th Archaeological Convention of the Israel Exploration Society in 1978. That year, 1978, coincided with the 30th anniversary of the founding of the state of Israel in 1948. Hence, the original title of the Hebrew edition, *Thirty Years of Archaeology in Eretz-Israel, 1948-1978.*

It soon became apparent that the book's immediate popularity was attributable not simply to the fact that it was dedicated to Joseph Aviram but also to the fact that it contained archaeological surveys and a scholarly overview that could be found nowhere else. At that point the Israel Exploration Society approached us to publish the English edition. We welcomed the opportunity and readily agreed.

It was originally our intention to bring out the English edition in six months. After all, how much could be involved in changing Hebrew words to English words? We now know differently. After three years of labor, we understand the difficulties of producing a readable, clear English text that also satisfies the scholarly commitment to precision and detail of 19 different scholars.

On the other hand, the delay enabled a number of contributors to update their texts so that they include even more recent materials. Some of those who chose for one reason or another not to update their work have requested that we note the date "1978" at the end of their chapters to indicate that later materials have not been included. We have of course acceded to those requests.

We are especially pleased and proud to include in the English edition two important contributions that were not in the Hebrew edition. The first is by Lee Levine, whose chapter on "Archaeological Discoveries From the Greco-Roman Era" fills a lacuna in the Hebrew edition. The second is a seminal paper by Yigael Yadin on the Lachish Letters that is sure to shake up our thinking about these sixth-century B.C.E. Hebrew documents and is likely to change drastically the way we understand them. This chapter replaces Yadin's contribution to the Hebrew edition, which was a considerably more technical paper on the Temple Scroll that will be published elsewhere in English. It is a special tribute to Joseph Aviram that Yadin chose to publish his new views on the Lachish letters in this volume.

The papers collected here provide an overview of archaeology in Israel that is unavailable elsewhere. Moreover, the impact of the whole is greater than the sum of its parts. Again and again, the reader will be amazed at how much is going on with respect to a particular area of scholarship. When the entire range of archaeological scholarship is confronted, the mind boggles. I know of no other single volume in which this broad range of archaeological scholarship, both artifactual and historical, is presented.

To the accolades of his Israeli colleagues, I should like to add a personal, American tribute to the man to whom this volume is dedicated. I have sat in Joseph Aviram's office and watched one major archaeologist after another traipse in despairingly, only to see Aviram deal with the problem of each calmly, diplomatically and imaginatively. He knows just what buttons to press. He always seems to solve the problem. Although he sits in the hotseat, I doubt that any member of the Israeli archaeological community is better liked and respected.

On November 1, 1983, Joseph Aviram retired as director of Hebrew University's Institute of Archaeology. He continues, however, to direct the activities of the Israel Exploration Society as its Executive Secretary. We wish him many more years of fruitful service.

I should like to acknowledge the contribution to this volume of Wendy Miller, Assistant to the Editor of the *Biblical Archaeology Review*. Her careful, detailed text editing is evident throughout, as well as her faithful attention to the countless production details. The overall supervision of the project was the responsibility of *BAR*'s accomplished Associate Editor, Suzanne F. Singer.

Hershel Shanks
Biblical Archaeology Society

Washington, D. C.
December 1983

I

Excavations
and
Discoveries

Research on Stone Age Archaeology in Israel Since 1948

By Ofer Bar-Yosef

T he last 35 years have seen enormous progress in research on the Stone Age in Israel and at various sites around the world. New methods of research have been developed. There have also been changes in approaches to problems considered enigmatic not too long ago. Radioactive methods, including "radiometric dating," as it is usually called, have made it possible to date human and animal remains and also to interpret socio-economic processes. These methods have even extended the timeframe in which the scholarly debate has been carried on. Moreover, the combination of potassium-argon dating with paleomagnetic readings has enabled scholars to fix the time period of the tool-making man who once inhabited East Africa approximately 1.8 million years ago.

Thanks to these paleomagnetic and radiometric dating techniques, along with the examination of deep sea cores, we are now able to discern more clearly the climatic changes of the past two million years. Indeed the discovery of the relationship between meteorological events and the glacial loess stratifications in Czechoslovakia and Austria was solely the result of paleomagnetic dating. Consequently, we no longer refer only to four Ice Ages during this time period but rather to a series of periodic glacial formations and retreats. Just 25 years ago, our knowledge of such matters was limited and quite general. Today, however, we possess much more detailed and precise information, which is of considerable importance in understanding how climatic conditions influenced ancient hunting and food-gathering cultures. The Last Ice Age, which was generally contemporaneous with the Last Pluvial period in our own region of the world, has been subject to especially minute scholarly scrutiny.

Carbon 14 tests enable us to date sites 40,000-45,000 years old, but they are ineffective for more ancient sites. Ironically, these more ancient sites are often too

3

young to be dated by the potassium-argon method, while the techniques that employ Uranium 234/Thorium 230 can be applied only to the dating of seashells and travertines (spring deposits) that are about 300,000 years old. However, sedimentological studies of cave accumulations, as well as geomorphological observations on ancient seashores in Israel and Lebanon, have helped to build a chronological sequence for the early part of the Last Ice Age.

A significant development in the methods of gathering basic excavation and survey data occurred simultaneously with the development of radioactive dating techniques. These new methods were inspired by the work of American archaeologists and became known as "The New Archaeology." Archaeologists had long attempted to establish their research on a sound methodological foundation, itself dependent upon general scientific principles as applied in the behavioral sciences. These attempts and the need for more precise data led to a more careful system of excavation. One example of this new system is marking the exact position of many artifacts. Another example is the opening of broader areas of excavation. This enabled us to determine the spatial distribution of the finds and to locate the smallest remnants of prehistoric dwellings. For another example, we no longer assign great importance to the random collection of varied flint stone items on this or that hill, for as soon as the succession of cultures has been accurately determined, these individual items no longer have any real significance. The need to calibrate the means used to interpret archaeological data has led to greater cooperation among archaeologists and anthropologists studying primitive societies and primates.

Methodical gathering of archaeological information about prehistoric societies includes determining their respective economic bases. We no longer ascribe significance to a list of animals hunted, unless it is accompanied by quantitative data. Now we attempt to determine the age of these hunted animals or the presence of certain species of birds, information that would help determine when the hunting season occurred. The new discipline of paleo-botany enables examination of food residues to determine the forms of plant life inhabitants once grew or gathered. Finally, the objective of recovering plant remains led to the introduction of various methods of sediment flotation.

To be sure, not all of these innovations in the scientific study of prehistory have been used in the Land of Israel. However, there is probably no country employing all of these new methods and techniques. Moreover the site's salutary preservation state is a prerequisite for the use of many of these methods. Ideally, a site would produce, *inter alia*, plant and seed residues, animal bones, artifacts *in situ*, and structural remains. Although there are few such ideal sites, excavations in Israel have made substantial contributions to research on ancient Near Eastern prehistoric periods.

I. The Lower Paleolithic Age

Radiometric dating proves that Lower Paleolithic Age is by far the longest period in prehistory. Radiometric dating has also emphasized the achievements as well as the failures of geological research. This research is the basis of our discussion of the Quaternary period, for it provides the geochronological framework for calibrating prehistoric cultures and sites.

Since 1948, explorations on Israel's coastal plain and in the Jordan Valley have increased dramatically. The sequence of geomorphological events is now more clearly distinguished, although the exact dates of several of these events are still disputed. Moreover, a dearth of basalt eruptions and volcanic tuffs has precluded extensive use of potassium-argon dating, as practiced, for example, in East Africa. Also, few paleomagnetic examinations have been conducted. Skepticism is there-

Excavation of inclining strata at Ubaidiya. These ancient deposits of a lake are stratified one on top of the other.

fore prudent when regarding the attempts to establish long-term chronologies with Europe and Africa.

The crowning achievement of the research on this period is the excavation at Ubaidiya, west of the Jordan River and about four kilometers south of Lake Kinneret. The late Professor Moshe Stekelis began this dig in 1960. More than 12 archaeological strata were discovered there containing many man-made artifacts. These included chopping tools, polyhedrons, spheroids, handaxes and flake tools. We may ascribe this assemblage to the Early Acheulean cultural tradition which began in East Africa some 1.5 million years ago. In addition to various artifacts made of flint, basalt and limestone, the excavators uncovered many broken pieces of bone, including those of several types of deer and horses, a hippopotamus, an elephant, a bear, and a wild ox. The few human remains consisted merely of two teeth and three small skull fragments. The importance of the site lies in its size—hundreds of square meters have already been excavated—and in the richness of its finds. When the final report is published, it will provide important comparative material for further research on the Levant and on ties between the Levant and the Euro-Asian and African continents. The crucial question, the site's age, has as yet not been definitively resolved. However, the local fauna, initial paleomagnetic examinations, and comparisons with the geological section already dated at Gesher B'not-Ya'acov, have encouraged various hypotheses. Thus, almost 25 years after the excavations were begun, we may now cautiously assert that the site is between 0.7 and 1.1 million years old.

Recently excavated sites that are identified with this lengthy span of human prehistory include Evron quarry, Tell El-Hesi, Holon and sites near Kfar Menahem. The various Acheulean cultures can be divided as follows: Ubaidiya, Evron, and probably the site near Kfar Menahem belong to the Early Acheulean culture;

the rest may be assigned to the Late Acheulean culture. The many sites dating to the Late Acheulean culture can be identified chiefly by concentration of handaxes spread over the areas' surfaces. Indeed, amateurs and professionals alike have gathered many of these handaxes. The site near Ma'ayan Barukh, boasting a rich bounty of well-worked handaxes is possibly the most important of these sites. Unfortunately, research on this phase of prehistoric society has not progressed to any great extent. This is because too few assemblages have been discovered *in situ*; also, systematic excavations at sites attributable to this period have been scanty.

Nevertheless, we do have some fresh insights into the transitional phase between the Late Acheulean culture and the Mousterian cultures. This is typical of the present scholarly inclination to solve problems raised by older excavations; indeed this is what usually motivates a return to a previous excavated site. The aim is to clarify this cultural sequence through analysis of the remnants left by earlier excavators.

Excavations of prehistoric sites in the Land of Israel began in 1925-26 with the exploration of the Zuttiyah Cave, located in the Amud Valley. The cave became famous when it yielded a fragmented human skull, later dubbed the "Galilee Man" and classified within the Neanderthal grouping. However the site was reexcavated in 1973, and the skull was reexamined. Stratigraphy clearly placed the skull earlier than the Mousterian culture, in the Acheulo-Jabrudian sequence. The skull is thus 120,000 years old and comes from the Last Interglacial period. Its morphological characteristics attest that it belongs to the later evolutionary phase of Homo Erectus. This skull is therefore the most ancient well-preserved human remnant found in the Land of Israel.

This cultural phase, in which we find both Acheulean and Jabrudian characteristics (epitomized, respectively, by handaxes and thick side-scrapers), is being explored anew in the ongoing excavations at the Tabun Cave. Dorothy Garrod excavated Tabun first in the 1930s. The new excavations have uncovered the longest stratigraphical sequence yet found in the Land of Israel, from the Late Acheulean Cultures to the later phases of the Mousterian. The goal of these new excavations initiated by A. Jelinek is to clarify the intricate stratigraphy in the cave, to reconstruct the chronological succession of climatic occurrences through paleontological and sedimentological studies and to ascertain the sequence of the cave's lithic assemblages. Since the site presents a stratified sequence ranging from the Lower to the Middle Paleolithic Ages, research is also directed to the problems posed by the Middle Paleolithic Age.

II. The Middle Paleolithic Age

The Paleolithic Age was first subdivided at the beginning of the 20th century. However, those precise temporal boundaries have little credibility today. My discussion here will include all those cultures whose provenance is the Last Interglacial period and the first half of the last Glacial (or Pluvial) Age. Dates determined by the examination of deep sea cores and by Carbon 14 tests attest that the Middle Paleolithic Age occurred between 42,000 and 120,000 years ago.

Several stratified sites have revealed remnants from the first phase of this period. Among these sites are the Tabun Cave, the Zuttiyah Cave, the Jabrud rockshelter in Syria, and the Lebanese Bezez Cave. These yielded assemblages of the Acheulo-Jabrudian, Amudian and Jabrudian cultures. The very paucity of the finds, however, mainly from old excavations, has rendered interpretation more difficult. Also, the finds were confined to a limited geographical area and apparently had been missing in the arid regions. The remains seem to be the material remnants of hunter societies from the Interglacial Age, in the Mediterranean climatic zone of the Levant and its environs. These hunter societies may have been coeval with those of the Early Mousterian or Later Acheulean cultures.

The stratigraphical sequences at the above four sites and those at Jaraf Ajalah near Tadmor and the Abu-Zif Cave in the Judean Desert indicate that the Mousterian culture made its appearance after the complex described above. Thus, we can deduce that the first Mousterian peoples inhabited our region between 75,000 and 110,000 years ago. A more precise determination is contingent upon calculating the age of the Lebanese shorelines and upon radiometric dating.

Our knowledge of the cultural sequence now referred to as "Mousterian" (previously called "Levalloiso-Mousterian" was formerly based totally on the Tabun Cave. Over the last 35 years, however, several other sites have been excavated: the Qafzah, Kebarah, Sefunim, Geula and Hayonim Caves, as well as several open-air sites—located mainly in the Negev—such as Rosh Ein Mor, Site D35 near Ein Akev, Farah B (in Nahal Besor) and Tirat Carmel (at Mt. Carmel). Two important conclusions were reached as a result of the new excavations at the Tabun and

Contracted burial of woman from the Natufian stratum at Hayonim Cave. The skeleton had been placed in a pit walled by stone slabs.

those at the Qafzah Cave near Nazareth: (1) A certain development, taking the form of technological innovation, is noticeable within the Mousterian sequence; this is especially obvious in the refinement of the Levallois flakes. (2) We should not assign all of the human remains discovered in the Mousterian strata of the Land of Israel to the Neanderthal grouping. Those hominids were palpably more advanced than their West European contemporaries. Indeed, the morphological characteristics of more than one of these "Homo sapiens" are indistinguishable from those of the human skulls discovered at Upper Paleolithic sites. The complete human skulls in the Qafzah Cave were discovered at the bottom of the layers ascribed, with some qualificaton, to the early phase of Israel's Mousterian sequence. A plausible estimate is that they are between 60,000 and 80,000 years old.

Although the exploration of Mousterian sites in the Land of Israel is not yet finished, finds to date indicate the existence of sites replete with large residential areas. This fact suggests that these sites may have been inhabited by small communities or by extended families. Orderly burial rites—exemplified by a child's grave at Qafzah covered by fallow-deer horns—suggest a tradition already old.

Unfortunately, because Mousterian cultures are outside the effective range of Carbon 14 dating, detailed research on them is difficult. On more than one occasion, the stratigraphical sequences in the caves had been disturbed by renewed Karstic activity, involving dripping and flowing water, and the collapse of fills into floor sink-holes. As a result, many layers have been either swept away or disturbed, and finds mixed together. We have even seen the formation of breccia—hardened layers that petrified after combining with calcium carbonate.

III. The Upper Paleolithic Age

In 1934, René Neuville, the French Consul in Jerusalem during the 1930s, and a colleague of Dorothy Garrod, published the first division of the Upper Paleolithic Age. This division, founded upon the notion of a linear development of cultures, could be challenged only during the last decade. Following publication of finds in Lebanon, the Negev and north Sinai, as well as the renewed Qafzah Cave investigation, scholars have been able to discern in this period—between 19,000 and 40,000 years ago—the parallel development of at least two technological traditions. The first one is based on flake production. In its early phase it is known as "Emiran." Its later manifestations are so similar to the French "Aurignacian" that this term was adopted by most scholars. The second technological tradition is known as "Ahmarian"; its main products were blades (long and slender flakes). Both technological traditions were contemporary but they varied in their geographical distribution—the Aurignacian is more common in Lebanon, the Galilee, and Mt. Carmel, while the Ahmarian is more frequent in northern Sinai, the Negev and the Judean desert. Because the Ahmarian is currently under study, it is as yet easier to describe the hunter-gatherer way of life in the Land of Israel on the basis of the Aurignacian sites.

Contracted burial of woman at Nahal Ein-Gev I, dating to the Late Aurignacian Period (approximately 17,000 B.C.E.).

Most Aurignacian material has been found in caves in Israel and Lebanon. Moreover, since the majority of these were discovered in old excavations, the task of interpreting the finds anew is more difficult. The residential levels rarely extend over the entire area of the cave, evidence that only a small number of hunters and food gatherers once inhabited the cave, perhaps merely a single family. The open-air sites, too, known chiefly from the latter phase of this culture, cover only a tiny area. At one of these sites, Nahal Ein Gev I, archaeologists uncovered a woman's grave. The deceased had been laid to rest in a contracted position. This is the only burial known from this period (see photo on p. 8). The paucity of human remains dating to the Upper Paleolithic Age in the Land of Israel is certainly unfortunate. The skull fragment from the Qafzah Cave, a leg bone from Hayonim Cave, and varied pieces of bone from the El-Wad Cave present too little material for a reconstruction of the morphological characteristics of this prehistoric population.

From the bones of the hunted animals—mainly fallow-deer, Palestinian deer, wild ox and roe deer—we may conclude that hunting was an important source of sustenance. Hunters used bone spearheads and, almost certainly, flint points. Scholars refer to these flint points as *Ksar Akil* and *El-Wad* points. The use of red ochre, customary even in earlier times, is attested to in grinding stones and grinding slabs dating to this period from Qafzah Cave and Hayonim Cave.

The production of bladelets with wooden hafts is evidence for the existence of composite tools. Here, we may detect an incipient technology typical of later eras.

Basalt mortar and pestle from the Ein-Gev I excavations (approximately 14,000 B.C.E.).

IV. The Epi-Paleolithic Age

During the last 30 years Israel, like other countries, abandoned the terminology used for Western Europe, which previously dominated Asian and African prehistory research. The term, "Mesolithic Age," for example, indicated flint assemblages typified by postglacial microlithic tools in Western Europe. In the north African context the term "Epi-Paleolithic Age," which includes the end of the

Pleistocene, is used instead. Later, this term was adopted in the Levant as well; today it encompasses the Levantine microlithic industries. Some of the cultures attributable to this period—for instance, the Kebaran and the Kebaran Geometric cultures—were originally included within the Upper Paleolithic Age. Similarly, the Natufian culture and its contemporaries had previously been incorporated in the Mesolithic.

The Epi-Paleolithic Age was a decisive period in human history. Hunters and food gatherers changed their modes of living and became farmers and shepherds. The transition normally would not be considered a quick one. Yet when contrasted with the preceding two million years, when humankind's only occupations were hunting and food gathering, the change to farming and animal husbandry may be viewed as a truly radical permutation.

The Eynan excavations. Note the structure's circular wall. Beneath the floor, burials consisting of round installations and pits were discovered—all of which point to the difficulty posed by the stratigraphy of a typical Natufian site.

Research on the Epi-Paleolithic era has been conducted chiefly during the last decade, except for initial defining of the Natufian culture. Excavations in Lebanon, the Jordan Valley, the Coastal Plain, the Negev Mountains and in northern Sinai, together with the results of many surveys, have provided a variegated socioeconomic picture of the Epi-Paleolithic Age. Climatic research, based upon fragmentary evidence of wadi terraces and upon paleontological and paleozoological factors, suggests that a significant change occurred at the end of the Pleistocene and the beginning of the Holocene eras. The sequence of events seems at present to have been as follows: During the time of the Kebaran culture, a dry, cold climate predominated. A moist period followed, which began during the Kebaran Geometric culture, close to 12,500 B.C.E., and continued to the latter part of the tenth millennium B.C.E. The ninth and eighth millennia witnessed an attenuation of the moisture, though it did not vanish entirely. Then during the seventh millennium B.C.E., moisture rose again. However, we still lack detailed knowledge of these events; thus, it would be premature to draw conclusions regarding the extent to which climatic changes influenced the socio-economic structure of these populations.

The Kebaran and Kebaran Geometric cultures reflect the first part of the Epi-Paleolithic Age. Remains from the Kebaran culture have enabled us to make a territorial division within the Land of Israel based, alternatively, upon tribal apportionment, or on a division between hunters and food-gathering communal entities. Sites from this period, usually only 150 to 400 square meters in size, have produced animal bones and the first grinding tools discovered in the Levant (see photo p. 9). The important Ein Gev I site has the only grave attributable to this period. A woman 30-35 years old was buried in a semi-contracted posture in this grave.

Kebaran sites are only located north of the Beersheba basin. Those of the Kebaran Geometric are found in this area and in the arid Negev Mountains, the western Negev, the northern Sinai, and even in Wadi Feiran in southern Sinai. These sites do not differ in size from those of earlier cultures; indeed, they attest to the perpetuation of a lifestyle appropriate to small hunting and food-gathering communities.

The remains of additional groups of hunters from this era have also been discovered in northern Sinai. Apparently, these groups had penetrated into northern Sinai from North Africa. The influence of these groups of hunters finally reached the Negev mountains.

Archaeological finds demonstrate that a fundamental social change occurred with the onset of the Natufian culture. The most ancient sites of Natufian culture, originally excavated in the 1930s, are the El-Wad Cave and its terrace, the Shukbah Cave, the Kebarah Cave and the Irq el-Ahmar rock-shelter in Wadi Khareitun. Later, other sites were found: Nahal Oren in the Carmel, Eynan in the Huleh Valley, and Hayonim Cave and the terrace in front of it in western Galilee. Smaller sites that served as seasonal camps were also uncovered. Some of these were used only on a single occasion. Others were permanent encampments. Examples of both types were discovered recently in the lower Jordan Valley.

Some of the villages at these Natufian base camps cover an area between 1,000 and 5,000 square meters. Remnants of circular buildings and an abundance of under-floor burials were found at these sites (see photo p. 10). Large quantities of grinding tools were also discovered. Many were made of basalt imported from far away. Microliths, especially lunates, characteristic of the flint assemblages, were found. Sickle blades appeared as well. The sickle blades were easily identifiable—harvesting wild wheat had put a luster on the edges.

Many individual and collective burials of various styles were discovered at these Natufian villages. Burial positions include semi-contracted, contracted and supine. Very few grave gifts were found. Some ornaments and jewelry which perhaps adorned the garments of the deceased were uncovered. But these burials do not indicate positions of the deceased in any social hierarchy. The Natufian culture, like other hunting and food-gathering societies, was quite likely egalitarian.

The most ancient art objects yet discovered in Israel come from these Natufian sites. They include animals carved on sickle handles and stone and bone figurines exhibiting stylized human and animal motifs. The Natufians may deserve credit for making the very first attempt to domesticate animals. Evidence of domesticated dogs, thought to be descended from Palestinian wild wolves, was recently found at Eynan and at the Hayonim terrace. Also, the Natufians herded goats and sheep.

The large sites of the Negev Mountains, such as Rosh-Zin and Rosh Horesha, belong to the latter phase of the Natufian culture; however, no comparable sites were found in the northern Sinai. These Natufian peoples, known for their hunting and intensive food gathering (especially of wild cereals) apparently were organized in larger social groups than those of preceding cultures. Although they ultimately confined themselves to the Mediterranean climatic region, small Kebaran-like hunter societies persisted in arid and semi-arid regions and in well-wooded areas such as the Lebanon Mountains. It is, thus, notable that the social change accompanying the domestication of wild grains and herd animals (a practice imported from the northern Levant) occurred within a particular ecological region.

This civilizing economic process continued at a brisk pace in the second half of the ninth and during the eighth millennia B.C.E. The above is, though, somewhat difficult to reconcile with the usual schematized archaeological division of the Ages. The Harifian culture succeeded the Natufian in the Negev and derived from the Late Natufian. However, it co-existed with the large village at Jericho that boasted walls and a tower. Fortunately, the many Carbon 14 datings carried out at Sinai, Negev and Jordan Valley sites help solve the problem. We can now better apprehend these dual societies that typify human history during the last 10,000 years.

V. The Neolithic Age

Usage of the term "Neolithic Age" attests to the necessity of separating the terms of relative chronology from those of the archaeological cultures. Today we are able to define prehistoric cultures within the framework of both radiometric time-scale and geographical space. Justification for the European term, "Neolithic Age," rests entirely upon the combined relevance of pottery, polished axes and domesticated animals. Yet, as early as the 1930s, Garstang's excavations at Jericho revealed that certain Neolithic layers lacked any pottery whatever. It was only in the wake of Kathleen Kenyon's excavations at the same site between 1954 and 1958 that the term "Pre-Pottery Neolithic" was coined. I would suggest that this expression reflects all too keenly the exaggerated importance ascribed to the presence of pottery. At the same time, it fails to accent the societal changes that characterized the Neolithic Age. Societal changes are more aptly recorded in Gordon Childe's phrase, "The Neolithic Revolution."

Carbon 14 datings have determined that the Neolithic spanned the period roughly between 8,500 and 5,000 B.C.E. Interestingly, when we compare the socio-economic system at the beginning of the Age to that of its latter phase, it becomes clear that a dramatic change had occurred. We can no longer, for example, refer to hunters, intensive food gatherers and owners of domesticated dogs, of the Natufian sort. Instead, we are confronted by a village society that cultivated wheat, barley, flax, legumes and olives (and possibly also dates and pomegranates), while it tended its goats, sheep, pigs, cattle and dogs. Further investigation may demonstrate that this late Neolithic society was organized into a series of tribal kingdoms. Also, they may have carried on internal trade of sundry items and raw materials imported from the Aegean, Anatolia, the southern Levant, Mesopotamia, Iran, and even the Indus Valley.

In the Land of Israel, we have explored various phases of the Pre-Pottery Neolithic A and B, and Pottery Neolithic Ages, with special emphasis on the Pre-Pottery epochs. The sites at Jericho, Nahal Oren, Munḥata, Abu Ghosh, Beisamon and Beidha (in Transjordan) represent our main sources of information. Most

Carbon 14 datings were obtained at sites in the semi-arid regions.

Dual societies, that is, the simultaneous existence of hunter and food-gatherer societies with those of the semi-agricultural peoples, were found at Neolithic sites. Hunter societies inhabited the semi-arid border regions. Examples are Harifian sites scattered chiefly in the Negev Mountain, northern Sinai, and western Negev. Some were also found in the high Lebanese mountain ranges and in the Antilebanon (such as the Nasharini Cave).

Like Jericho and Nahal Oren before them, the Jordan Valley sites of Gilgal and Netiv Ha'Gdud have failed to yield evidence of systematic wheat and barley cultivation. Information about agriculture in the seventh millennium B.C.E. is rather clearer. But the paucity of finds, and the very late introduction of "flotation" technique have made tracing the precise process of grain and vegetable domestication difficult. We can state that sites belonging to this age were larger than those of the preceding Natufian.

Structure and building techniques evidence the Late Neolithic social structure. Construction of round buildings persisted, but we now see the introduction of bricks. The presence of defense walls testifies to some sort of concerted social effort. These walls may have been erected to deter attacks by neighboring societies. Their principal task, however, was to prevent the inundation of settlements situated on alluvial fans.

Hunting weapons, for example, aerodynamically designed arrowheads, point to the consistent use of the bow. Axes and adzes were also in use. Further, the many grinding tools shaped like flat bowls show a new method of food preparation. The gazelle was the most-hunted animal. Pigeons, waterfowl and migratory birds were also prey. Apparently, goats and sheep constituted the main meat source. As noted, these animals were domesticated in the northern Levant throughout the eighth millennium B.C.E. and reached the Land of Israel only in the late years of this period.

The coextensive but dichotomic socio-economic phenomenon referred to earlier was intensified during the Pre-Pottery Neolithic B Age, which lasted from the middle of the eighth millennium B.C.E. until the beginning of the sixth. Small hunter communities still inhabited the border regions and the semi-arid regions— for example, the Transjordanian and Sinai wildernesses. But the seventh millennium B.C.E. saw intensified grain cultivation. This larger-scale agriculture with its accompanying social and economic development was located mainly in the Jordan Valley, which boasts the largest sites dating to this era—the Hill Country and Coastal Plain.

Another facet of Late Neolithic socio-economic development was obsidian, or volcanic glass, trade.* Glass working led to the construction of rectangular brickwork dwellings, and other technological processes, for instance, the flint heat treatment in order to produce pressure flaking.

Jericho, Munḥata, Abu Ghosh, Nahal Oren and Beisamon are the best-known excavations of this period. Most prominent among the discoveries were the brickwork or stonework rectangular buildings (see photo p. 14), especially those with plaster floors, sometimes painted red. Although the plastered skulls from Jericho and Beisamon have been well publicized, a fully satisfactory interpretation of their function has proved elusive. Nonetheless, the consensus today is that they evidence ancestor worship. Under-floor burials—a custom that originated in the Natufian culture—were a common occurrence at these sites and were intended to strengthen the population's claim of ownership over the settlement and its territory. The economy was based on agriculture, mainly growing cereals. From the

*Vestiges of obsidian trade were discovered at the western Negev site of Nahal Lavan and even in Beidha in Transjordan.

General view of the Neolithic Pre-Ceramic II buildings at Munhata.

middle of the seventh millennium B.C.E., herding goats and sheep occupied a good part of the daily routine at Neolithic villages. Hunting remained as important as it was in the Natufian period. With the introduction of sheep into the Land of Israel, spinning probably followed, although we do not possess much direct evidence to that effect.

We still do not fully comprehend the scope of barter during this period. For, in addition to obsidian blades and cores from Anatolia, greenstone axes from the northern Levant, shells from the Red Sea, and turquoise, malachite and haematite from the Sinai were also discovered. Although Jericho's wealth and size were attributed to its trade in asphalt, salt and sulphur, we should point out that it does not appear so large when compared to other contemporary sites on the Euphrates or in Anatolia. For the time being, we must admit that our knowledge of the economies of the Neolithic settlements in the Land of Israel is quite deficient.

As early as the 1930s, researchers were beginning to appreciate the wide distribution of sites from this era in the desert regions, but it was only in the wake of the excavations in the southern Sinai and Transjordan that the true extent of their dispersion was realized. This lends credence to the assumption that relatively humid conditions prevailed in this area during the seventh millennium B.C.E.

Compared with the rich remains left by the people of the Pre-Pottery period, the remnants from the Pottery Neolithic appear rather impoverished. There are, for instance, the pit-dwellings—such as those at Jericho, Munḥata and sites in the Coastal Plain—and settlements, like those at the Sha'ar Ha-Golan site, comprising only flimsy huts. The above seems to support the assumption that the climate warmed at the beginning of the sixth millennium B.C.E. and that precipitation decreased. The accepted view regarding the long hiatus in the settlements in the Jordan Valley has not yet been sufficiently examined, but the question itself has effectively highlighted discussions of the changes in social structures. These are expressed archaeologically in the new types of dwellings, site locations, and their distribution.

One of the most important developments of this period was the appearance of pottery. In the Syro-Lebanese area, vessels were made first of a mixture of ash and

DATES IN B.C.E.	ARCHAEOLOGICAL AGE	CULTURES IN THE LAND OF ISRAEL	PRINCIPAL SITES
	Pottery Neolithic	Yarmukian	Sha'ar Ha-Golan, Munḥata
6,000			
	Pre-Pottery Neolithic	Pre-Ceramic Neolithic B	Jericho, Beisamon, Abu Ghosh, Nahal Oren
		Harifian and Sultanian	Har Harif sites, Jericho, Gilgal I, Nahal Oren, Netiv Ha'Gdud
8,300			
		Khiamian	El Khiam, Selibivah IX, El-Wad, Kebarah, Nahal Oren, Eynan,
	Epi-Paleolithic	Natufian	Hayonim Cave and Terrace, Rosh Huresha
		Kebaran Geometric	Haon, Hefzibah, Ein Gev III, Hofith, Iraq-Zigan
		Kebaran	Ein Gev I, Nahal Hadera V, Kebarah Cave, Hayonim Cave
17,000			
	Upper Paleolithic	Aurignacian and Ahmarian Traditions	Ein Akev, Nahal Ein Gev I, El-Wad, Kebarah, Sefunim, Hayonim Cave, Irq el-Ahmar, Boker, Qafzah Cave, Jebel Legama sites.
		Transitional Industries	Lower Boker site, Emirah Cave
40,000			
		Late Mousterian	El-Wad, S'hul Cave, Kebarah, Hayonim Cave, Farah B
	Middle Paleolithic	Early Mousterian	Qafzah, Hayonim Cave, Tabun Cave, Rosh Ein Mor, Abu-Zif, Ein Akev
		Acheulo-Jabrudian	Tabun Cave, Zuttiyah Cave
125,000			
	Lower Paleolithic	Late Acheulean	Ma'ayan Barukh, Kissufim, Holon, Gesher B'not Ya'acov, Umm Qatafa Cave
		Early Acheulean	Kfar Menahem, Evron Quarry, Ubaidiya
1,000,000			

gypsum and are called "Vaisselle blanche." But it seems that within a relatively short period—not more than several hundred years—the skills needed to create pottery from clay became prevalent throughout the entire ancient East.

During the Neolithic Pottery Age we witness the simultaneous existence of hunters and food gatherers on the one hand, and tillers of the soil on the other. Domesticated pigs and cattle, however, do not augment the numbers of goats and sheep. We must admit that, because few sites belonging to this period have been excavated and because plant remains are not well-preserved, we have been unable to construct a total picture of the age.

Among the significant advances in recent years in the research of the Neolithic Age in the Levant is the attempt to digress from the old chronological framework and define cultures in the context of their geographical regions. By using an ecological approach, as well as by viewing the cultures as interrelated systems, we try to understand the various causes and developments of this period's major social and economic changes. These changes within the Neolithic societies have led to the establishment of the threefold aspects of Near Eastern life: urban centers, farming communities and pastoral nomads. However, sedimentological studies of cave accumulations, as well as geomorphological observations on ancient seashores in Israel and Lebanon, have helped to build a chronological sequence for the early part of the Last Ice Age.

At the Dawn of History—the Chalcolithic Period and The Early Bronze Age

By Amnon Ben-Tor

The year 1948 marked the beginning of a new chapter in the study of the third and fourth millennia B.C.E.—roughly the Chalcolithic Period and the Early Bronze Age—in the Land of Israel. In 1948 a comprehensive report was published on the Early Bronze remains from Megiddo.[1] This was followed, in 1949, by a report on the Ai excavations[2]—one of the key sites in understanding the third millennium. Excavations at another key site, Tell Farah (N), began in 1946.[3] Excavations at Beth-Yerah, another important site, also started at about the same time.[4]

Excavations at Chalcolithic sites in the Beersheba region began in 1951.[5] During the mid-1950s excavations were conducted at Tell Irani,[6] Jericho,[7] and at the Chalcolithic cemetery at Azor.[8] One year after the discovery of the Chalcolithic "treasure" in a cave in the Judean Desert in 1961,[9] excavations were begun at Arad, another key Early Bronze site.[10] At the present time, both the important Chalcolithic site at Gilat and the Chalcolithic culture of the Golan are in the process of being uncovered.[11]

In light of this impressive, and only partial, list of excavations since the mid-1940s, it is appropriate to ask what was known of the Chalcolithic and Early Bronze Ages before these excavations. The most authoritative, if summary, treatment of the subject is contained in William Foxwell Albright's now classic book, *The Archaeology of Palestine,* which was published, coincidentally, in 1948.

To borrow the terminology of the building industry, we can say that until the late 1940s, the foundations were being laid for research on the Chalcolithic and Early Bronze Ages; the framework was constructed during the years that immediately followed, and recent years have seen an effort to complete the project. In the years to come, scholars will continue to work toward completion. Yet as we strive toward this end, we sometimes need to move the frame slightly or, less often, to

Basalt idol of a house deity from the Chalcolithic Period, found in the Golan.

shake the very foundations a little.

The topic of this short survey includes the term "The Dawn of History." Perhaps it would be more accurate to refer to the periods under discussion as "The Beginning of Civilization and Urbanization." Neither phrase is wholly unequivocal, and without getting into a debate over precise definitions, let us simply observe that the Chalcolithic and Early Bronze Ages in the Land of Israel are essentially prehistoric.

During the last several years, with the discovery of the Ebla tablets from the mid-third millennium B.C.E., the Dawn of History can be said to have burst forth upon the Syrian scene. But the Land of Israel has not yet yielded a comparable revelation. Perhaps the rays of Syria's historic dawn might, in the meantime, illuminate at least some dark corners in the annals of the Land of Israel during this period. For the present, however, we must base our history of the Land of Israel during this period almost entirely upon the testimony of mute artifacts from excavations. Regrettably, this method of interpretation is frequently disconcerting; as soon as one arranges the materials in an apparently logical pattern, one becomes aware that the same artifacts could just as logically be ordered in another pattern. But the effort must be undertaken nonetheless.

Three central questions confront the researcher:

1. When? What is the relative and absolute chronology of the period?
2. Who? Who were the peoples who inhabited the country at that time?
3. What? What were the elements of their culture? Where did they live? What were their living conditions? What were their sources of sustenance? What kinds of social institutions did they have? Did they maintain ties with their neighbors? What were the elements of their religion and what were the rituals in which it was expressed? Questions of this kind can easily be multiplied.

Turning to the first question, "When?," a more or less accurate relative chronology of the period had already been determined in the years before 1948. The absolute chronology of the Chalcolithic Age was computed primarily by means of Carbon 14 datings, while the chronology of the third millennium—that is, the Early Bronze Age—was based mainly on synchronisms with the cultures of nearby countries, especially Egypt and Mesopotamia, as well as on Carbon 14 readings. Although fourth-millennium synchronisms with Mesopotamia have been quite scarce, this is apparently simply a matter of chance; indeed, indications in recent years are that we shall soon be able to make synchronistic comparisons between the Land of Israel and Mesopotamia in the fourth millennium, as well as in the third.

Bronze crown dating to the Chalcolithic Period found in the "Cave of the Treasure" at Nahal Mishmar.

Among the most difficult questions, one for which we have no satisfactory answer is "Who?" Moreover, we are at an impasse, chiefly because of factors beyond our control—for example, the lack of written sources. Nevertheless, we should be able to make some progress if we conduct a fundamental and extensive examination of the abundant skeletal remains discovered in cemeteries from both the Chalcolithic Period and the Early Bronze Age. This task has not yet been undertaken, even though scholars have been much troubled by questions of the origin of these peoples and of their ultimate fate. Such a study may indicate not only who the inhabitants of the Land of Israel were during the Chalcolithic Period, but where they came from; whether they were all immigrants, or whether some were long-term residents; and what happened to them at the end of the era, whether they simply disappeared, were destroyed, or were assimilated. Probably a synthesis of several historical processes will be found to be at work here. Similar questions may be posed with regard to all phases of the Early Bronze Age.

Another interesting question concerns the number of people living in the Land of Israel during these periods. The answer involves not only some guesswork but also a certain amount of supposition and calculation. For example—in the Chalcolithic Period, approximately 5,000 to 10,000 people inhabited about 50 settlements in the Land of Israel. Each settlement comprised, on the average, between 100 and

200 people. In the Early Bronze Age, the population increased to between 40,000 and 80,000 people living at about 150 different sites, an average of nearly 3,000 people in each settlement. The number of settlements did not increase significantly during the course of the Early Bronze Age. The increase in population—estimated at 0.5 to 1.5 people per thousand each year—did not, in general, lead to the establishment of new settlements but rather to an increase in population density at existing settlements. This is an enormously important datum for understanding the urbanization process.

About 90 percent of all Early Bronze Age sites are located in regions whose mean annual levels of precipitation exceeded 300 millimeters. This presents a striking contrast to the distribution of Chalcolithic sites, which are centered mainly in the semi-arid regions of the Land of Israel, where the average annual precipitation is less than 300 millimeters. This reflects an important economic difference: The economy of the Chalcolithic settlements was based on goats, sheep, and to some extent, cattle, as well as minor agricultural cultivation. On the other hand a so-called "Mediterranean Economy," in which the economic base combined pasturage, particularly sheep, and more intensive cultivation of agricultural produce such as wheat, barley, grapes and olives, crystallized at the beginning of the Early Bronze Age and remained the typical pattern until modern times.

Cache of Chalcolithic Period bronze objects in situ from the "Cave of the Treasure."

A picture of the quality of life during these periods can be sketched according to several components:

Type of Settlement

During the Early Bronze Age we find a gradual transition from the typical Chalcolithic settlement—open, with a comparatively sparse population—to enclosed and fortified settlements, inhabited by increasingly dense populations. Indeed, one is tempted to refer to the latest of these Early Bronze Age settlements as "cities."

Ceramic Industry

Domestic pottery predominated during the Chalcolithic Period. During the Early Bronze Period, vessels for storing and marketing the now diversified agricultural yield were added to the pottery repertoire. Also during the Early Bronze Age, the technology used in the manufacture of pottery improved noticeably.

Foreign Relations

Ties with Egypt clearly existed during the Chalcolithic Period. Recent finds indicate contacts with more distant cultures as well, for instance, Iran. Scholarly opinion is splintered with regard to the precise role of Egypt in the Land of Israel at the beginning of the Early Bronze Age. Did Egypt govern the country, or do the finds merely reflect mutual commercial ties? The further we get into the Early Bronze Age, the more evidence we find of relations with other countries in addition to Egypt, including lands to the north such as Anatolia.

Metallurgy

The treasure trove of beautiful copper artifacts from the Chalcolithic Age—scepters, standards, tools, and weapons—found in 1961 in a cave in the Judean Desert near the Dead Sea reflect the apex of ancient metallurgic art. We have yet to determine, though, whether these objects were manufactured locally or were imported. Metallurgy during the Early Bronze Age was, surprisingly enough, less sophisticated. The finds are primarily work implements and weapons that have been found at various sites, most particularly at Kfar Munash.

Art

In art too, especially in the carving of ivory, the craftspeople of the Chalcolithic Age excelled. The artistic achievement of the Early Bronze Age, on the other hand, was relatively modest and was limited, in the main, to the engraving of cylinder seals used in the decoration of pottery.

General view (looking south) of the Chalcolithic temple at Ein-Gedi.

Ivory statuette from the Chalcolithic Period discovered at Beer Tzefed near Beersheba.

Cult

The temple at Ein Gedi reflects Chalcolithic religious architecture at its highest point. Early Bronze Age buildings of similar design suggest that people of the same ethnic character continued to inhabit the land and even had some of the same religious customs.

The cultic objects that have been found eloquently reflect the intimate relationship between the economic life and religious conscience of the community. For example, the shepherds' culture of the Chalcolithic Age, which depended on sheep, cattle and dairy products, is palpably reflected in the cultic paraphernalia discovered at Ein Gedi and Gilat. Some of the cylinder seals and diverse religious objects unearthed at Ai and at Arad from the Early bronze Age reflect the "Mediterranean Economy," in which agriculture and animal husbandry become equally important. In these artifacts we find frequent depictions reflecting notions of the earth's fertility and of the harvest.

As I noted earlier, contemporary research on the Chalcolithic and Early Bronze Ages focuses primarily on interpreting mute artifacts from excavations. I have presented one such interpretation here. I am fully aware, however, that others might offer equally plausible interpretations. What is important is that in recent years we have been asking more of the right questions, for that is where all research must begin.

[1]G. Loud, *Megiddo II* (Chicago, 1948).
[2]Judith Marquet-Krause, *Les Fouilles de 'Ay (et-Tell) 1933-1935* (Paris, 1949).
[3]R. de Vaux, O.P., A.M. Steve, O.P., "La première campagne des fouilles à Tell Far'ah, Près Naplouse," *Revue Biblique* LIV (1947), pp. 394-433, 571-589.
[4]B. Maisler, M. Stekelis, M. Avi-Yonah, "The Excavations at Beth Yerah (Khirbet el-Kerak), 1944-1946," *Israel Exploration Journal* 2 (1952), pp. 165-173, 218-229.
[5]J. Perrot, "Excavations at Tell Abu-Matar, Near Beersheba," *Israel Exploration Journal* 5 (1955), pp. 17-40, 73-84, 167-189.
[6]S. Yeivin, *First Preliminary Report on the Excavations at Tel "Gat," 1956-1958* (Jerusalem, 1961).
[7]Kathleen M. Kenyon, *Digging Up Jericho* (London, 1957).
[8]J. Perrot, "Une Tombe a Ossuaires du IVᵉ Millenaire à Azor, Près de Tel-Aviv," *Atiqot* III (English Series)(Jerusalem, 1961), pp. 1-83.
[9]Pessah Bar-Adon, *The Cave of the Treasure* (Jerusalem, 1980).
[10]Ruth Amiran, *Early Arad I: The Chalcolithic and Early Bronze City* (Jerusalem, 1978).
[11]David Alon, "A Chalcolithic Temple at Gilat," *Biblical Archeologist* 40 (1977), pp. 63-70. Claire Epstein, "The Chalcolithic Culture of the Golan," *Biblical Archeologist* 40 (1977), pp. 57-62.

"At That Time the Canaanites Were in the Land . . . "

By Moshe Kochavi

I shall briefly survey here the history and culture of the "land of Canaan" during the millennium preceding the conquest by Joshua. Archaeological excavations clearly demonstrate that this millennium, from 2200 to 1200 B.C.E., can be considered as three distinct historical periods. Each differs from the others in its history and in its material culture.

I. Intermediate Bronze Age

The Intermediate Bronze Age is the most problematic of the three periods. There is no scholarly consensus even regarding the term itself, and to a lesser degree, there is a disagreement as to its chronology. Opinion differs on the question of whether this period belongs to the last phase of the Early Bronze Age, to the first phase of the Middle Bronze Age, or to an intermediate period which is distinct, and which might appropriately be called the Intermediate Bronze Age. Moreover, since we do not possess a single find from this period that synchronizes with absolute chronology, the dates for this period can be based only on the dates for the periods that precede and follow it. The dates suggested by the *Encyclopedia of Archaeological Excavations in the Holy Land*—2200-2000 B.C.E.—have, however, been accepted by most scholars, although there are some indications for an earlier date for the Early Bronze Age. My discussion will assume this chronology and will use the term "Intermediate Bronze Age" (abbreviated to IBA).

As early as the first excavations at Jericho, at the turn of the century, archaeologists saw that the IBA constituted a distinct archaeological period. Only during the 1930s and '40s, however, following publication of the excavations at Tell Ajjul, Megiddo, Lachish, and Tell Beit Mirsim, did its material culture become known. Research since 1948 has built on the foundations laid by earlier scholars. In this way, a new view of the period emerged. The essential change came with the

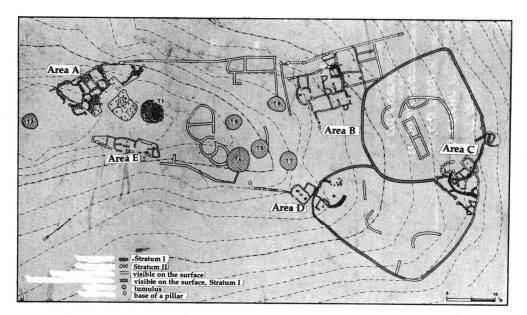

Plan of settlement at Har Yeruham.

realization that the period is characterized by a semi-nomadic culture, unlike the preceding and following periods, whose cultures can be described as urban-agricultural.

Three factors brought about this new view:

(1) Archaeological surveys in the arid regions, in the desert fringe areas of eastern Transjordan, in the Golan, the Negev mountains, and in the northern part of the Sinai peninsula all demonstrated a wide distribution of settlements dating to this period.

(2) IBA peoples inhabited caves or lived in temporary structures such as those found at Har Yerucham in the Negev mountains, Jebel Qa'akir in the Shephelah and other sites. These "shelters" were obviously occupied only for short periods of time, and their remains were, not surprisingly, scanty.

(3) Extensive cemeteries like those at Jericho, Ein Samiyah, Dhahar Mirzbaneh and other places indicated that these semi-nomads maintained large central cemeteries to serve a widely distributed nomadic population. In the shaft tombs of these cemeteries and in the cairn graves of the Negev and Golan there were double burials in a single grave. The great variety of burials attested to a tribal structure.

Other sites dating to the IBA were discovered in the Galilee and on the coastal plateau. Scholars were able to divide pottery from these sites into typological-regional sub-groups. The precise chronology of these groups, however, is still energetically disputed, but a portrait of tribal egalitarian society is emerging. A comparatively large number of copper items, mainly weapons, were found. At different sites, excavators discovered copper bars, evidence that coppersmiths worked at these sites.

The IBA peoples had few ties with foreign countries. What little contact there

Entrances to the burial shafts dating to the Intermediate Bronze Age, discovered at Jebel Qa'akir in the Hebron mountains.

was was almost entirely with lands to the north and northeast. Pottery from Megiddo, Hazor and Kadesh in the Galilee and from other sites in the northern part of the country indicate ties with central Syria—for example, Hamay in the Orontes valley. Some of the weapons are of types that were common throughout the Fertile Crescent. The unique silver goblet from the Ein Samiyah cemetery, decorated with mythological scenes, reflects a prototype that originated in the Mesopotamian and north Syrian cultural milieu. The influence of these distant regions is discernible, too, in the pottery assemblages from southern parts of the country.

To understand the IBA fully, we must find answers to several key questions:

(1) The internal division of the period. At the moment we have only very sparse stratigraphical data. More data of this kind would allow us to make internal divisions within the period. This, in turn, would help us understand the various historical processes that occurred throughout the period.

(2) Understanding the period's ecology. Very few scholars have dealt with this subject. Thus we have almost no data with which to reconstruct either the economic life of the IBA peoples or the manner in which they related to their environment.

(3) The queston of ethnic identity. When the key questions in the first two paragraphs have been answered, we will be able to proffer a better response to this question. Most scholars are inclined to equate the IBA peoples with the Amurru, the desert brigands mentioned in contemporaneous Sumerian documents. Others have gone even further, suggesting that the IBA peoples are the biblical Amorites. Some scholars have even maintained that the archaeological remains of the period in the Negev should be dated specifically to Abraham's time. Unfortunately, we do not, at present, have enough data to provide a positive answer to this difficult question—especially since we have no historical information whatever about the period. We can say, though, that research thus far does not confirm the identification either with the Patriarchal period, or more specifically, with the period of Abraham. I maintain that even the currently accepted identification with the tribes of the Amurru needs further proof, particularly in light of the great difference between the material culture of the IBA and that of the Middle Bronze Age, when

Intermediate Bronze Age silver goblet from Ein-Samiyah.

28

Intermediate Bronze Age communal building uncovered at Har Yerucham.

the Land of Israel was host to peoples speaking a Western Semitic language whom one might associate with the Amurru (see below).

II. Middle Bronze Age II

In order to avoid the confusion that results from using the ambiguous term "Middle Bronze Age I," most scholars use the term "Middle Bronze Age II" to designate the entire period following the IBA; that is, the first half of the second millennium B.C.E., between approximately 2000 and 1550 B.C.E. Firm foundations for research on this period were laid by the large-scale excavations conducted between the two World Wars at such sites as Megiddo, Jericho, Tell Ajjul and Tell Beit Mirsim. Research since 1948 has added considerably to our knowledge of the material culture of this period. These achievements were the result of excavations, archaeological surveys, and extensive analysis of all the new, as well as old, data. Let us look first at some of the new data:

(1) The unearthing of large urban complexes, which include fortifications, public buildings and private dwellings. The largest city in the country during that period, Hazor, is a characteristic example.

(2) Research into the nature of the settlements located in regions that had not been previously investigated. These settlements include Shechem and Tell Farah North (Tirzah?) in the central mountains; Dan and Hazor in the Upper Galilee; Nahariya, Akko, Tell Poleg, Tell Aphek and others in the coastal plain; and Tel Malhata and Tel Masos in the eastern Negev.

(3) The discovery, through surveys, of small sites—some fortified and some unfortified—or isolated buildings associated with the cult. At some of these sites, excavations were conducted—for example, at Nahariya, Tel Mevorakh, Khirbet Zorekiyeh, Kfar-Shmaryahu and Sdeh-Dov in the coastal plain; Tell Kitan in the Beth Shean Valley; and Givat Yeshayahu near Beth Shemesh in the Shephelah.

(4) Excavations at certain tells in the coastal plateau—for instance, Kabri, Akko, Burga, Zeror, Poleg, Aphek and Yavneh-Yam—that allowed us to understand better the way of life during the first phase of this period, that is, Middle Bronze Age IIA.

(5) The uncovering of six strata belonging to the first phase of the period, at

Aphek-Antipatris. The earliest layer was built directly on top of the strata of the Early Bronze Age, while the latest was covered by a stratum from Middle Bronze IIB. These discoveries taught us how to differentiate between the earlier and later phases of this period and even to isolate the transitional stage that bridges the two principal phases of the period.

(6) The discovery in the Jericho cemetery of the daily household materials made of organic material enabled researchers to reconstruct more fully the daily life of peoples of the period.

(7) Archaeological sections in the earthen ramparts around Jericho, Gezer, Shechem, Yavneh-Yam, Tell Nagilah, Tel Zeror, Hazor, Akko and Dan revealed new data that allowed us to appreciate these peoples' extraordinary building methods. Some of these earthworks were dated to the beginning of the period.

(8) New evidence allowed us to study the form of worship of the period. This evidence came from the excavation of temples in Nahariya, Kfar Shmaryahu, Hazor and Tell Kitan, as well as the reexamination of temples that had been

Aerial photograph of Tel Hazor (looking north).

excavated at Shechem and Megiddo, and that could now be positively ascribed to the latter part of Middle Bronze II. At Nahariya and Givat Yeshayahu near Beth Shemesh, excavators found evidence of worship on *bamot* (high places).

(9) Regional cultures were identified, principally through pottery finds, so that we can now distinguish between the coastal plain and the interior of the country, and between the northern and southern parts of the country.

(10) We can now determine the early date of the beginning of commercial activity and the provenance of various imports. For example, imports from northern Syria were found in the Dan excavations; Kabri finds demonstrated Anatolian influences; at Achziv and Akko imports from Cyprus dating to the beginning of Middle Bronze II were found. Egyptian influence on the material culture is attested mainly during the second phase of the period.

During recent years there have been many attempts to establish a comprehensive view of the period, based on an abundance of historical and archaeological evidence. Determining the nature of the relation between Middle Bronze IIA and Middle Bronze IIB has, however, remained a knotty problem. This is an archaeological-historical and chronological problem and is therefore inevitably complex. The principal questions that must be asked are these: Is there, in fact, a cultural-historical gap between these two phases, or is the transition between them a gradual development? What is the nature of the difference between these two phases, and when and how did the transition from one phase to the other occur? What were the relations between the Land of Israel and Egypt during this period? What is the significance of the ties between the Land of Israel and the countries to the north and northeast? Do archaeological finds indicate ethnic changes that might have occurred? Do archaeological finds in the Land of Israel provide any data relevant to the chronology of the ancient East as a whole? These are some of the questions that will intrigue researchers of the Middle Bronze Age in the coming years.

View of Middle Bronze cyclopean wall uncovered at Shechem.

Small dolmen comprising three stones, from the Intermediate Bronze Age.

III. The Late Bronze Age

Of the three distinct periods comprising the millennium preceding Joshua's conquest, the Late Bronze Age (approximately 1550 B.C.E. to 1200 B.C.E.) most deserves the appellation "Canaanite." The period can thus be distinguished for two reasons: (1) The inhabitants of the country called themselves "Canaanites." Moreover, as contemporaneous documents attest, even foreigners referred to the country as "Canaan." (2) Scripture uses this name for the country prior to the coming of the Israelites; indeed, the country continued to be known as Canaan for many generations thereafter. With the Late Bronze Age we enter the horizon of "biblical archaeology." This is the period that illuminates the background of the biblical traditions on the Holy Land and its inhabitants just before the conquest and settlement by the Israelites. The number of historical records increases to such an extent that the period can be called the first historical period. Interest in archaeology and the Bible has always been a major driving force in archaeological research in the country. It is not surprising, therefore, that archaeological research on the Late Bronze Age since 1948 has been characterized by quantity rather than by new trends and innovations.

Settlement during the Late Bronze Age was quite sparse compared to that of the preceding period. The small, unfortified communities of the mountain areas disappeared, and permanent settlements became concentrated in the more fertile regions of the country.

The most important data relevant to the Late Bronze Age have been uncovered at Hazor, the largest city in Canaan at the time. Hazor dominated the entire Galilee area. Middle Bronze Age fortifications used at Hazor and those used at many other cities in Canaan were still used during the Late Bronze Age. This is

The Late Bronze Age orthostat temple from Hazor.

especially clear in the continuity of the location and design of the city gates, whose main feature was an entrance that allowed direct access into the city.

Hazor also provides us with our most complete picture of temples from this period. On the northern corner of the tell was a magnificent temple used throughout this period; it was originally built in an even earlier time—in the Middle Bronze period. At the height of its splendor, this temple was decorated with orthostats along its walls and columns and lion reliefs on either side of the entrance. Another temple, situated on the Acropolis, apparently joined the royal palace, while a third temple was much smaller and more modest, intended apparently for the local population. In general, Hazor's architecture and art strongly reflect the influence of central and northern Syria.

Remains at the Rabat-Ammon temple show that imports reached inland as far as eastern Transjordan, evidence of burgeoning trade with Cyprus and other foreign lands. Further witness to this trade are the flourishing harbor cities—for instance, Akko, Shikmonah and Ashdod. Modern, sophisticated neutron-activation techniques have shown that bichrome ware vessels, which were so widespread at the beginning of the Late Bronze Age, especially along the coastal regions, originated in Cyprus.

The cultural influence of Egypt, which ruled over the Land of Israel for this entire period, was especially noticeable in the south. At Timnah, the Egyptians utilized the copper mines in partnership with the Midianites (who came there from the Hejaz) and other local residents. At Timnah the Egyptians even built a temple to Hathor, the goddess of mines. Mining operations in this area continued from the reign of Seti I (beginning of the 13th century B.C.E.) until the reign of Ramesses V (mid-12th century B.C.E.). Ornamented and variegated pottery called ''Midianite'' has been found not only at Timnah but at more distant sites as well—at Tel Masos in the Negev, and even at Tell Gedor in the Judean Hills. The handmade ''Negev'' type of pottery is rare north of the Negev mountains; there,

The ''stele temple'' from the Late Bronze Age, uncovered at Hazor.

however, it was used throughout the Iron Age. In the sands of Deir el-Balah, on the southern border of Canaan, excavators unearthed a large town and an extensive cemetery containing many local, Egyptian and imported vessels. Anthropoid coffins, consistent with Egyptian custom, were also found there.

Evidence of Egyptian rule was also discovered in other places: the Egyptian citadel at Tell Mor; the temple and citadel at Tell Shera, where hieratic inscriptions were found; the Tel Lachish temple, which embodied Egyptian architectural features and contained hieratic inscriptions. A bronze cartouche of Ramesses III indicates that Egyptian rule over Lachish continued until the reign of that king (beginning of the 12th century B.C.E.). Ramesses II, Egypt's greatest 13th-century king, certainly left his mark in the Yarkon basin, for his seal is impressed on the Jaffa Gate. And in Aphek, archaeologists found the dedication plaque of a temple that Ramesses II erected to the goddess Isis.

Only one archive from the Late Bronze Age, a small one uncovered at Taanach at the turn of the century, has been found in the Land of Israel. However, many important documents have been discovered at a number of other sites. In addition to the Egyptian documents described above, we should mention the Akkadian documents found at Hazor and Aphek. Most important is the letter sent from Ugarit to a high Egyptian official at Aphek during the second half of the 13th century. This letter is the only direct synchronism between the two great powers of the period, Hati and Egypt. It throws light on the nature of the commercial relations between these two empires and dates the destruction of the Egyptian base at Aphek to c. 1240 B.C.E. Additional finds include documents written in alphabetic Ugaritic, documents in an as yet undeciphered script from Deir-Alahah and Aphek, and several inscriptions written in Proto-Canaanite.

The accumulated quantity of documents written in a variety of scripts, sometimes discovered lying side by side, has shed new light on the internationalism of the period that preceded as well as on the period that followed the El-Amarna archives.

As new data are gathered, the precise date of the destruction of the Late Bronze Age culture becomes easier to pinpoint. We can now say that both Jaffa and Aphek were destroyed at the end of the reign of Ramesses II (1240/30 B.C.E.) Deir-Alla was destroyed during the reign of Queen Twosre (approximately 1200 B.C.E.), at the earliest; and Lachish and Tell Shera (Ziklag?), during the reign of Ramesses III, at the earliest (1175 B.C.E.).

Concurrent with the destruction of Canaanite culture, Israelites and other peoples characterized by the culture of the Iron Age began settling in the Land. This settlement process had already begun by the 12th century—the Israelite Age was ushered in.

In the Days When the Judges Ruled— Research on the Period of the Settlement and the Judges

By Trude Dothan

During the second half of the 13th and the beginning of the 12th centuries B.C.E., a wave of destruction and decline swept over the lands bordering the Aegean Sea and the eastern Mediterranean. Great powers and small states alike succumbed. The Hittite kingdom in Anatolia collapsed. The states of the Syro-Canaanite coast were so sorely affected that some never recovered. Even Egypt weakened toward the end of the New Kingdom; except for a momentary revival during the 20th dynasty, she would never again be a major power in the region.

A principal, though not exclusive, reason for this fateful decline was the advent of the "Sea Peoples." After destroying extensive areas in the Aegean countries as well as on the Syrian and Canaanite coast, the Sea Peoples invaded Egypt. Although the Sea Peoples were initially successful, Egypt was to be the scene of their final defeat. A part of the Sea Peoples then settled in the southern coastal areas of Canaan.

These events profoundly altered the political and cultural make-up of the entire region. The Arameans descended into Canaan from the northeast and became a significant political force. Hebrews, Edomites, Moabites and Ammonites took possession of the eastern Transjordan.

During this period the main phase of the Israelite settlement of Canaan also occurred. The Israelite newcomers apparently united with Hebrew tribes that had been long-time inhabitants of the Promised Land.

The Israelite settlement required a prolonged and persistent struggle against the Canaanite city states. A few of these city states were able to retain their independence until Davidic times, but the rest succumbed to the Israelites earlier. This historical process surely included the use of force as well as peaceful settlement.

Clay anthropoid coffin **in situ** *at Deir el-Balah.*

Since the turn of this century, the sole purpose of many excavations has been to confirm the scriptural version of the Conquest and Settlement, reflecting early interest in this historical process. Since the founding of the State of Israel, interest in the earliest Israelite settlement of the Land understandably intensified.

Excavations led by Israeli archaeologists prior to the establishment of the State concentrated in the main either at sites belonging to later eras—for example, synagogues and cemeteries—or at sites dating to prehistoric or protohistoric epochs. Since 1948, however, the period of the Settlement and Judges has been a major focus and much basic work has been done.

It is interesting to note that patterns that later marked the subsequent settlement and material culture of the Israelites in the Land of Canaan are discernible in the very early period of the Settlement and Judges. Only after the process of settlement had been completed, however, did the divided and disparate elements in the country become consolidated into a unified political, ethnic and religous entity.

Before 1948, remains dating to this period were uncovered chiefly at large tells, such as Tell Beit Mirsim, Beth Shemesh, Beth El and Megiddo. Since the founding of the State, however, investigators have concentrated their efforts mostly on surveys and exploratory excavations, hoping in this way to get a better understanding of the *process* of settlement. Especially important in this connection is the work of the late Yohanan Aharoni at Kadesh and Tel Hareshim and his survey of the upper Galilee. At the same time, however, major excavations were conducted by others at key sites such as Tell Farah (North), Dan, and particularly Hazor. This combination of broad surveys and exploratory excavations with major site excavations has shed much new light on various phases of the Israelite settlement.

A number of scholars believe that the first wave of Hebrew tribes took possession of the Land as early as the second half of the 14th century. According to these scholars, this was especially true in mountainous regions like the Upper Galilee. The valleys, however, remained in Canaanite hands. The most important phase of the Settlement, according to this scenario, was the second wave of immigrants, who occupied the country during the latter half of the 13th century B.C.E. at the latest. Most Israelites then lived in small settlements that were organized along tribal and patriarchal lines. Their chief source of sustenance was pasturage and agriculture. Although their material culture was poor, as we know from finds both in surveys and in excavations, the Israelites nevertheless had a unique ceramic culture that enables us easily to distinguish their settlements from those of their Canaanite neighbors.

The surveys seem to suggest that at the same time Israelites were settling the northern part of the Land, there might have been a parallel Israelite settlement in the mountains of Ephraim and Benjamin. Sites like Izbet Sartah have allowed us to trace this settlement to the lower western slopes of Mt. Ephraim, to the area to the south, and to settlements in Benjamin. Moreover, in this area, we can quite clearly detect the transition from dwellings typical of the initial Settlement Period, mostly pit-dwellings, to the houses that characterized later Israelite history, specifically, the four-room house.

Hazor is the key site in our effort to understand the historical events associated with the process of settlement in the large Canaanite cities. The last Canaanite city at Hazor covered both the Upper City on the tell and the adjacent Lower City. Total destruction of both is recorded in stratum XIII at the site. The Lower City was never occupied again. On top of the ruins of the Upper City (stratum XII), which, incidentally, Yadin has identified with the Conquest of Joshua, we find a meager Israelite settlement. The finds indicate that the Israelite settlers were a semi-nomadic community. Their settlement here was contemporaneous with the small Israelite settlements from the end of the 13th and the beginning of the 12th centuries B.C.E. in the Galilee.

Lid of clay anthropoid coffin from Deir el-Balah.

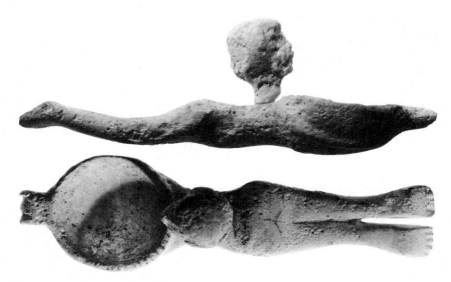

An alabaster cosmetic spoon shaped like a swimming girl, from Deir el-Balah.

Remains from stratum VI at Tel Dan attest to the nature of the Israelite settlement in the Canaanite city of Laish, following the migration of the Tribe of Dan from the coastal Plain. Most prominent in this stratum are the dwelling pits. The ceramic artifacts are varied and diverse.

The evidence is clear that all of the early Israelite settlements in the north were both small and unwalled. The structures, if we can call them that, in which the Israelites lived, were very modest, mostly pits. In the central region and in the Negev, on the other hand, we find the crystallization of the Israelite house-type: that is, the four-room house. Moreover, as can be seen at sites like Izbet Sartah, Tell Ashdod and Tell Masos, a kind of defensive wall was created by stringing the houses together in a circle to form what might be called a security cordon.

The pottery from the Israelite settlements in both the northern and central parts of the country includes some figurines, which seem basically to perpetuate local Canaanite traditions. No pottery imported from either Mycenae or Cyprus is found in the Israelite settlements. This is in striking contrast to pottery assemblages from earlier Canaanite settlements. Indeed, this imported pottery is now regarded as one of the distinguishing characteristics of the preceding period, the Late Bronze Age. In Iron I, we find jugs and jars with decorated necks instead, which seem to be especially characteristic of Israelite pottery. Pottery from the Negev settlement sites, however, more nearly resembles the earthenware previously prevalent in the region.

We should also mention the presence of a metal industry, particularly of bronze, at Israelite settlements such as Tel Hareshim and Khirbet Radana. Iron artifacts also appear sporadically, for example at Mt. Adir. There is some evidence for the use of alphabetic writing, apparently a continuation of the Proto-Canaanite script. An abecedarium, or alphabet, was discovered in one of the storage pits at Izbet Sartah. A few letters on pottery from Khirbet Radana tend to confirm the use of alphabetic writing.

As noted earlier, the Philistine occupation of Canaan occurred more or less simultaneously with the main wave of the Israelite Settlement. Excavations and surveys prior to 1948 helped scholars discriminate between the various phases of

Philistine settlement and to understand the evolution of their material culture within the wider context of historical events in the eastern Mediterranean and particularly in the Land of Israel. Research since 1948 has added substantially to our knowledge and has broadened our understanding of certain facets of Philistine settlement and culture. Two sites in Israel's coastal region are especially important: Tell Qasile, on the Yarkon River on Philistia's northern border, and Ashdod in central Philistia. (See "What We Know About the Philistines," *Biblical Archaeology Review,* July/August 1982.)

At Tell Qasile—site of the very first excavation to be conducted after the establishment of the State of Israel—archaeologists sought to establish an exact stratigraphical sequence of the Philistine strata (strata X, XI and XII), and the chronology of the sequence. Tell Qasile was founded by these "Sea Peoples," apparently during the first quarter of the 12th century B.C.E. The remains of this city reflect a sophisticated urban organization as well as a comprehensive and precise plan for residential areas, industrial sections and religious quarters. The variety of finds at Tell Qasile reflects not only the beginning of Philistine culture but also its consolidation.

Yet, as early as the second half of the 11th century B.C.E., we notice a new development in the northern provinces, reflected in ceramics and cult objects that differ from artifacts discovered at Ashdod in central Philistia.

Ashdod alone among the cities of the Philistine pentapolis mentioned in the Bible has been excavated in a sufficiently large area to establish a stratigraphical sequence. Finds from Ashdod reflect the process of Philistine settlement and subsequent establishment of the city, which arose on the ruins of an earlier Canaanite city. Stratum XIII—the first Philistine city—revealed the remnants of an unwalled settlement that differed significantly from the late Canaanite city immediately beneath it. Not only was stratum XIII a smaller settlement than the Canaanite city, it also reflected an entirely different material culture. The typical pottery in the Philistine city, for example, was a late Mycenaean type, resembling the ceramic style common to the eastern Mediterranean Basin and the Aegean Sea region following the destruction of Mycenaean civilization. Remains from the stratum XII city, which was also Philistine, testify to a quiet transition from one city to the next.

Apparently, Ashdod was occupied by the same Philistines who were defeated by Ramesses III in 1190 B.C.E. A strongly fortified and well-planned Philistine city existed at the site for several generations. Here, we encounter for the first time a mode of worship that was clearly inspired by the cult of the great Mycenaean Mother Goddess.

The Philistine city in the next layer (stratum XI) is still not as large as the city in stratum X, which branches out a considerable distance from the acropolis. The stratum X city was fortified with a massive wall and gate that, the excavators discovered, surrounded a Lower City too. The material culture of the stratum X city no longer bears the characteristics of the original Philistine traditions. The stratum X city, during the peak of Philistine power in the second half of the 11th century B.C.E. has assimilated local cultural elements instead.

The principal phase of Philistine settlement—reflected in stratum XII at Ashdod and in stratum XII at Tell Qasile—is now thoroughly understood as a result of research on the finds at these two sites and in surveys in the coastal plain. These excavations and explorations have demonstrated that even in the initial stage of their occupation, the Philistines exerted influence far beyond Philistia proper; indeed, this influence reached as far as Tell Masos in the southeast and Tel Dan in the north.

The earliest settlements that can definitely be associated with the Philistines are

General view of the Late Bronze Age settlement beneath the sand dunes at Deir el-Balah.

located chiefly on the southern coast of Israel and in the coastal plain. Because the road to and from Egypt passed through this area, it was naturally regarded as important strategically as well as commercially. The densely populated area the Philistines encountered upon their arrival was hardly monolithic. The various settlements they found there differed from one another in size, in material culture, and in the way they functioned. Stratigraphic analysis of these Philistine sites, together with surveys of the area, have enabled us to trace the evolution of Philistine settlement.

The principal wave of Philistine occupation, and the period during which Philistine culture exerted its maximum influence, occurred after the crushing defeat of the "Sea Peoples" by Ramesses III in 1190 B.C.E. At this same time, the invaders became established in Philistia—which stretched from the northwestern Negev to the Yarkon River, and from the Mediterranean to the western slopes of Judah—and established their league of cities. At first this alliance comprised only Gaza, Ashkelon and Ashdod, but later it included Ekron and Gath as well—the so-called Philistine pentapolis. At several sites in Philistia—for example, Ashkelon, Tell Jemmeh, Tel Sippor and Tell Gerisa—the Philistine settlement continued to thrive even after the destruction of the Late Bronze Age cities.

The Egyptians played a significant role in this settlement process. As is well-known, for example, the Philistines in certain cities served as mercenaries for the Egyptians, but despite the different character of these settlements (for instance, Deir el-Balah, Tell Mor and Tell Farah (South) in Philistia, and Lachish and Gezer on its borders, as well as Beth Shean and Megiddo in the north), all of these settlements had two things in common: the perennial Egyptian presence and a newly acquired ethnic element (i.e., the Philistines).

Toward the end of the main phase of Philistine settlement, the conquerors' pottery reached sites far beyond Philistia itself. Philistine pottery has been found at such Israelite settlements as Tell Masos, Izbet Sartah, Tell Qiri, Hazor and Dan. This does not necessarily imply Philistine occupation at these sites, but merely that commercial or military ties were maintained between these Israelite cities and Philistine cities.

The next phase of Philistine settlement, which occurred during the latter part of the 12th and the 11th centuries B.C.E., saw an expansion of Philistine hegemony to its greatest extent. In addition to the information we have from a large number of sites in Philistia itself, we also have evidence of Philistine control, or at least influence, in the northern Negev, and in certain parts of the territories of Simon, Judah and Dan. At Dor, pottery that can be identified with the Tjekker, one of the constituent groups of the "Sea Peoples" mentioned in the Egyptian Tale of Wen-Amun, was discovered dating to this phase. Near Dor, at Tell Zeror, excavators found Philistine pottery from the 11th century B.C.E., as well as metal artifacts that should probably be associated with the culture of the western Mediterranean.

Precisely during this period of great Philistine expansion, Philistine culture began to intermix with that of the local population, as can be seen in stratum X at Ashdod and stratum X at Tell Qasile. This period of expansion ended during King David's reign, when Philistine settlements were restricted to the southern coastal regions of Canaan.

Archaeological Research on the Period of the Monarchy (Iron Age II)

By Amihai Mazar

Excavations between the two World Wars at Samaria, Megiddo, Lachish, Tell en-Nasbeh, Beth Shemesh, Tell Beit Mirsim, and elsewhere laid the foundations for the archaeological research on the Period of the Monarchy (Iron Age II) in the Land of Israel. These excavations and the subsequent studies provided much basic data regarding the Israelite culture of this period. From them we learned about urban planning, fortification systems, the architectural styles of both public and private buildings, and the evolution of the pottery industry as well as other small craft industries. Since 1948, archaeological research of this period has gathered considerable momentum. Many sites hitherto unknown were excavated systematically using the new methodologies that have been developed. The research expanded to include geographical regions that previously had been neglected, like Upper Galilee, Philistia, the Negev and the Judean Desert. In addition to the excavations, archaeological surveys added vast new data concerning the pattern of settlement during this period. In the following paper we will discuss some of the major achievements of the research since the modern state of Israel was founded.

I. The United Kingdom

The Bible describes David's 40-year rule in several lengthy chapters. Ironically enough, despite David's major conquests and the consequent founding of the Israelite empire, we have very few archaeological remains from the Davidic period. There are no monuments that can positively be identified as Davidic. The late Professor Yohanan Aharoni suggested that the city gates at Dan and Beersheba as well as the two "palaces" built of ashlar masonry in stratum V (IVB-VA) at Megiddo should be ascribed to David's reign. This thesis failed to win much support, however, for the proof was quite weak.

In fact, the meager archaeological finds from this period should not be surprising. This was essentially a time of war and the establishment of a seminal royal apparatus rather than a time of extensive royal building. In the more peaceful Solomonic era that followed, on the other hand, scripture emphasizes Solomon's various building activities both inside and outside Jerusalem.

The detailed biblical descriptions of Solomon's various buildings in Jerusalem have always presented a special challange to archaeologists. Although no actual remains of these buildings have been found, various scholars have suggested reconstructions based on comparisons to other monumental structures found in Israel and Syria.

Although archaeological remains from the Solomonic era are not numerous, what has been discovered is of great interest, especially when set beside the biblical text. Before 1948, some suggested that the remains of two major groups of buildings were Solomonic: (1) the complex of buildings in stratum IV at Megiddo, including the solid wall, the six-chambered gate, and the cluster of buildings that the excavators had suggested were royal stables; and (2) the building complex at Etzion-Geber (Tell el-Khaleifah) excavated by Nelson Glueck, and interpreted by him as Solomon's copper refineries. Israeli scholars have revolutionized our views on these subjects.

Aerial photograph of the strata from the Period of the Monarchy at Hazor's Area A.

The excavations at Hazor between 1954 and 1958, and in 1968, demonstrated that the city was built anew during Solomonic times after a long period of abandonment. During the Solomonic period the city was circumvallated by a casemate wall and was entered through a six-chambered gate identical in plan and measurement to the gate found in stratum IV at Megiddo. Following this discovery, and in the light of the statement in the Bible that Solomon built cities at Hazor, Megiddo and Gezer (1 Kings 9:15), Yadin returned to Megiddo and closely examined the buildings there. His exploratory excavations (in which he was assisted by the architect I. Dunayevsky) led him to suggest a new interpretation for the development of Israelite Megiddo. The offset-inset wall and the stables previously attributed to Solomon's time were now pushed forward to the ninth century B.C.E., to the time of King Ahab, while a newly discovered palace (building 6000) was attributed to King Solomon's time, together with another palace excavated in the 1930s. The Solomonic city was fortified, according to this suggestion, by a casemate wall related to the early phase of the six-chambered gate.

Following his work at Hazor and Megiddo, Yadin proposed that the "Hasmonean Fortress" uncovered by Macalister at Gezer at the beginning of this century is, in fact, part of a Solomonic six-chambered gate to which a casemate wall was joined. This proposal was later confirmed by the American expedition at Gezer digging under the auspices of the Hebrew Union College. This expedition unearthed the entire Solomonic gate and positively established its date. Today this is one of the most impressive architectural remains from the period of the United Kingdom.

The Solomonic "palace 6000" that Yadin excavated at Megiddo was built on the "Hilani Building" plan, a typical Syrian Iron Age palace plan. D. Ussishkin has proposed that the southern palace at Megiddo excavated in the 1930s was built according to a similar plan. All of this seems to point to cultural relations between Israel and the Aramean and Neo-Hittite cities of northern Syria. The two Megiddo palaces are the earliest examples of Israelite monumental buildings built of ashlar masonry and decorated with beautifully carved "Proto-Aeolic" stone capitals. This characteristic royal architectural style continued to be used in the kingdoms of both Judah and Israel after the division of the United Kingdom.

Archaeological research in the Negev has changed previous conclusions. Beno Rothenberg's work at Timnah and new analyses of the Tell el-Khaleifah finds have demonstrated that Nelson Glueck's identification of "King Solomon's mines" located in the Aravah was mistaken. The archaeological remains found at Timnah actually belonged to Egyptian mines from the New Kingdom (13th to 12th centuries B.C.E.), while the finds at Tell el-Khaleifah should probably be dated to a later phase of the Iron Age and are not related to copper industry in any way. Extensive exploration of the central Negev mountains, north of Machtesh Ramon, revealed, however, a net of small settlements with eitherfortresses or large fortified central buildings.

Excavations at several sites, such as Ramat Matred, Atar Haro'ah, Horvat Halukim, Horvat Retamah and Ein Qadesh, have demonstrated that they were established either at the end of the 11th century B.C.E. or at the beginning of the 10th century. Shortly afterward, however, they were destroyed.

Scholarly opinion is divided as to the historical context in which these settlements were established and the cause of their destruction. B. Rothenberg and A. Negev argue that they were established by nomadic tribes like the Amalekites who inhabited the Negev and were destroyed in the wars Saul and David fought against these tribes. Y. Aharoni, on the other hand, argued that these sites were established by the Israelites as a result of their need to expand geographically during the latter part of the period of the Judges. B. Mazar, R. Cohen and Z. Meshel believe that these Negev sites were established as a result of royal Israelite initiative to settle the Negev during the United Kingdom. Some think that this expansion southward began as early as Saul's reign, while others insist that it began later, in the time of either David or Solomon.

The relationship between the establishment of these settlements and Solomon's trade with southern Arabia by way of Etzion-Geber is still unclear. Most scholars do see a connection, however, between the destruction of these settlements and the Egyptian Pharaoh Shishak's campaign in the fifth year of Rehoboam's reign. Shishak's march into the southern part of the country was undoubtedly aimed at the destruction of this system of forts and settlements, which had been established throughout the Negev by the Israelite kingdom. This is clearly demonstrated by the fact that many of these Negev sites are probably specifically mentioned in Shishak's monumental victory inscription at Karnak.

II. The Divided Kingdom

The material culture of Israel following the division of the United Kingdom can be divided into a number of regional geopolitical units: Judah, the Northern Kingdom of Israel, Phoenicia, Philistia and the Transjordanian kingdoms of Moab, Ammon and Edom. Obviously, these different material cultures have much in common, yet modern research has made great advances in identifying the unique aspects of each. We shall briefly examine the new data.

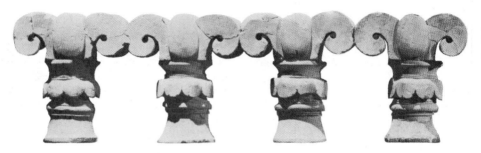

Stone parapet of window from Ramat Rahel.

A. Judah

Since 1948, a number of excavations have been carried out within the boundaries of the ancient Kingdom of Judah, answering several basic questions that had remained unsolved from the previous generation of research and opening new horizons for research in previously unexplored areas, especially the Judean Desert and the Negev.

Jerusalem, the capital of Judah, has naturally been a focus for intensive archaeological work, which is summarized elsewhere in this book. Here we should mention the important site of Ramat Rahel, south of Jerusalem, where Aharoni exposed a palace-citadel built by one of the kings of Judah. This imposing building stands isolated in the middle of a fortified area covering the top of a hill overlooking the Judean mountains. It is a rectangular building circumvallated by a casemate wall. Inside is a large courtyard and various other structures. The architecture is superior. Some of the walls are built of hewn ashlar stones like those in the royal palace at Samaria dating to the reigns of Omri and Ahab. The Proto-Aeolic capitals at Ramat Rahel are a local variant of the style used in northern cities of the kingdom, like Samaria, Megiddo and Hazor. Fragments of a unique window balustrade repeat a window design depicted on Phoenician ivories. The precise nature of the building and its exact date are a question of debate. The excavator suggested that the building was constructed during the latter part of the period and identified it with the palace of Jehoiakim described by the prophet Jeremiah (22:13-19). Y. Yadin suggested a much earlier date (see below). The evidence is rather complicated, since many stamped jar handles of the *lmlk* type (see below)

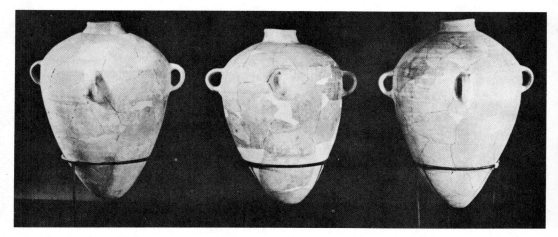

Three jars from eighth-century B.C.E. Lachish, on whose handles "lmlk" is inscribed.

were found in the fill of the building's main courtyard pavement, thus suggesting that the building had two major construction phases. Because the jar handles have now been clearly dated to the time of Hezekiah, the later construction phase must be dated to the seventh century B.C.E. The nature and date of the earlier phase of this important site has yet to be investigated.

D. Ussishkin's continuing excavations at Lachish have resolved some of the major questions left from previous excavations of this important Judean city. The destruction of stratum III has now been securely dated to 701 B.C.E., when the city was sacked by Sennacherib. This conclusion seems to end a long debate on the chronology of the site, which is of great importance to our understanding of the archaeology of Judah in general. The date of the sealed jars of the *lmlk* type, bearing royal seal impressions, was also fixed. Previously the seal impressions had been divided into three types and attributed to different periods. The new excavations make clear that all the types were used simultaneously during the reign of Hezekiah, on the very eve of the rebellion against Assyria. The evidence from the Lachish excavations is unequivocal and relegates to irrelevance a whole array of previous studies based either on the erroneous assumption that stratum III had been destroyed during Nebuchadnezzar's campaign against Judah in the days of Jehoiakin (597 B.C.E.), or on the assumption that the various *lmlk* seal impressions were not used simultaneously.

The new finds also throw some light on the nature of the *lmlk* jars themselves, as well as on the seal impressions. It seems to me that the great number of these jars found at Lachish, running into the hundreds, were produced and sealed as part of Hezekiah's preparations for his revolt against Assyria. That is, the jars were used to store huge amounts of food for the troubled times ahead that the Judean king tried to anticipate. The storage jars were probably assembled in four different administrative districts as reflected by the names of the four cities referred to in the impressions: Hebron, Ziph, Sochoh and Mmsht. The filled jars would be sent to their destination, where the front against the Assyrian army could be expected to be located: Jerusalem and its vicinity, and the Shephelah. Indeed, most of the sealed jars discovered so far were found in destruction levels caused by the Assyrian devastation of Judah. Thus at Tel Batash—biblical Timnah—in the northern Shephelah we found many *lmlk* jars in a destruction level caused by Sennacherib's invasion of the city, which is mentioned in his annals. The few cities not destroyed during Sennacherib's campaign—most prominently Jerusalem—probably continued to use these jars in royal warehouses, perhaps even during the seventh century B.C.E. This accounts for the sporadic appearance of *lmlk* seal impressions at various sites in occupation levels dating to the latter part of the Monarchy.

Another important achievement of the Lachish excavations was the recovery of the city gate of stratum III, a small part of which had been previously exposed by the British expedition in the 1930s. The gate has six chambers and therefore resembles the Solomonic gates at Hazor, Megiddo and Gezer, although it is larger than any of these. It appears to have been built in the post-Solomonic era, possibly during the reign of Rehoboam who, according to the Bible, fortified Lachish (2 Chronicles 11:9).The gate continued to be used until the destruction of the city by Sennacherib.

The acropolis of Lachish was also investigated by the Israeli expedition. East of the huge palace-fortress explored by the British expedition, the Israeli excavators identified a large rectangular compound, surrounded probably by a stable or storage buildings. West of the palace-fortress a very massive wall separated the northern part of the mound from its southern part, probably dividing the city into various zones with separate functions. Outside the city exposed by the excavators they found the remains of the only Assyrian siege rampart known thus far anywhere in the Assyrian empire.

Excavations in the Judean Desert and in the northern Negev have given us a comprehensive picture of the material culture of these areas during the Monarchy. During the 1960s, B. Mazar, working at Tel Goren in the Ein Gedi oasis on the shore of the Dead Sea, uncovered an Israelite city established toward the end of the Monarchy, probably during Josiah's reign. Among the finds were workshops for the production of the spices for which Ein Gedi was noted. Smaller Iron Age sites have been discovered elsewhere in the Judean Desert—along the northern shore of the Dead Sea, in the Bukiah Valley, and between the Dead Sea and Jerusalem. All point to economic and military activity in the desert during the last decades of the Judean Kingdom.

The extensive excavations and surveys conducted for 15 years by Y. Aharoni in the Beersheba and Arad regions of the northern Negev contributed much new material to the study of the archaeology of Judah. In the course of his detailed surveys, many previously unknown settlements were discovered, such as the fortified city of Tell Ira (Khirbet A'arah) as well as the Israelite citadel at Khirbet Uzza. Extensive excavations were conducted at the royal citadels of Tel Arad and Tel Beersheba, and more limited excavations were conducted at other sites, such as Tel Malhata and Tel Masos in the Beersheba Valley. At Arad, almost the entire massive royal citadel, comprising six strata, was excavated. The crowning achievement of this dig was the discovery of dozens of Hebrew letters inscribed on potsherds, the largest collection of ostraca yet found in the Land of Israel.

At Beersheba, Aharoni excavated almost in its entirety an Israelite provincial administrative center. The city has a circular plan which covers 16 dunams (four acres). Four separate strata reflect alternate destruction and rebuilding from the United Kingdom until the final destruction of the city, which, according to Aharoni, occurred during Sennacherib's Judean campaign of 701 B.C.E. The two older strata (IV-V) were fortified with a solid wall; the two later strata (II-III) by a casemate wall that was reinforced with an earthworks rampart. The chambers in the wall were joined to the line of houses built on the inside of the wall. In front of these houses ran a circular road from which other streets radiated toward the city center. Other Judean cities, such as Tell en-Nasbeh (Mispah), Beth Shemesh, and

Aerial photograph of Tell Beersheba, with a view of the remains from the Period of the Monarchy.

Tell Beit Mirsim, had a similar plan. Apparently, this was the characteristic city plan for Judean cities during the Monarchy. The Beersheba excavation also uncovered a city gate, flanked by towers, that held four guardrooms. On the inside of the gate was a public square, near which was a complex of royal storehouses. The storehouses reflect the importance of the city for the royal administration of the Negev region.

Unique archaeological evidence for Israelite religious practices discovered at Beersheba and Arad has aroused considerable interest. At Arad a local temple was unearthed. In the courtyard a sacrificial altar was revealed; the temple itself consisted of one broad room with a niche used as a holy of holies, containing a sacred stone (*massebah*) and two small altars. At Beersheba, hewn stones from a monumental sacrificial altar were found in secondary use inside walls of the last Israelite city. They originated in an altar which was in use in one of the earlier phases of the city's history.

Naturally, these unique discoveries relating to Judean cult practices led scholars to suggest various interpretations of the finds. Thus, B. Mazar suggested that the building of the temple of Arad was associated with the wanderings of the descendants of Hovav the Kenite, Moses' father-in-law. "The descendants of [Hovav] the Kenite, Moses' father-in-law, went with the Judahites from the City of Palms to the wilderness of Judah, which is south of Arad" (Judges 1:16). Aharoni proposed that the destruction of the Arad temple was the result of the religious reforms of Josiah and that the Beersheba altar was torn down during Hezekiah's religious reforms a century earlier. Aharoni found parallels to the architecture of the Arad temple in the scriptural specifications for the wilderness Tabernacle and for Solomon's Temple in Jerusalem. He also suggested a location for a hypothetical temple that once, so he thought, stood at Beersheba yet was totally obliterated during Hezekiah's religious reform. Yadin, however, suggested an alternative chronology for the Beersheba strata and attempted to locate the high place destroyed by Josiah at this city. In spite of the sometimes imaginative character of the interpretations, there is no doubt that Aharoni's discoveries opened a new chapter in the research of the northern Negev and of the material culture of Judah in general.

Research in the Negev has recently intensified. The excavations at Aroer, directed by A. Biran and R. Cohen, revealed a fortified desert town dating to the seventh century B.C.E. including objects that reflect contact with Edom during this period. Intensive excavations at Kadesh Barnea, the oasis on the border between Sinai and the Negev, directed by R. Cohen, revealed the continuous history of this important Israelite fortress throughout the period of the Kingdom. The interrelations between the Israelites and the desert nomads is reflected here in the mixture of "northern" type and local "Negev" ware, produced probably by the nomads. A sophisticated planning and water system turned this site into one of the mightiest Israelite fortresses known so far.

The most exciting discovery in the area was made at the remote Israelite site of Kuntillet-Ajrud, located between Kadesh-Barnea and Eilat. Z. Meshel uncovered a citadel-like structure here with a central courtyard around which was a series of rooms. The entrance was through a broad room with plastered benches. The building yielded an abundance of finds, including numerous pottery vessels and everyday articles, some made of well-preserved organic material such as a sieve made of animal sinew and date palm fiber, fragments of cloth and various foodstuffs. The most significant discovery, however, was the collection of Hebrew inscriptions written in ink on wall plaster and on large pottery jars, as well as a number of ink drawings. The site was apparently destroyed toward the end of the ninth or beginning of the eighth century B.C.E. The obvious cultic nature of the epigraphic material indicates that the place must have had some religious importance, but the interpretation of the inscriptions is still subject to discussion. The pottery and the artistic motifs on the large storage jars reflect a mixture of cultural elements originating in Judah, Israel and Phoenicia.

Research in the Judean heartland—that is, the Hebron and Jerusalem mountains, and the Shephelah—has been more limited. In addition to the exploration of Jerusalem and its vicinity and to the Lachish excavations, various surveys have discovered a number of new sites. This has demonstrated the density of settlement in Judah during the last two centuries of the First Temple Period. Various citadels and forts discovered in the Judean mountains might well be the "fortresses and towers" built in Judah by Jehosaphat and Jotham (2 Chronicles 17:12; 27:4). One of these citadels, located at Khirbet Abu et-Twein, west of Kfar-Etzion, was excavated by the author.

B. The Kingdom of Israel

The important aspects of the material culture of the kingdom of Israel were familiar to us before 1948 principally from the excavations at Samaria and Megiddo. Since 1948, however, important excavations have been conducted at two cities in the northern part of the kingdom of Israel: Hazor and Dan. The Hazor excavations revealed a great amount of material concerning the development of the city from Solomonic times until its destruction by Tiglath-Pileser III in 732 B.C.E. During Ahab's reign (mid-ninth century), the area of the city expanded to twice the size of the Solomonic Period city. Strong walls now encircled the new section of the city. In the west end of the mound, a large, well-planned citadel was built. The gate of this citadel was ornamented with Proto-Aeolic capitals. Massive communal storehouses and granaries were also built at this time, and an impressive water tunnel was dug, evidence of considerable engineering skill and hydrological knowledge. The excavators were able to synchronize the destruction of

Aerial view of ninth-century B.C.E. waterworks at Hazor. Note the access building above the shaft and the steps around the shaft.

several occupation levels from the ninth to eighth centuries B.C.E. with known historical events. This, in turn, provided a basis for understanding the development of the material culture of the northern part of the country and especially of its pottery. In Hazor's last phase, just before its destruction by the Assyrians, several houses that had been built against the citadel were torn down, and a solid wall was built on the site of the former residences to reinforce the city's fortifications. Despite these defensive measures, however, the city could not withstand the onslaught of Assyria's siege machines. Following their conquest of the city, the Assyrians completely destroyed it and then built an administrative fortress on its ruins.

During the course of eleven years of excavations at Tel Dan, A. Biran exposed two groups of monumental buildings from the Israelite Period. The city gates and walls were uncovered in the southern part of the tell. The lower gate is one of the handsomer examples of an Israelite gate with its various installations. A decorated structure in the open space in front of the gate may have had some cultic function, or, as the excavator himself proposed, it could have been a base for a canopy used by judges or rulers sitting in the gate square. This open square must have had an important function in the city's daily life. The plan of the gate and the ornamentation of the small structure in the gate area show clear North Syrian artistic traditions, characteristic of the Neo-Hittite cities of this region.

The most interesting discovery at Tel Dan is the sacred precinct, which may be identified with the sacred area erected by Jeroboam I at Dan, where he placed one of the golden calves. This sacred precinct had a complicated architectural history. During its main construction phase, probably in the ninth century B.C.E., it was built of ashlar stones, in the characteristic Israelite royal style. The precinct included a square courtyard surrounded by walls with a sacrificial altar inside; north of this precinct a large rectangular platform was erected, ascended by a flight of steps. The excavator thought that this platform remained open to the sky, a kind of open cult place (*bamah*), while others claim that the platform was just the foundation of a large temple.

Several excavations at minor sites produced important data concerning daily life in the northern kingdom of Israel. Of these, we should mention the tenth-century village at Tel Amal, the fortified town at Ein Gev, the port town of Shikmonah (near Haifa), and a series of sites along the Sharon valley (Tel Zeror, Tel Mevorakh, Tell Qasile, Aphek).

In addition to the Israeli research, considerable important data concerning the Kingdom of Israel was added by foreign expeditions working in Jordan prior to 1967, and in Israel. Of these the excavations of Taanach, Tel Dothan, Tell Farah (Tirzah), Shechem, Gibeon and Gezer added much to our knowledge of city planning, the art of fortification and water systems of Israelite cities. Studies in pottery typology and of other artifacts coming from these excavations added new horizons to the archaeological study of this heartland of the Israelite kingdom. Israeli research in this area since 1967 has been limited mainly to extensive surface surveys, which revealed dozens of previously unknown sites. Some of these sites were excavated and revealed some new phenomena, like circular isolated defensive towers, rural architecture and agricultural installations.

III. Israel's Neighbors

A. Philistia

Research since 1948 on Iron Age II Philistine material culture has seen important breakthroughs, pincipally thanks to M. Dothan's excavations at Ashdod. During the tenth century B.C.E. the city expanded to about 400 dunams (100 acres) and became one of the largest independent city states in Philistia. The city gate was uncovered in the excavations. In its fully developed phase it resembled the six-chambered Solomonic gates at Hazor, Megiddo and Gezer as well as Lachish. Like the Lachish gate, the one at Ashdod remained in use until the capture of the city by the Assyrians in 714 B.C.E. Sargon II, king of Assur, celebrated this capture on a victory stele, fragments of which were found during the excavations. Ashdod's material culture in the eighth to ninth centuries B.C.E. is unique and is epitomized by the pottery and pottery figurines of a peculiarly local style. During this period, Ashdod was a city-state with a king of its own, like its neighbors Gaza, Ashkelon and Ekron (Tel Miqneh).

Finds from Philistia's minor cities have also revealed much of its material culture. At Ashdod-Yam, the harbor city of the Ashdod metropolis, J. Kaplan discovered the city's ancient earth ramparts. This city is mentioned in the description of Sargon's campaign against Ashdod in 713/712 B.C.E., mounted because its local ruler, Yamani, had revolted against Assyrian hegemony. Timnah, a city within the boundaries of greater Ekron, to which reference is made both in scripture and in the annals of Sennacherib's devastating 701 B.C.E. campaign, is identified with Tel Batash in Nahal Sorek. Excavations at this site during the past decade, conducted by G. L. Kelm and the author, have unearthed the city gate and walls and several dwellings. The last phase of this city dates to the seventh century B.C.E., when it was restored after the destruction by Sennacherib. At Tell Ser'a (Ziklag?) in the southeast corner of Philistia, E. Oren uncovered tenth-century residential

General view of gates from the Period of the Monarchy uncovered at Tel Batash.

houses and sections of two large buildings built of ashlar stones and wooden beams. R. Gofna's surveys in southern Philistia brought to light many small settlements also dating to the tenth century. These discoveries attest to the flourishing of Philistia during this period. On the coast, north of Ashdod, at a site named Mesad Hashavyahu, J. Naveh discovered a well-planned fortress dating to the late seventh century B.C.E. A long Hebrew inscription found at this site indicates Israelite presence, while Greek-Oriental decorated pottery sherds indicate that Greek mercenary forces may have been stationed at the site. Perhaps this fortress was built when the kingdom of Judah was expanding towards the Mediterranean coast during the reign of Josiah.

B. Phoenicia

The boundaries of the present State of Israel include the southern edge of the ancient Phoenician coast, where Phoenician culture thrived during the Iron Age. Near Tell Achziv, one of the most important Phoenician sites in the region, I. Ben-Dor and M. Prausnitz unearthed Phoenician burial fields rich in finds. These burial fields comprised both familial burial caves and unique burial jars containing the ashes of the deceased. Remains of meals eaten in honor of the dead were also found. Other important Phoenician finds were discovered at Tel Kisan, Shikmonah and Tel Mevorakh, all along the northern coastal plain of Israel. These finds can be integrated with finds in Lebanon (Tyre and Sarepta) and Cyprus (Salamis and Kition) to provide a new picture of the development of the Phoenician culture.

IV. The Period of Assyrian Rule

The effect of Assyrian rule on the northern part of the country and on the coastal plain, beginning in the late eighth century B.C.E. constitutes a special chapter in Iron Age archaeology of Israel. Several sites yielded remains typical of this period. At Hazor, the Assyrian rulers built a new fortress on top of the devastated Israelite fortress. The new fortress on the peak of the tell was built in Assyrian style, with chambers arranged along the four sides of a large inner courtyard. At the foot of the mound, a large building excavated years ago was recently identified by R. Reich as part of a large Assyrian residency. Two large Assyrian buildings were discovered in the northern Negev—at Tell Jemmeh and at Tell Ser'a. The building at Tell Jemmeh, excavated by G. van Beek, includes unique brick vaults, while the building at Tell Ser'a is a large military fortress. Both buildings point to the Assyrians' powerful military hold along Nahal Gerar at the edge of the northern Negev. All these sites, along with those in the Judean mountains, yielded delicate Assyrian pottery vessels that local potters had copied from Assyrian palaceware.

V. Methodological Problems

One of the more difficult problems in the study of the Iron Age of Israel, as in any archaeological venture, results from the time gap between the actual dig and the publication of its results. The minute examination of the finds, the processing of the material for publication and the composition of the final report necessarily constitute an exhausting and prolonged process. Sometimes the project continues for many years; indeed, on some rare occasions the full report is never published at all! The delay in publication of finds creates a gap between the achievements in the field and the up-to-date synthesis and interpretation of the finds. New methods to deal with the masses of material must be developed, so that we can provide scholars with the full results of a given excavation as quickly as possible.

In the final phase of archaeological research the finds are integrated into the fabric of current knowledge of the culture and history of the particular period involved. This stage of the research has its own far-from-simple problems, for despite scholars' diligent efforts to make research methodologies precise, archaeology is still far from being an exact science. Scholarly conclusions often depend on subjective—sometimes even speculative—interpretations. Most of the controversies concerning our period involve this phase of interpretation, especially in the area of relating the archaeological finds to written sources, in particular to the biblical sources. Such were the debates between Yadin and Aharoni on a series of major topics in the archaeology of the period of the Monarchy, such as the interpretation of the finds at Megiddo, the stratigraphy of the last phase of the Arad fortress, the dating of the last phase of the city at Beersheba, the location of the sacred place in that city, and the dating and interpretation of the large building at Ramat Rahel.

The lack of any objective criteria to aid in the confirmation of the various theories posited (especially dated epigraphic material) inevitably invites contradictory interpretations of a given find. Ultimately, it is the scholar's mastering of the archaeological finds themselves or of the pertinent biblical or external sources that necessarily determines the validity of his or her interpretation. Unfortunately, although our information has greatly increased, the archaeologist's way of thinking about these issues has changed hardly at all since the 1930s. On too many occasions the relationship between the archaeological finds and the written sources is based on intuition rather than on facts. Some solution to this problem may be achieved in the future by refining our methods of analysis of the finds, particularly of pottery, which comprises the bulk of the finds in any excavation. Unfortunately, methodological difficulties complicate this area of research. The evolution of pottery vessels within individual geopolitical units was a slow process. Thus, for example, the development of the pottery style in ninth- to seventh-century B.C.E. Judah was slow and therefore difficult to trace in detail. It is a simple task, however, to differentiate between a cache of pottery originating in Judah and a contemporaneous one from the northern kingdom of Israel. We should persevere, however, in our attempts to investigate the slow but definite changes that occur in the pottery of each geopolitical entity, by constructing a series of exact typologies and by using quantitative analysis. Overcoming these difficulties is important for the application of archaeological data derived in the Land of Israel to research in other countries. For instance, the chronologies of Iron Age Cyprus and of Greece depend to a large extent on the dating of certain archaeological strata in Israel.

VI. What Distinguishes the Material Culture of the Land of Israel During the Iron Age?

During the period of the Israelite monarchy most of the Hebrew Bible was written. The term "People of the Book" may be applied to the Israelites of this period more than in any other period. Did these people have any unique Israelite material culture at this time? Were the Israelites creative in the material realm as well as in the spiritual? When we glance at the material remains left by Israel's neighbors—the Aramean and Neo-Hittite kingdoms of Syria, the Phoenicians in Cyprus and in their various overseas colonies, and especially those dominant powers, Assyria and Babylon—we realize that the extant material remains in the Land of Israel are poor indeed by comparison. In Israelite sites dating to the Period of the Monarchy we never encounter statues or monumental reliefs. Neither do we find magnificent palaces or delicately carved ivories, jewelry, or skillfully crafted metal objects or vessels of local manufacture. In fact, the vast majority of art objects discovered in the Land of Israel were imported. Admittedly, scripture does make reference to certain precious treasures in Jerusalem and Samaria, but we have as yet only been able to trace a few isolated items, such as a group of ivories in Samaria discovered in the 1930s.

The material culture of the kingdoms of Judah and Israel as archaeology has revealed it to us is, in the main, the everyday sort of culture typical of a dense but well-organized population concerned rather prosaicly with matters of agriculture, work, commerce, and with its own self-defense. Surveys conducted in recent years attest to the obvious density of the settlement at this time, particularly within Judean boundaries, between the eighth to seventh centuries B.C.E. Additional investigations continue to demonstrate that the sites were actually more crowded and numerous than had previously been thought. Soil cultivation and general agricultural and irrigation knowledge reached a high degree of development during the period, as recent research in the Negev and the Judean Desert testifies. Indeed, the archaeological finds clearly reflect the initiation of various projects on a truly regal scale throughout the kingdom. Large areas in the fortified cities were generously given over to royal institutions, as the royal granaries and storehouses and stables at Hazor, Megiddo, Lachish and Beersheba illustrate.

The series of fortresses and towers both in the desert regions and in Judah itself point to a highly developed system of defense and to a well-defended road network. The urban planning of the cities—especially in Judah—indicates a sophisticated ability to prepare plans and to make maximum use of a given area. The same design and construction expertise is evident in private dwellings. The four-room house plan typical of private residences in Judah and Israel for some five hundred years at least was appropriate to the living style of an average Israelite family at the time. This house plan, moreover, allowed for the construction of dwellings of different sizes to suit the needs and social status of a variety of families. The use of monolithic stone masonry is characteristic of all Israelite architectural structures

Aerial photograph of the fort from the Period of the Monarchy at Tel Arad.

and shows that the builders sought to adjust their methods of construction to the prevailing rock found in their land.

We find that even Israelite burial customs of the time were unique, exemplified by hewn stone burial caves with benches arranged according to a fixed plan. The resourcefulness and engineering ability of these ancient people is amply evidenced by impressive water systems found in a number of cities: these water systems are exceptional and unparalleled in contemporaneous states. Thus, in these manifestations of Israelite material culture, we detect distinctly original Israelite elements. Uniquely Israelite elements also appear in the design of certain fortifications, such as the casemate walls and six-chambered gates from the tenth century B.C.E. This is not true, however, of walls and gates from the ninth century on, which generally resemble the fortifications of neighboring Syrian cities. It is conceivable that the common regional threat, namely the danger of conquest by the Assyrians, brought about the development of a uniform style of fortification in a larger geographical area.

The monumental architecture of the Monarchy, which characterizes the palaces at Samaria, Megiddo and Ramat Rahel and which is also present in the sacred precincts at Dan, is worthy of consideration in itself. These splendid buildings were made of cleanly smoothed hewn stones, some with chiseled margins. The buildings were decorated with Proto-Aeolic carved capitals, and the windows were ornamented in the typical contemporary fashion. The view once current among scholars was that this style had originated in Phoenicia and was subsequently introduced into Israel by Phoenician artisans. This process supposedly began during Solomonic times but was especially true of the Omride dynasty, when ties with Phoenicia were particularly close. Y. Shiloh's special study of the subject, however, concluded that this architectural style was actually an Israelite development of originally Canaanite-Phoenician elements and motifs. His theory was based on the fact that there are no extant architectural remains in Phoenicia itself that exactly parallel this style, while these elements are widespread in Israel beginning in the tenth century B.C.E. However, this new thesis is not yet universally accepted, and only further excavations—especially in Phoenicia—will confirm or refute it.

We have already mentioned the significant contribution archaeology has made towards a better understanding of the era's cultic life. The Arad temple, the altar at Beersheba, the sacred precincts at Dan and the finds at Kuntillet-Ajrud constitute important new discoveries in this area of research. To these must be added incense altars, clay figurines and sundry cultic vessels and appurtenances, some of which came to light in special cultic chambers such as the one discovered by Aharoni at Lachish.

Great advances have been made in the archaeological research on the period of the Monarchy during the last several years. Extensive excavations continue to be conducted at many sites throughout the country, and our knowledge about the era is consequently growing at a fast pace. We hope that this ongoing work in the field will bring about a more profound appreciation of this all-important period.

Inscriptions of the Biblical Period

By Joseph Naveh

The corpus of written material from the biblical period includes cuneiform inscriptions in Sumerian, Akkadian, Hittite and Elamite, Egyptian writings (in hieroglyphic and derivative scripts) and alphabetic inscriptions in the various Canaanite and Aramaic dialects. The subject is vast and for this reason the present survey will deal only with alphabetic inscriptions originating in the Land of Israel and Trans-Jordan. Even with such a limitation, the period to be considered still spans some 13 centuries. This stretch of time may itself be further divided into three parts: (1) the second half of the second millennium B.C.E., (2) the period of the First Temple, and (3) the period of the return from the Exile, and restoration.

To be sure, I will refer here to most of the inscriptional material known to date, and in particular to inscriptions discovered since 1948. However, my main purpose is to describe the present state of epigraphic research and the advances made since then. I must point out at the start that my remarks may be somewhat subjective, and I apologize beforehand for perhaps overemphasizing my own views.

I. The Second Half of the Second Millennium B.C.E.

The first period to be considered is that in which alphabetic script first came into being, beginning around the 17th century B.C.E. Modern epigraphic inquiry into this period starts with the discovery of the Serabit el-Khadem inscriptions in Sinai in 1905. These inscriptions, still known as "Proto-Sinaitic," are written in a script that is principally pictographic-acrophonic, i.e. a picture writing in which each picture represents the intital consonant of the word depicted. During the 1920s and 1930s, scholars debated whether these inscriptions were written by Semites—including Hebrews—or by non-Semites, and there were those who claimed that alphabetic writing was actually invented in the Sinai. The designation "Proto-

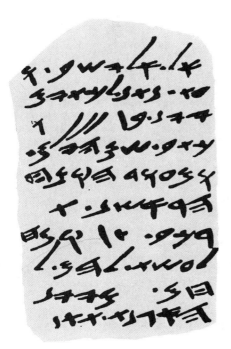

"Yein Ha-aganot" ostracon from late eighth-century Arad—facsimile and original.

Sinaitic" is still in use today, but the terms "Proto-Sinaitic script" and "Proto-Sinaitic alphabet" are no longer satisfactory. It appears that the Proto-Sinaitic inscriptions are only a part of the family of Proto-Canaanite inscriptions now known from various Canaanite sites.

Three inscriptions discovered at Gezer, Shechem and Lachish are actually older than the Serabit el-Khadem inscriptions. This script first appeared and was developed in Canaan and was used at Serabit el-Khadem by miners who were apparently Semites. The script, a picture writing, was created under the influence of Egyptian hieroglyphics, but the Canaanites successfully reduced the number of signs to a mere 27. Whereas the Egyptian script contains tri-consonantal, bi-consonantal and mono-consonantal pictographs, the Proto-Canaanite signs are exclusively mono-consonantal. That is to say, only the initial sound of the word depicted is represented. The Proto-Canaanite script emerged and evolved in southern Canaan but its mechanical aspects—drawing with paint and incising on stone—were borrowed from Egyptian writing. At Ugarit, an alphabetic script was employed which consisted of 27 + 3 wedge-shaped signs written by impressing a stylus on soft clay. The encoding principle is the same, yet the graphic technique is borrowed from cuneiform writing, which was ubiquitous during the second millennium B.C.E., for at this time Akkadian, written in cuneiform, was the *lingua franca* employed in international correspondence. Most of the known material written in alphabetic cuneiform originated at Ugarit, but the dispersal of this mode of writing was not confined to Ugarit and northern Canaan alone. In four places in southern Canaan—Sarepta, Nahal Tabor, Taanach and Beth Shemesh—short inscriptions in the alphabetic cuneiform usually designated "Ugaritic writing" were found.

The alphabetic inscriptions discovered at Ugarit are instructive about early Canaanite poetry and about the Ugaritic language of the 14th to 13th centuries B.C.E.

In contrast, the Proto-Canaanite writings, including those from Serabit el-Khadem, have contributed practically nothing to our knowledge of literature and language. All suggestions about the decipherment of the Sinai inscriptions have remained conjectural, and, apart from isolated words and phrases such as *lbˁlt* and *rb nqbnm*, the Proto-Sinaitic inscriptions remain undeciphered. The significance of the Proto-Canaanite inscriptions, be they the ones found in Sinai or the ones discovered at various sites within Israel, is limited to the realm of paleography. With the help of these finds, we are able to trace the initial steps in the evolution of alphabetic writing from pictographs to linear signs and letters. In the 13th century B.C.E. the number of phonemes in the south Canaanite dialect decreased so as to leave the alphabet with only 22 signs. In the 12th and 11th centuries, the linear signs developed into well-defined letters and the direction of writing stabilized so that from the 11th century onward writing was executed in horizontal rows from right to left. The writing used subsequently, i.e. from around 1050 B.C.E., is no longer designated "Proto-Canaanite" but "Phoenician."

The preceding summary is based largely on the studies of Professor Frank Moore Cross, which began to take form nearly 25 years ago, and especially those concerning the short, 12th century inscriptions etched on three arrowheads found at El-Khader. Since then the corpus of Proto-Canaanite inscriptions has not increased significantly. In 1962, a seal inscribed with the word *l'b'* was found in the fields of Kibbutz Revadim. In 1969, a piece of a jar handle was discovered at Khirbet Raddana in the Benjamin district. On the basis of two letters and a fragment of a third letter incised on this handle, several scholars tried to date the Israelite settlement in the hilly region. The most recent discovery in the realm of Proto-Canaanite inscriptions was an ostracon found at Izbet-Sartah near Aphek and published in 1978. This ostracon, from around the 12th century B.C.E., was inscribed faintly with more than 80 signs. The sherd was discovered at a site designated by archaeologists as a "settlement site" and as a result there has been a tendency to exaggerate its importance. In my opinion, this ostracon is disappointing. The first row contains a faulty 22-letter abecedary while the remaining four lines are no more than an agglomeration of letters that do not comprise any coherent text, or at least not a Semitic one. It seems that these scratches were produced by a semi-literate person—perhaps a student, and if so, not a very good one. It would be prudent, therefore, to refrain from any far-reaching conclusions based on the writer's errors, and one should certainly avoid—at least at this stage—basing on this find any conjectures concerning the history of the alphabet. Furthermore, one should not assume that the writing on the sherd reflects a scribal tradition different from that of the other Proto-Canaanite inscriptions known so far.

II. The Period of the First Temple

This phase in the development of writing actually begins prior to the construction of the First Temple. It starts around 1050 B.C.E. when the 22 letters were already stabilized and written only in horizontal lines from right to left. This script is called from here on "Phoenician" but it was used as well by settlers in Canaan and the immediate vicinity towards the end of the second millennium. These people learned the writing system from the Canaanites. Thus, a Hebrew used it for writing the Gezer calendar towards the end of the tenth century. Only in inscriptions from the middle of the ninth century is it possible to discern the initial evolution of the Hebrew (= old Hebrew) script, and only in the middle of the eighth century does the Aramaic script begin its independent development.

Eighty years ago, when scholars already had access to numerous Phoenician and Aramaic inscriptions, the land on both sides of the Jordan had yielded up in addition to several seals, only two inscriptions from the First Temple Period: the Mesha stela, written in Moabite, and the Siloam inscription in Hebrew. In 1908 the Gezer calendar was discovered. The year 1910 marks the discovery of the Samaria ostraca, which list quantities of wine and oil. These were published in 1924, and in the same year the Ophel inscription was discovered. In 1932 additional ostraca were found at Samaria but these differed in type from the first. The discovery of the Lachish letters in 1938 was the high point of Hebrew epigraphic finds between the years preceding the Second World War and the 25 years following it.

In 1945 and 1946 two Hebrew ostraca were discovered at Tell Qasile and these were published in 1949. In 1952 a piece of papyrus containing a Hebrew palimpsest was found in a cave in Wadi Murabba'at. Bullae—individual seal impressions on pieces of clay which had been used to seal papyrus scrolls—had been found

Ink-written papyrus document from the middle of the seventh century, discovered at Wadi Murabba'at.

earlier. This showed that Hebrew had also been written on papyrus during the First Temple Period. A bulla from Lachish is impressed with the seal of *gdlyhw'šr 'l hbyt* (Gedalyahu who is in charge of the royal house). Today dozens of such bullae are know to us. In 1953 Professor Avigad deciphered the burial inscription of *"[. . .] yhw 'šr 'l hbyt,"* which had been discovered in 1870 in Siloam Village. Since 1956 approximately 60 jar handles with inscriptions have been found at Gibeon. In 1960 the Yavneh-Yam (Mesad Hashavyahu) inscription was discovered. Between 1962 and 1967 more than 100 inscriptions—mostly ostraca—were found at Arad. With their publication in 1975 the focus of scholarly attention passed from Lachish to these new finds. In various places ranging from Tel Dan and Hazor in the north to Beersheba and Kadesh-Barnea in the south, many dozens of inscriptions have been found both incised and painted on jugs. These usually indicate ownership. In addition, numerous Hebrew, Ammonite and Moabite seals of unknown provenance have reached the antiquities market during the last 30 years and have become available for scholarly scrutiny.

The vast majority of Hebrew epigraphic material from the First Commonwealth is written on ceramic—either on whole ceramic vessels as an indication of ownership or contents—or on ostraca. Ostraca could be inscribed with relatively long letters or with shorter memoranda. They could also serve as administrative documents such as lists of names and goods, bills of lading or receipts. In my opinion, the Samaria ostraca were merely labels meant to accompany the jars of wine or oil. We also possess inscriptions that were chiseled or engraved on stone, including some burial inscriptions. The Siloam inscription is *sui generis* and cannot be in-

Late seventh-century B.C.E. ostracon discovered at Mesad Hashavyahu near Yavneh-Yam.

cluded among the well-known genre of royal inscriptions, for the epigraphic remains of the Kingdoms of Judah and Israel have yet to provide any clear evidence for the existence of royal monuments and stelae.

The most common literary type represented in Semitic epigraphic remains is the dedicatory inscription. Until a few years ago no dedicatory inscriptions from the periods of the First or Second Temples had been found, and the genre was known only from ancient synagogues. The Kuntillet-'Ajrud excavations provided the first ancient dedicatory inscriptions. The rim of a stone basin found at the site is inscribed with the words *l 'bdyw bn 'dnh brk h' lyhw*—"(dedicated) by 'Obadyahu . . . may he be blessed by Yahwe." The Tetragrammaton appears to be written in this inscription in the defective spelling, without the final *he*.

Another type of inscription well attested in early Semitic epigraphic finds is the *graffito* or the *dipinto*. These are usually found chiseled on rocks or painted on walls. Such inscriptions were previously unknown among Hebrew epigraphic finds and have been found in Israel only recently. In the burial caves of Khirbet Bet Lei and El-Kom in southwest Judea—which seem to have been used as places of hiding—graffiti have been discovered. A dipinto has also been found in a rock crevice near Ein Gedi.

In the Ein Gedi inscription one must read and complete the formula *brk X lyhwh* three times. The El-Kom inscription reads *'uriyāhū ha-śar keṭābō bārûk 'uriyāhū leYHWH*. "Uriyahu the governor wrote it. May Uriyahu be blessed by Yahweh." The third line contains additional letters, several of which do not belong to the original inscription. I suggest reading this line *nôserŷ wela-'aśēratô*—". . . my Guardian and by His Asherah." The formula "May Uriyahu be blessed by Yahweh my guardian and by His Asherah" resembles the dedicatory inscription from the

Kuntillet-'Ajrud basin but it is especially reminiscent of the formula found on the large pithoi from that site: *brkt'tkm lyhwh šmrn wl'šrth*, to be understood "I bless you by Yahweh our Guardian and by His Asherah." These inscriptions contain two examples of defective writing at the ends of the words—*brkt* and *šmrn* (*bēraktî* and *šôm^erēnû*). The connection between the dedicatory inscriptions and the graffiti in general and the relationship of the 'Ajrud and the El-Kom inscriptions in particular has been dealt with in *BASOR* 235 (1979), pp. 27-30.

The inscriptions from Kuntillet-'Ajrud which are attributed to around 800 B.C.E. are the oldest known Hebrew inscriptions. In addition to their paleographic and epigraphic importance, they are also of utmost significance for other areas of study, and they will certainly be the focus of much additional research.

To complete the survey of the Hebrew epigraphic finds from the period of the First Temple, mention must be made of an inscribed ivory fragment discovered in 1961 at Nimrud. The fragment bears a Hebrew inscription and seems to have been among booty taken from Samaria. A similar discovery had been made in 1906 at Susa where two fragments of an alabaster vessel were inscribed with the words *hn wḥṣy hlg wrb't hlg*—"a hin and half a log and quarter of a log." The letters on the alabaster vessel—which was apparently brought from Judah—date to the seventh century B.C.E.

Phoenician and Aramaic inscriptions from the period of the First Temple have been found in several border towns of Israel. A jar found in 1961 at Ein Gev is inscribed on the shoulder with the Aramaic word *lšqy'*—"belonging to the cup-bearers." A bowl fragment discovered recently at Tel Dan is inscribed on the base with the Aramaic word *lṭbhy'*—"belonging to the cooks." It seems that these two inscriptions—both dating to the ninth century B.C.E.—were incised on utensils used in a large kitchen and they designate the function of the men charged with preparing and serving diners beverage and food. The eighth-century Hebrew inscription found in 1955 on the shoulder of a jar from Hazor is very likely of the same type. There, I prefer the reading *lmkbdm* (lam^ekabb^edîm), "belonging to the food-server," to the generally accepted reading *lmkbrm* (l^emakbîrām), "belonging to (a person named) Makbiram."

A jar fragment discovered at Tel Dan is inscribed with the Phoenician inscription *lb'lplṭ*. South of Tel Aviv a similar inscription was found: *lšlmy*. These two inscriptions, along with the Aramaic inscription *'lsmk* on the base of a bowl from Tel-Zeror near Hadera, date from the period between the destruction of Samaria and the fall of the First Temple.

We turn now to the Ammonite, Moabite and Edomite inscriptions. The stela of Mesha, king of Moab, has been known since 1868. This is a monument the likes of which has yet to be found in Judah and Israel. In 1958, some 90 years after the discovery of the Mesha stela, a fragment of an additional monumental inscription of Mesha was found at Kerak, the site of ancient Qir Moab. From this piece it was learned that Mesha's father was named Kemošyat. The two inscriptions date to the ninth century B.C.E. and are written in the Moabite language. However, the script is Hebrew. Sometime following the Assyrian takeover of the area along the King's Highway, Aramaic elements started penetrating the script of the Moabites, and several independent forms developed, such as, for example, the shape of the large-headed *mem*. This *mem* appears in seals containing characteristically Moabite names such as *kmš 'm (bn) kmš'l hspr* (Kemoš'am, son of Kemoš'el the scribe). Incidentally, a similar *mem* also appears in seals which do not bear typically Moabite names, such as the seal *'mṣ hspr* (Amos the scribe). The Moabite origin of these latter seals may be determined on the basis of the similarity in writing between them and the *Kemoš'am* seal.

Ancient inscriptions like that of Mesha, king of Moab, have yet to be discovered in Edom. However, the great similarity and perhaps absolute identity between the scripts of the Moabites and the Edomites may be attested by two ostraca and several seal impressions from Umm el-Biyara near Petra and Tell el-Khaleifah near Eilat. At the former site, among other things a bulla was discovered belonging to *qwsgbr mlk 'dm*—"Qausgabri king of Edom." A sixth-century ostracon from Tell el-Khaleifah contains a few letters that preserve the Hebrew form, but most of them have already adopted the Aramaic shape, and the *mems* resemble those found on the Moabite seals.

The Moabites and Edomites learned their scripts from the Hebrews when they were politically subjugated to the Kingdoms of Judah and Israel. However, when they liberated themselves from this political and cultural sphere of influence, their writing started to absorb Aramaic features. Today we have at our disposal several Ammonite inscriptions and we know that the Ammonite language was a Canaanite dialect related to Hebrew and Moabite, but its script had always been Aramaic.

Until 1948 only three Ammonite seals were known: one from Amman, one from Irbid and one of unknown origin but inscribed: *l'dnplt 'bd 'mndb*. An inscription of Ashurnasirpal, king of Assyria, from the year 667 B.C.E. mentions Amminadab king of the Ammonites. Around 1950, in a grave near Amman, three seals were discovered, one of which bears the name *'dnnr 'bd 'mndb*. A small statue bearing the name *yrḥ 'zr* has been discovered in Ammon. The script of these texts is very similar to the Aramaic script and ever since their discovery almost every seal written in Aramaic script but containing the word *bn* rather than *br* has been considered to be Ammonite. So far, many dozens of Ammonite seals have been discovered. In the last decade several Ammonite inscriptions have come to light, verifying the conclusions about the Ammonite language and script that had been reached previously solely on the basis of the seals.

Ten years ago an inscription from the Amman Citadel was published. This inscription seems to be contemporaneous with the Mesha Stela. In 1972 a bronze juglet was discovered at Tell Siran on the campus of the Amman University. The inscription tells of the works of Amminadab, king of the Ammonites, the son of Hissel'el, king of the Ammonites, the son of Amminadab, king of the Ammonites." This text may be attributed to the second half of the seventh century, the time of the grandson of the Amminadab mentioned by Ashurasirpal. In 1973 an ostracon was discovered at Heshbon with an ink inscription from the same period. There are today no longer any doubts that the Ammonite script in the Ammonite inscriptions is very similar to the Aramaic script, but it has not yet been determined whether the Ammonite and Aramaic scripts are totally identical or whether there are slight differences between the Ammonite and the Aramaic.

This question of similarity of identity between Ammonite and Aramaic writing arose over a decade ago when part of a plaster inscription found at Deir 'Alla was published. If this inscription is considered to be in the Aramaic script, it must be dated to the eighth century, but if it is actually Ammonite it may be dated to about half a century later. The text was published recently, and it contains a prophetic story about none other than Balaam the son of Beor. The publishers of the *editio princeps* claim that the text is Aramaic. However, the text that can be read from the published photographs offers no proof that the language of the inscriptions is in fact Aramaic. It is possible that the language of the inscriptions is a Canannite dialect related to Moabite—perhaps Gileadite or Ammonite. Admittedly, the personality mentioned in the Deir 'Alla inscriptions is entitled *bl'm br b'r* and not *bl'm bn b'r*, but this indicates nothing about the language. Whatever the case may be, these inscriptions are an extremely important find and will be the subject of much future study. Incidentally, small plaster fragments bearing similar but somewhat earlier writing have been found at Kuntillet-'Ajrud.

A survey of the epigraphic remains from the neighbors of Judah and Israel during the first Commonwealth should also mention three short Philistine inscriptions. These inscriptions reveal a peculiar writing tradition that bears affinities to Hebrew on the one hand and to Phoenician on the other but is not completely identical to either one of them. Hopefully in the near future additional inscriptions will come to light at Philistine sites that will teach us something about the Philistine script of the first Temple period.

III. The Period of the Return from the Exile and the Restoration.

In this period the use of the Aramaic script and language was on the rise. As early as the eighth century B.C.E. the Assyrians had employed Aramaic as an official language, especially in their western provinces, and it achieved the position of a *lingua franca*. This status became more deeply entrenched during the rule of the Babylonians and especially under the Persians. Most of the epigraphic corpus from the period of the Return is written in Aramaic, which served as the official language of Judea as well.

The epigraphic material in the Hebrew language and script includes only a few coins and seals. These finds seem to date to the part of the Persian period when an anti-Persian nationalistic movement erupted. In 1970 a small silver coin was found at Tell Jemmeh bearing the words *yhzqyh hphh*—"Yehizqiya the governor" in Hebrew characters. Thanks to the writing on this coin it is now possible to read the word *hphh* on a coin found 40 years earlier at Beth Zur. In recent years there has been an increase in the number of coins inscribed in Hebrew script with the word *yhd*—"Yehud," the official name of the province of Judea. It seems that the solitary extant coin bearing the word *yhd* in Aramaic script was minted prior to the minting of coins with *yhwd* written in paleo-Hebrew script. In a cave near Wadi Daliyeh, along with the Aramaic documents from Samaria written on papyrus between 375 and 335 B.C.E., a bulla was discovered inscribed "[. . .] yhw bn [sn] blt pht šmrn." This impression, produced by the official seal of ". . . Yahu the son of Sanballat governor of Samaria," is written in Hebrew language and script. At Tel Michal on the Herzliyah seashore another seal with Hebrew script was discovered, probably from the same period. It is difficult to decide whether it is a Samaritan or a Jewish seal.

The collection of Aramaic inscriptions from the Persian period is richer. So far, as we have said, only one coin bearing the inscription *yhd* in Aramaic letters has been found. In 1955 a seal impression *yhwd 'wryw* was discovered on a piece of a jar from Jericho. Several years later a similar fragment was found at Ramat Raḥel, this one inscribed *yhwd ḥnnh*. Also found at Ramat Rahel were handles stamped with the inscriptions *yhwd, yhw'zr phw'* and *'ḥzy phw.* These impressions may be added to the dozens of previously known Aramaic impressions of the type *yhwd, yhd* and the shorter form *yh*. Stamping with these seals apparently confirmed the exact volume of the wine jars. Similar seals bearing the inscription *mṣh* or *mwsh* seem to have been impressed on jugs containing wine produced at Motza.

Several years ago a group of 65 bullae of 12 seals as well as two actual seals was published. One seal is incised with the three letters *yhd* while on the other hand we finds the words *lšlmyt 'mt 'lntn ph[w']*. The seal impressions include the inscriptions *yhd, yhd ḥnnh, l'lntn phw', lyrmy hspr, lbrwk bn šm'y, lyg'l bn zkry, l'l'zr bn nhm, [l]'l'zr* and *lmykh*. In light of this find there is no longer any doubt about the reading *phw'*—"the governor"—and we must reject the suggestion that the seal impression of Yehoezer and Ahazay referred to above contain the word *phr'*—"the potter." At the same time, I doubt that the word *phw'* in these cases is the title of the governor of Judah as indeed it is in the coin inscribed *yhzqyh hphh* and in the bulla from Wadi Daliyeh which contains the title *pht šmrn*. In Aramaic the definite form of the word *pḥh* is *pḥt'*. The form *pḥw'* seems to be derived (a back formation) from the plural *pḥwt'*. The vocable *pḥwt'* appears, among other places, in a fifth century Aramaic papyrus from Egypt and means "the officials." It is therefore not obligatory to conclude that Elnatan, Yehoezer, Aḥazay, Urio and Ḥanana were governors of Judah and it may be assumed, rather, that they were mere civil servants. It is even likely that the bullae and the two seals came from the private archive of Shelomit, the maidservant of the Judean official Elnatan and did not originate in a royal archive as is usually thought.

Recently, there has been a vast increase in the number of Aramaic ostraca discovered in Israel. About 100 Aramaic sherds were found at Arad, but only 50 of them are legible. These sherds are some sort of dockets concerning the barley rations distributed to horsemen and donkey drivers and their animals. They seem to be related to the Persian postal system, which is described in great detail by

"Ramat Negev" ostracon (left) from the beginning of the sixth century B.C.E. and "Nehemiah" ostracon (right) from the latter part of the eighth century B.C.E., both found at Arad.

Herodotus. Arad may have been one of the waystations of this sytem. The ostraca from Beersheba contain indications of a date—apparently the regnal year of Arta-xerxes III who ascended the throne in 359 B.C.E.—and stipulate as well quantities of wheat and barley that were brought as taxes to royal strorehouses of the administrative center in Beersheeba. The ostracon from Tell el-Farah, discovered during the 1920s, testifies to the extensive sown areas then found in the northern Negev. Individual Aramaic ostraca have been found as well at Ein Gedi, Ashdod, Yoqne'am and Eilat. An ostracon with Phoenician writing was discovered at Eilat, and it contains a list of Phoenician names. Phoenician inscriptions on jars were found at Shikmonah and Bat-Yam.

Most of the ostraca originate from sites that were outside the territory of Judea during the period of the restoration, but many of them contain Hebrew names: *'qbyh* at Yoqneam; *zbdyh* at Ashdod; *dlwy* at Beersheba; and *yhwntn, ydw', 'lyšb, 'qbyh, 'nny* at Arad. The ostraca from Arad and Beersheba contain many Edomite as well as Arabic names, reflecting the ethnic composition of the population at these sites during the Persian period.

The most outstanding epigraphic find from the Persian period is undoubtedly the Wadi Daliyeh papyri, found in a cave used as a place of refuge by well-to-do people from Samaria who fled from the armies of Alexander the Great. As far as this is concerned, one may draw an analogy between Wadi Daliyeh during the Persian period and Wadi Murabba'at and Nahal Hever at the time of Bar Kokhba. The Aramaic papyri from Wadi Daliyeh have yet to be published.

I have attempted to describe here in a summary fashion the present state of epigraphic research on the basis of the corpus of Palestinian inscriptions from the biblical period. This material poses a host of problems, only a few of which I have been able to discuss briefly. Many crucial problems, such as the change of script during the age of the Return, have not been touched upon at all. In order not to encumber the presentation I refrained from mentioning by name the many scholars instrumental in the discovery, decipherment and interpretation of the finds. Many are the scholars who may be credited with bringing the field of ancient Hebrew epigraphy to its present state. Were I to single out the individuals responsible for every decipherment, interpretation or opinion the list would have been dominated by the names of Nahman Avigad and Frank Moore Cross. The prominence of these two scholars was accordingly noted at the outset.

During the 1960s the claim could still be heard that the Land of Israel was poor in written remains from the biblical period. It seems that this allegation may now safely be laid to rest.

JERUSALEM, October 1978
Translated by Dr. Avigdor Hurowitz

Archaeological Research on the Period of the Return to Zion

By Ephraim Stern

Archaeological research since 1948 has greatly contributed to our knowledge of the settlement in the Land of Israel during the Persian Period, the time of the Return to Zion. Before 1948, our information about this period was very scanty; we certainly knew much less about it than we did about earlier periods. Since 1948, occupation levels from the Persian Period have been discovered at many sites, and the great amount of material accumulated from these excavations has made possible, for the first time, a careful typological comparison and an examination of clean strata to which the finds can be attributed. It should be noted, however, that much of the material of the new excavations is either unpublished or has been published only in preliminary form.

Of special value are the excavations at Hazor, Shikmonah, Tel Megadim, Tel Mevorakh and Ein Gedi, both because their Persian levels are much better preserved than at other sites and also because these excavations paved the way for an examination of regional cultures. Indeed, the Persian level at Hazor sheds light on the Galilean culture; rich finds at Shikmonah, Tel Megadim and Tel Mevorakh complement our knowledge of the culture of the coastal settlements, and thanks to the excavations at Ein Gedi, we can reexamine the results of previous excavations in Judea and Samaria. In addition to the Ein Gedi finds, three homogeneous discoveries were later made in the same region: in the Wadi Daliyeh cave, the Sheikh Ibrahim cave near Bar-Giora and the burial cave at Ein Arub, north of Hebron.

At some of the sites (Akko, Shikmonah, Tel Megadim, Dor, Tel Mevorakh, Mikhmoret, Tel Michal, Ashdod, Tell el-Hesi, Tell Jemmeh, Tell Ser'a and Ein Gedi), the Persian stratum included two or more stages; at other sites only part of the period was involved (the end of the Persian Period at Hazor, and only the fourth century B.C.E. at Wadi Daliyeh). Thus, for the first time it is now possible

Remains of buildings from the Persian Period uncovered at Tel Mevorakh.
Above—the wall skillfully constructed of hewn stones and filled in with rough stones.
Below—two stages of the central building at the site.

to trace the development of the period's material culture and to classify finds as early or late.

Various surveys have yielded data concerning the distribution of settlements during the Persian Period. Surveys were conducted in the Galilee, Beth Shean Valley and Nahalat Issachar, at Nahal Manasseh and Sharon; in the Nahal Rubin region, the Negev, and in various surveys in the Sinai by "The Israel Survey," in the Haifa and Carmel coastal region, and in Judea, Samaria and the Golan. In recent years "regional excavations" have been initiated—the dig is not limited to a single "tell" but includes an entire region. Regional excavations have been conducted at Yoqne'am and Aphek and at a great number of sites in the Beersheba plain. As a result, we have a clear picture of hundreds of sites dating to the Persian Period and now have new data to estimate what the map of the settlements and populations was like during the Persian Period. Consequently, the notions prevalent in the archaeological world before 1948 have been totally revised.

The epigraphic finds from this period are no less notable. Two discoveries in particular shed light on the historical background of Judea and Samaria—the principal provinces in the Land of Israel at the time. In the early 1960s Ta'amireh Bedouin found Aramaic papyri in the Wadi Daliyeh cave in Samaria. Apparently, remnants of Samaritans who had rebelled against Alexander the Great's commissioner had fled to this cave. Paul Lapp, who excavated the cave after the Bedouin discovery, fully published his work; however, only a few provisional reports published by Frank Moore Cross describe the Bedouin discoveries. About 40 fragments of papyri, written in Aramaic, were discovered in the cave, which also contained more than 100 seal impressions and rings. According to the dates on these documents—which were reckoned according to the reigns of the Persian kings—it appears that the earliest document dates to 375 B.C.E., and the latest to 335 B.C.E. Not only do these documents provide us with information about the variegated elements of the Samaritan population in the fourth century B.C.E., but they also shed light on the dynasty of rulers from the House of Sanballat. We can now reconstruct this succession of rulers *in toto*, from the days of Sanballat I, a contemporary of Nehemiah, until the Macedonian conquest when this Sanballat dynasty ended.

The second crucial discovery, published in full by Nahman Avigad, was the trove of bullae and seals from an unknown site near Jerusalem, which turned up in a private collection. The trove included bullae and seals from a post-exilic archive. This find has, to some extent, filled in our knowledge of the Jewish dynasty that ruled in Judea at the time. Much interest was aroused by the unique seal belonging to "Shulamit, the maidservant of Elnatan, the Governor," which suggests that women too fulfilled responsible functions in the administration. This discovery complemented earlier information from seal impressions and inscriptions found at Ramat Rahel, Jericho, Ein Gedi, Jerusalem, Motzah, and other sites in Judea, and ended the long dispute over their date and meaning. Thanks to the work of Frank Moore Cross, Joseph Naveh and Avigad (the latter at his excavations in the Jewish Quarter of Jerusalem), we are now able to classify "Yehud" stamps with considerable certainty. The various Hebrew "Yehud" and "Yerasalem" impressions can no longer all be attributed to the Persian Period, as was earlier thought.

Excavations conducted after the founding of the State of Israel have also yielded a very rich booty of ostraca and inscriptions. Especially important are those found at Arad and Beersheba that tell us about the military and administrative organization of the Persian government in southern Israel. Ostraca and inscriptions also turned up at many other sites all over the country. On the whole, the messages are short and concise, since these were only "notes," intended to give information about the transfer of food supplies. On occasion, however, they include a list of names or some other bit of information that helps us understand the variegated population elements in various parts of the Land of Israel. Most of the ostraca are written in Aramaic, but a few are written in Phoenician or a mixture of the two. An ostracon found in Ashdod seems to be written in a language peculiar to the province of Ashdod.

Numismatic discoveries have provided the basis for the solution of several long-disputed chronological and historical problems. The most important discovery in this area was made by chance; a small cache of coins was discovered on the surface at Tell Jemmeh. After the coins had been cleaned, it became apparent that they belonged to the characteristic "Yehud" coin type, but instead of the word "Yehud," the name and title of one of the Jewish rulers, "Hezekiah the Governor," appeared on these coins.

The number and different types of "Yehud" coins has grown considerably. A few have been discovered in excavations—especially in Jerusalem—but the majority have turned up in private collections. A most surprising discovery, and one to which we must ascribe great historical significance, is the Hebrew expression "Yehuda" which occurs on a new type of coin whose provenance is unknown. These date to the beginning of the Ptolemaic period.

More coins of various types common to the Land of Israel during the Persian period continue to be discovered. First and foremost are the coins that had been incorrectly identified as "Philisto-Arabian." We can now confirm that these coins should be considered local coinage. The names of provincial capitals, such as

Clay flask in the form of the god Bes, discovered in the Persian level at Tel Mevorakh.

Lower part of a clay **rhyton** *from Gaza in the form of a ram.*

Samaria and Ashdod, are imprinted on several of these finds. The large number of these coins has permitted us to be very precise in our comparative research.

Our collection of Greek coins has also been enriched. Two Greek coins from Jerusalem and one from Shechem, dating to the sixth century B.C.E., attest to coin usage in the Land of Israel as early as the first part of the Persian Period—and perhaps even several years earlier. We now also have a much richer collection of Phoenician and Cypriot coins.

A Persian silver coin from Samaria, which probably dates to the reign of Darius III, the last ruler of the Persian Empire, is the only Persian coin discovered in the country; its very existence, though, attests to the fact that Persian coins from the royal mint were in use in the Land of Israel during this period.

Several impressive assemblages of statuettes and figurines—of stone, clay and bronze—give us an opportunity to perceive the nature of the various national cults throughout the Land of Israel during the Persian Period. These collections of statuettes and figurines seem to have originated in temple favissae. The most important collections come from Tel Michal, Tel Erani, Tel Sippor and Tel Dor. Many more figurines that enhance our understanding of these cults have been discovered at excavations and in ancient cemeteries.

Even underwater exploration has contributed to our knowledge in this area. A shipwreck discovered on the Shavei Zion coast yielded a cargo of various clay statuettes. Rumor has it that a similar ship has been discovered in the harbor at Tyre. What distinguishes the latter find is that several of the figurines had been impressed with the symbol of the goddess Tanit Pene Baal, who was, so far as we know, the sole goddess of the Phoenician colonial settlements.

These finds enrich our knowledge of figurine types and the nature of the popular cult in the Land of Israel. They also enable us to comprehend those alien influences that became indigenous during the Persian Period and to understand the degree to which the religious traditions of earlier periods were preserved.

Obviously, no field of research dealing with the Persian Period, the time of the Return to Zion, has failed to profit from the extensive archaeological activity of recent years. No wonder so much scholarly effort is now being devoted to analyzing the new knowledge from this period—studies re-examining the entire complex of historical problems pertaining to this period as well as detailed treatments of one or two aspects of the culture, for example pottery, coins or seals.

Thanks to the vast accumulation of archaeological material since 1948, we can now draw a completely new and comprehensive picture of Israel's material culture during the Return to Zion. The evidence presented by this material affects almost every aspect of the Persian Period culture. It necessitates a few radical changes in our previous views—about the relative importance of the period in the country's history and about the size and distribution of settlements then. We cannot discuss all these points here; we will instead concentrate on one major new conclusion drawn from the archaeological evidence.

As early as the beginning of the Persian Period, the country was divided into two regions: the hilly area of Judea and the Transjordan (and also, to a lesser degree, Samaria) on the one hand, and the Galilee and the coast on the other. The borderline between these two cultural regions was often very sharp, almost like the boundary between two nations. Without an understanding of this regional division, it is almost impossible to comprehend the internal development of the culture of the period.

Analysis of the cultures of these two regions reveals that the culture of the hilly areas was basically "eastern," a combination of the local culture (the outgrowth of the Israelite tradition) and of such eastern cultural influences as Assyrian, Babylonian and Egyptian. The coastal culture by contrast was basically "western," showing eastern Greek, Cypriot and Athenian influence. It would seem, therefore, that the Greek material culture was present long before the Macedonian conquest. This influence, however, was merely on the surface: the products of Greek culture were adopted without their original meanings and were adapted to local traditions and customs. The principal bearers of this new culture in Palestine were probably the Phoenicians. The Greek soldiers and settlers played only a secondary role.

It follows, therefore, that William Foxwell Albright's designation of this period as "Iron Age III" is correct as far as the limited region of the hills is concerned, but not with regard to other regions of Palestine. Moreover, we can now attribute the difference between the "coastal" and "hill-region" cultures not to a time gap, as Albright suggested, but rather to differences in cultures—"eastern" and "western"—that dominated the two regions.

Archaeological Discoveries From the Greco-Roman Era

By Lee I. Levine

S ince Israel achieved statehood, we have witnessed a remarkable increment in our knowledge of the classical period in the Holy Land. Some finds have been brought to light by chance—from urban construction, kibbutz agricultural work or the paving of new roads. Other finds have been uncovered while continuing earlier explorations as, for example, in Beth She'arim and the Nabataean cities of the Negev. In many cases an excavation has been undertaken because of an awareness of a new opportunity. Chance finds from the Judean Desert led to the discovery of a series of caves from the Bar Kokhba era. This was followed within a few years by extensive exploration of nearby Masada. These last excavations and their historical significance riveted the attention of the entire country.

Of late, Christian archaeologists have turned their attention to the Palestinian background of the New Testament. What, in fact, can we know about Judea in the New Testament period? Attempts to answer this question have led to excavations in regions as far-flung as Caesarea, the eastern Galilee, Jerusalem and the Transjordan area. Since 1967, Israeli archaeologists have been especially active in areas that previously had been inaccessible: Jerusalem, the Golan Heights and the West Bank. Undoubtedly the single most significant discovery during this last generation has been at Qumran. The scrolls, discovered in caves high above the Dead Sea, have had a startling impact on a plethora of scholarly disciplines. Our perceptions of ancient Judaism have been radically realigned, as has our understanding of the Jewish background of early Christianity.

The quantity and diversity of discoveries from the years since statehood are indeed remarkable. Fortresses, ports, necropolises, synagogues, churches, villages and cities have been explored. This last category has undoubtedly been the most fruitful. Buildings of political, social, economic and religious importance have been discovered, as well as private dwellings. Given the quantity of literary material available from this period, more than from any other period of history before or after until modern times, archaeological data can often be related to what is known from other sources. Sometimes archaeological material will confirm extant literary data to a remarkable degree, as was the case with Masada. In other instances, archaeology will supplement and complement literary data, adding new and important dimensions to our understanding of the past. Urban discoveries are mostly of this order. In certain cases, archaeological material has raised new questions and issues, at times even revolutionizing our understanding of the past. As noted, examples are Qumran and, to a lesser extent, Beth She'arim.

The Early Hellenistic Period

The 150 years or so between the conquest of Alexander and the Hasmonean revolt marked a watershed in the history of ancient Palestine. No longer was the country a province on the periphery of a large empire as it had been under Assyria, Babylonia and Persia. With the Macedonian conquest of the East and the ensuing rivalry between the Ptolemaic Empire of Egypt to the south and the Seleucid Empire of Syria to the north, the country was now subjected to wrenching political and military pressures. It was also exposed to a heavy dose of Hellenistic cultural influence. One expression of this outside presence was the stationing of foreign troops, both permanent and temporary, throughout the length and breadth of the land. Garrisons of Ptolemaic troops were to be found in most large cities (including Jerusalem), and the five major third-century B.C.E. wars between the rival empires brought many more soldiers into the country.

Archaeological evidence of Seleucid military presence is found in the Hefzibah inscription, first published in 1966. Written on a stone column, this inscription is, in fact, a copy of a series of letters sent by local officials to the Seleucid king around the year 200 B.C.E. A number of these letters speak of difficulties that the presence of a foreign army caused the local population—towns raided, food requisitioned, and soldiers quartered in various homes against their owners' wishes. In these letters, residents pleaded for removal of troops from their homes and for distancing these troops permanently from the towns.

Such sustained contact with foreign troops undoubtedly had a serious cultural impact on the local population. Language, dress, food and mannerisms might all too easily be aped. When added to the ubiquitous presence of the Ptolemaic bureaucracy and the generally close commercial ties with Egypt, channels for such influence were indeed numerous. A fascinating, though still enigmatic, expression of this influence is provided by 'Araq al Amir, a site east of the Jordan. In 1961-62, American archaeologists explored and excavated the area, identified as the home of the Tobiads, one of the leading families of pre-Hasmonean Jerusalem society. The structures there can now be dated with confidence to the beginning of the second century B.C.E. These activities and other finds corroborate Josephus's assertion that the last of this clan, Hyrcanus, lived the life of a typical Hellenistic prince. A large building has been identified as a temple. It was graced with large figural representations of lions carved along the outer walls; on its side, a fountain in the shape of a lioness was carved into a stone.

Hellenistic influence can also be traced in Jerusalem as well. Large numbers of Rhodian jar handles found in excavations attest to extensive commercial contacts with the Hellenistic world. Recently, a number of coins bearing the inscription *Yhdh* have been identified. They were minted in the late fourth to early third century and bear images of Ptolemy I, Cleopatra and an eagle with spread wings. These coins not only confirm the fact of Ptolemaic dominance and influence in Jerusalem, but indicate that the scrupulous avoidance of images, characteristic of the later Second Temple Period, had not as yet become the practice among Jews. Thus as late as the third century, the use of images *per se* was not interpreted in most circles as an infringement of the Second Commandment. This had been the case in biblical times as well (for example, the cherubim over the ark, the bronze serpent, etc.); only figural representation that reflected idolatrous worship was banned (and even then lines were not clearly drawn—see Jeremiah 44:16 ff.).

Yet Hellenistic influence, as profound as it was, was not the only cultural force at work in Jerusalem. There were many who took a dim view of outside influences, resisting foreign ideas and practices, and reasserting what they considered traditional Jewish values. Thus, from extant literary sources, Ben Sira balances Ecclesiastes (Qohelet), and the words of Simeon the Just (Avot 1, 2) the Song of Songs. Archaeologically, too, a number of stamped jar handles have recently been discovered bearing the inscription *Yehud* and *Yerushalem*, dating from the third and early second centuries. They reflect either a continuation or a resurgence of local pride and loyalties.

Hasmonean Era

The rise of the Hasmonean dynasty and its conquests, almost equaling those of David and Solomon, have left their mark on archaeological discoveries. Unfortunately, however, remains are not as extensive as might be expected. During the immediately succeeding period under Herod, building activity was so extensive and monumental that most earlier strata were destroyed or reused. Only here and there does one gain a glimpse of significant Hasmonean remains.

The enlarged Hasmonean kingdom had a profound impact on the capital city, Jerusalem. The city grew enormously in size, quadrupling its territory. This expansion to the west incorporated the entire area known as the "Upper City" in the late Second Temple Period. Today it is almost universally accepted that the "first wall" of Josephus, which encompassed all of this area, is to be attributed to the Hasmonean dynasty.

Contrary to popular opinion, the Hasmonean revolution was not so much a confrontation with Hellenism *per se*, but rather a response to the political and religious program of certain extremist Jewish Hellenizers who had the ear of the Seleucid king, Antiochus IV. The Hasmoneans themselves were never anti-Greek. Thus, the appearance of Hellenistic influences in later Hasmonean society should not be perplexing. An example of this kind of influence is the several tombs dating from the period. One of the best-known is that of Jason, discovered in the Rehavia section of Jerusalem in 1956. The style here is Greco-Egyptian: a series of forecourts, a single Doric column between two antae and a pyramidal monument. Moreover, the form of burial, in *kukhim* (niches large enough to hold bodies, cut perpendicularly to the wall of the cave), is new to a Jewish context. It first appears in Egypt in the late fourth to early third centuries. A Greek inscription further attests to the cultural proclivity of the interred, as does the name Jason, which referred to the leading member of the family.

Jason's tomb is significant in other ways as well. Wall representations, although primitive by modern standards, are nonetheless revealing. A gazelle is depicted, as is a series of menorahs—the first such archaeological evidence we possess of this Temple appurtenance that was soon to become the classic symbol of Judaism. On another wall, two ships appear, a warship pursuing a merchant vessel. It has been suggested that this depiction might reflect piratical activities of some members of this particular family. Finally, in addition to a room of *kukhim*, a second room served as a repository for bones. Here we find evidence, for the first time, of the practice of secondary burial that was to become the norm in late Second Temple Jerusalem (see below).

Hellenistic and Jewish components of society are reflected in other archaeological data as well. Hasmonean coins often bear Greek inscriptions along with symbols borrowed from the Hellenistic world. Yet these same coins also bear Hebrew inscriptions (and in palaeo-Hebrew script, no less!), and the decorations are strictly aniconic. Clearly, by the early first century B.C.E., Jewish aversion to figural representations, characteristic of the late Second Temple Period, was already well rooted.

In a bulla (seal) of Jonathan the High Priest, recently published by Avigad, a club of Heracles appears, along with a Hebrew inscription. Uniquely Jewish finds of this period are the ritual baths (*miqvaot*) which appear in Hasmonean Gezer and Jericho. These are stepped cisterns connected to water channels facilitating the collection of naturally flowing waters, as required by Jewish law. The priestly Hasmonean family located in Jericho and the pious settlers of Gezer (I Maccabees 13:48) were evidently concerned about the purity laws of Judaism.

The ritual baths of Jericho are only one element in a Hasmonean palace complex discovered in Tulul Abu el-Alayik along the banks of Wadi Qelt just southwest of the city. Excavated in the early 1950s by an American team and for the last ten years by the Hebrew University, the Jericho excavations have uncovered an impressive series of buildings and installations. The Hasmonean stratum is dominated by a monumental swimming pool measuring 34 meters (112 feet) long and 20 meters (66 feet) wide, and divided into two parts by a kind of podium some 6 meters (20 feet) wide. Stairs lead down to the pool on both sides. Connected to the pool on the south was a kind of pavilion, built in Doric style. The central building of this complex, only very partially excavated, was located just southwest of the pool. Located on a mound, this palace is about 50 meters (164 feet) square and may have been two stories high. It was built around a large open courtyard and the walls in many rooms appear to have been decorated with painted and molded stucco. Recently, twin residences have been discovered just south of this Hasmonean complex. Built according to an identical plan, these complexes may have served two Hasmoneans of equal rank. It has been suggested that these residences may have belonged to the brothers Hyrcanus II and Aristobulus II during the reign of their mother, Salome Alexandra.

The Jericho complex served as a winter palace for the Jerusalem-based Hasmonean rulers. Although the most elaborate, it was not the only installation built by the Hasmoneans in the Judean Desert. To date we know of at least six fortresses that existed at that time, from Alexandrium (Sartaba) in the north to Masada in the south, and including Duq, Threx and Taurus in the Jericho region, and Hyrcania (Khirbet Mird) east of Bethlehem. Most of these sites are known from preliminary surveys; in only a few cases have archaeological excavations been carried out. These fortresses have much in common; all are located on relatively isolated mountains in the desert and are almost inaccessible from three directions. In each case, a low ridge connects the fortress to another hill to the west. Water appears to have been provided by aqueducts coming across this ridge. These fortresses served a variety of purposes: vacation sites, administrative centers, burial places, treasure stores, prisons and observation posts.

Archaeological evidence in the Judean Desert attests not only to the activities of the Hasmonean dynasty, but to the activities of the dynasty's opponents as well. The upheavals of the mid-second century that gave rise to Hasmonean rule also led to the formation of other (and at times antagonistic) political-religious groups that flourished throughout this period and beyond. Archaeologically, we know next to nothing about some of them, for example, the Pharisees and Sadducees. However, regarding the Essenes of this period we are very well informed. The sensational discoveries of the Dead Sea Scrolls written by the Qumran sect—now

Aerial view of Qumran.

almost universally identified as the Essenes—have opened up new vistas in the study of Jewish society, beliefs, and religious groupings. The hundreds of scrolls and fragments discovered have revealed a tightly organized sect whose members lived in caves and whose activities were carefully regulated by communal discipline. The beliefs of this group are strikingly different from anything hitherto known (dualism, determinism, angelology, theory of the soul, etc.), and appear to derive, in one fashion or another, from outside influences. Sect members viewed themselves as the Sons of Light in constant conflict and tension with the rest of mankind (including other Jews), described as the Sons of Darkness. The denouement of this conflict was imminent and the members of the Qumran sect lived in expectation of a soon-to-be-born messianic era.

While some finds (other than scrolls) have been made in the surrounding caves, the most important Qumran archaeological remains are centered in the community complex, Khirbet Qumran, located at the northwest corner of the Dead Sea. The major periods of settlement date to Hasmonean and Herodian eras (ca. 150 B.C.E.-68 C.E.). The complex (illustrated on p. 80) measures 100 meters (328 feet) long and 80 meters (263 feet) wide and is divided into several distinct areas. In the center of the northern wall is a defense tower (4). Immediately to the south are rooms for the assembly of elders (5) and a scriptorium where scribes copied the various scrolls (6). The northeastern part of the complex was a kitchen and service area (7); the western sector, a series of storage rooms. On the southeast, several potters' kilns were found (10, 11); presumably Qumran was self-sufficient with regard to dishes and utensils—undoubtedly a result of the sect's stringent purity requirements. The southern part of the complex contained a large room (8) used for the daily meals of the sect. Members gathered after purifying themselves to break bread together and to listen to the reading of scriptures and the words of their leaders. A small room nearby (9) served as a pantry; some 1,000 vessels were

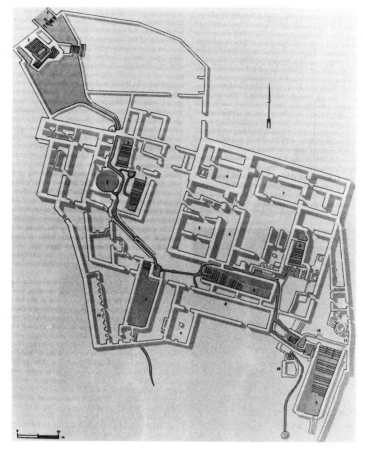

Plan of Qumran Settlement

(1) *entrance of aqueduct*
(2), (3) *reservoirs*
(4) *tower*
(5) *room with benches*
(6) *scriptorium*

(7) *kitchen*
(8) *assembly room and refectory*
(9) *pantry*
(10) *potter's workshop*
(11) *kilns*
(12) *animal pen*

found there. Throughout the whole complex was a series of cisterns (2, 3). Some stored water for daily use during the long, hot, dry summer months, but several of them appear to have been specifically designated for purification purposes. The steps of these latter cisterns show traces of partitions. Thus those ascending, who had just immersed and were ritually clean, could be separated from those descending, who were still impure. Immediately to the east of the Qumran complex was a cemetery containing some 1,100 graves, and several kilometers to the south, at Ein Fashkha, remains of an agricultural settlement associated with this sect have been identified.

Not all discoveries from this period relate to the Jewish population. A striking example of a Hellenistic pagan town is Tel Anafa in the Upper Galilee, excavated throughout the better part of the last 15 years. The site itself is not large, measuring 160 meters (525 feet) long and 110 meters (361 feet) wide. The town flourished during a clearly delineated period, from the mid-second century B.C.E. to about the year 80 B.C.E. Parts of the town wall, a street and several large residences have been excavated. These buildings made use of columns, pilasters, niches and windows. The walls of these homes were often painted or paneled, and the floors decorated with finely made mosaics. Hundreds of coins and stamped Rhodian jar handles have been found as well as decorated stucco and moldings carved with gold leaf. Of utmost significance is the large number of glass vessels found and the variety of lamps, many of which depict two figures of Erotes. These small finds not only allow us to date this Hellenistic town with certainty, but they also attest to the high standard of living enjoyed by the inhabitants. It would appear that Tel Anafa was destroyed by Alexander Jannaeus when he incorporated the Golan area into his kingdom.

Herodian Period

The final 133 years of the Second Temple Period—from the conquest of Pompey to the destruction of Jerusalem (63 B.C.E-70 C.E.) are referred to most often as the Herodian period, despite the fact that Herod ruled for only 33 of these years (37-4 B.C.E.). The reason for this nomenclature is not difficult to understand; Herod was indeed a monumental builder. A product of his age when the Roman emperor as well as other client kings engaged in massive building programs, Herod and his grandson, Agrippa I—41-44 C.E.—viewed the construction of edifices, water installations, fortress-retreats, palaces and entire cities not only as utilitarian and functional, but also as a means of self-aggrandizement and immortality. Thus, throughout his entire kingdom—in Jewish as well as pagan areas, in urban and desert settings—Herod built an enormous variety of structures. These buildings were usually of such solid dimensions that any earlier strata were almost entirely obliterated. As in other areas of life, Herod displayed an enthusiasm for adopting Roman architectural and artistic styles, as well as building techniques. It appears that Herod even brought Roman architects and engineers from Italy to carry out some work. Styles usually found only in Italy and almost unknown throughout the Roman east (for example, opus reticulatum) were used in several Herodian structures. Overall, the years since Israeli statehood have done more than the previous 100 to establish Herod's credentials as an imaginative and indefatigable builder.

Evidence for the scope and scale of Herod's building activity is nowhere better illustrated than in Jerusalem. Excavations conducted since 1968 have demonstrated the massiveness of Herodian construction (see "Jerusalem—'The City Full of People'" by Nahman Avigad, p. 129). The Temple Mount itself is a striking example. Herod doubled the size of the previous Temple Mount area by extending the wall to the south, west and north. In doing so, he was oblivious to natural topography. The western wall of the artificial podium was placed beyond the central Tyropoeon Valley and ran along the eastern slope of the Upper City. To the north, the wall was placed beyond the wadi, along the southern slope of the adjoining hill. The mountain was steep—to extend the Temple podium south, Herodian architects had to construct a mammoth retaining wall at the southeast corner.

Benjamin Mazar's excavations along the western and southern walls have revealed other examples of Herodian construction (see "The Royal Stoa in the Southern Part of the Temple Mount" by Benjamin Mazar, p. 141). First and foremost is the size of the Temple podium itself. Archaeologists have known that most of the remaining outer wall lay below ground level. However, it was only when these courses were exposed at the southwestern corner that the magnitude of the undertaking was fully appreciated. Five Herodian courses represented the "Western" wall prior to 1967. After the Six Day War, two more courses were exposed, and yet another 19 remained underground. Only now can these 19 courses be seen, in whole or in part, at the excavation site at the southwestern corner of the Temple Mount.

Remains of an enormous arch, some 13 meters (43 feet) north of this southwestern corner along the western wall, have been visible for centuries. In the mid-19th century, an American minister Edward Robinson identified these stones as part of a bridge connecting the Temple Mount with the Upper City. Recent excavations have uncovered a massive pier on which this arch came to rest. However, no further piers were detected. Rather, a series of smaller arches grading downward was found just south of this one pier, as well as a series of steps, some *in situ*. It can now be confidently asserted that a monumental staircase led up from the Tyropoeon Valley, affording access to the Temple Mount in general and to the Royal Portico located at its southern extremity in particular. A second monumental staircase of 30 steps, each some 75 meters (246 feet) in width, was uncovered in the southern sector leading to the western Hulda Gate. Part of this entranceway has been recently investigated. The monumental columns, large domed ceiling and ornate stucco decorations give us some idea of what other Herodian gateways must have looked like.

Important small finds were also uncovered. A number of *miqvaot* were discovered in the southern sector between the Hulda Gates. This is not surprising since Jews were required to be ritually pure before entering the Temple precincts. As the monumental staircase attests, the southern approach was one of the most important in general, but was especially so for those wishing to gain immediate access to the Temple itself. The passageway noted above leads under the Royal Portico and ascends to ground level just before the Temple precincts. Thus, placing *miqvaot* just outside the Hulda Gates would be most functional for pilgrims seeking to enter the Holy Sanctuary.

It has been suggested that the monumental southern staircase may indeed have been the location of the first of three higher courts that sat on the Temple Mount. It is reported that at this same place R. Simeon b. Gamaliel and R. Yohanan b. Zakkai, two Pharisaic leaders from the generation immediately preceding the war against Rome, dispatched letters to Jewish communities throughout Israel and the Diaspora. This suggestion gained further credence when archaeologists found a fragment of a monumental inscription near the Hulda Gates (another fragment of this same inscription was found 100 years ago). The first line appears to refer to "elders," perhaps those belonging to this very tribunal!

Another inscription found near the southwestern corner of the Mount reads "To the Place of Trumpeting, to herald . . .". This has been correctly related to the report of Josephus (*The Jewish War IV*, 502) that a priest would sound a trumpet from the Temple Mount at the inaugurations and conclusions of Sabbaths and holidays. Presumably this priest stood at or near the southwestern corner of the Temple Mount (the point must be accessible to the vast majority of the population of the city), and the stone bearing the inscription fell to the street below in the destruction of 70 C.E.

To return to Herod's monumental building activities—during these past few decades three sites in the Judean Desert have offered new and ample evidence of the scope and grandeur of his program. Masada immediately comes to mind. Yigael Yadin's excavations in 1963-65 have shown the extent to which Herod invested everything necessary in order to make this mountain, though located in a remote corner of the desert, an attractive and comfortable place to vacation. The water system, with its dams, ducts and 12 enormous cisterns along the side of the mountain, is a striking example of what can be accomplished with ingenuity, technology and resources. On the mountain itself, the storage rooms were huge, and could feed 10,000 people. The baths were typically Roman in their layout and in their ornateness.

The *pièce de résistance* of Herodian Masada was Herod's two palaces. A western one apparently served as an official residence, and is impressive for its extensive administrative area, service quarters, storage facilities and residential section—altogether occupying some 4,000 square meters (13,123 square feet). The focus of the building was a throne room in the southeast sector. Exquisite mosaic floors graced these rooms. The northern palace was intended for more private use and was built on three tiers on and just below the crest. Each tier had a unique plan; the uppermost contained four rooms set around an open courtyard with a semi-circular porch facing north. Frescoes covered the walls of these rooms; the floors were black-white mosaic. The middle tier, 20 meters (66 feet) below, contained a round room or monument (some 15 meters [49 feet] in diameter). The lowermost tier—15 meters (49 feet) below the middle one—was built in a rectangular area (17.6 square meters [58 square feet]) with a central courtyard surrounded by a stoa. A small bath was off to one side. Herod's desire to build on the northern side of the mountain in order to benefit most from winds, shade and a majestic view reflects the egotism, daring and resourcefulness that have become his hallmarks.

Excavations at Herodium, first by Italian and then by Israeli archaeologists during the past two decades, have revealed another example of Herod's ambitious undertakings. The mountain itself was augmented so as to give it much greater height. According to Josephus, Herod intended this site as both a mausoleum and a palace-retreat. A circular wall protected a royal residence composed of a large courtyard (with exedrae at each end), a triclinium, bedrooms and a bath. Of special interest at Herodium is the extensive building carried out at the foot of the mountain. A race course, palace, large pool and several monumental buildings have been identified. To date, Herod's mausoleum has never been found, although the search for it has served as the incentive for much of the exploration carried out at the site.

The Herodian complex at Jericho is of a different order entirely. As was the case under the Hasmoneans, Jericho often served as Herod's winter retreat. Here there were no defensive walls or fortresses, only buildings and installations intended to offer the king rest, relaxation, and entertainment. It is here at Jericho that we can best compare the scope and grandeur of Herod's building activities with those of his predecessors, the Hasmoneans. In part, Herod continued to use previous structures. The pool and some of the *miqvaot* were preserved, the nearby pavilion was retained and a smaller building was erected over the Hasmonean palace. However, it was to the east and south that Herod set his stamp on the site. At first he was content with building a large palace 86 meters (282 feet) long and 46 meters (151 feet) wide across Wadi Qelt to the south, along with a large pool, 175 meters (574 feet) long and 146 meters (497 feet) wide, to the east. Not long afterward, however, this palace proved inadequate and Herod embarked on an ambitious program on both sides of the wadi, far beyond anything known before. To the south he built a pavilion on an artificially raised hill. Below the pavilion he constructed a sunken garden with a long facade, decorative niches and a terraced hemicycle in the center. A stoa was built on either side of this garden. Directly opposite, on the northern side of the wadi, Herod erected a large complex, 85 meters (279 feet) by 35 meters (115 feet), including a reception hall, 29 meters (95 feet) by 19 meters (62 feet), two peristyle courtyards and a large bath complex. The most impressive room in this bath, and one almost fully preserved, is the round frigidarium, 8 meters (26 feet) in diameter, with its four semi-circular niches. Excavations continue at Jericho, and it is already clear that few other sites offer a comparable scope of Herodian building activity.

Finally, a word on Herod's building activities in urban settings other than Jerusalem. Josephus offers a detailed listing of buildings and monuments erected by the king in cities both in his own kingdom and in those of Syria, Asia Minor and Greece. Within his own kingdom Herod founded two cities, Caesarea and Sebaste. Since 1948, numerous excavations have been carried out in Caesarea. Josephus speaks of a mammoth harbor; to date, finds have largely substantiated his claim. The artificial podium on which a temple to Rome and Augustus was erected has been found, as has the sewerage system also noted by Josephus. In the early sixties, Italian archaeologists excavated the ancient theater, dating its earliest stratum to Herodian times. The Caesarean hippodrome has been dated in recent probes to the third century. An earlier hippodrome or stadium has not yet been located. Finally, two city walls and two aqueducts have been discovered. On the basis of these discoveries, it would seem that Josephus's description of Herodian munificence is well substantiated. Indeed, Herod was considered the founder of the city by later generations. In the conflict between the Jews and pagans of Caesarea in the mid-first century—two generations after Herod—each side appealed to him as a precedent in order to substantiate its claim.

Focusing on the excavations of Herodian structures these past decades has led to an emphasis on Hellenistic influences in Jewish society. Herod's palaces, baths, aqueducts, temples, cities, etc., all reflect the agenda of Hellenistic-Roman architecture (plan, style and technique) in the Imperial City itself as well as in the outermost provinces. The fact that Jerusalem possessed the three standard Greco-Roman entertainment arenas—theater, amphitheater, and hippodrome—indicates just how widespread these social and cultural patterns had become. Excavations in Jerusalem to date have revealed that more than one-third of the inscriptions from late Second Temple times were in Greek.

However, with regard to earlier periods, as noted above, Hellenism does not tell the whole story. Archaeological finds have revealed certain uniquely Jewish phenomena. We have already spoken of the *miqvaot* and the absence of Jewish figural art. Perhaps a further comment on each is warranted.

Concentrations of *miqvaot* in this period have been found in Jerusalem (especially near the Temple Mount to the south and in the Upper City), Masada, Jericho and Qumran. The latter two sites are carry-overs from the Hasmonean era; the Masada remains reflect the very last years of the period (66-74), when the mountain fortress fell into the hands of the revolutionaries. Concentrations of *miqvaot* at these sites were to be expected. They were designed to serve pietistic religious groups (Qumran and Masada), priestly families in the royal entourage (Jericho) and those about to visit the Temple, or wealthy priestly residents of Jerusalem's Upper City. (Priests were required to immerse themselves ritually before partaking of their *terumah* [free will] offering.) We have already noted the problem of identifying a ritual bath from other stepped cisterns. Three criteria, intended to separate the pure from the impure, have been suggested: a partition or two down the steps (Qumran, Jerusalem); double doors to separate those entering from those exiting (Gezer, Jerusalem); a system where collected rainwater is brought into contact with drawn water, making the latter permissible for use in a *miqva*. This last type has been found at Jericho, Masada and Jerusalem.

The absence of figural art in this period is indeed striking. From the hundreds of fragments of frescoes, mosaic floors and stone moldings found in Jerusalem and its environs these past 15 years, there is only one example of figural representation—several birds appearing on a mosaic floor from Mt. Zion. In this respect the norms of Jewish society were far removed from those of other Greco-Roman cities where figural representations were ubiquitous. Of no less interest, however, is the fact that such a prohibition was unique in terms of Jewish history as well. In no other period of antiquity do we read of such inhibitions regarding figural images.

Among the reasons suggested for such a strict application of the Second Commandment at this time are the dominance of Jewish political and religious life by the Sadducees, who espoused an approach that often tilted towards a restrictive, conservative interpretation of biblical injunctions, and that this strict observance was an expression of the traumatic effects in the wake of the persecution under Antiochus IV, when Jews were coerced into idolatrous worship and images were introduced into the Temple precincts. Whatever the reason may have been, it is becoming more and more evident just how deep a mark this avoidance of figural represntation left on Hasmonean and Herodian societies.

A most fascinating kind of discovery during this period is the numerous stone chests (ossuaries) used for secondary burials. There was a custom among Jews— sometime after death, probably about a year or so when the flesh already had decomposed—to gather the bones of the deceased and place them in this kind of repository. There were special customs in this regard and a religious association existed in Jerusalem for this purpose. Such a custom is *sui generis* to this period and place. No other contemporaneous society appears to have adopted such a practice. It was not the custom in biblical times, nor during the last 1,800 years. Yet this was not a sectarian phenomenon; it had widespread appeal. Over 2,000 such ossuaries have been discovered in Jerusalem alone, as compared, for example, with about 15 or so full-sized coffins (sarcophagi). We are well informed about some aspects of this practice but our knowledge of certain details is sketchy. We know exactly when this burial custom first appeared—during the last half of the first century B.C.E. We know when it began disappearing—following the destruction of the Temple, and where its practice was centered—in Jerusalem and environs, including Jericho. The origins of this custom are, however, enigmatic: internal development or a result of foreign influence, and if the latter, what foreign influence? Who introduced this custom, and why? Were there religious ideas behind this practice or only social norms? Was it opposed, and if so, for what reasons? Why did it disappear? As yet, we have no definitive answers to these questions. When we do, there is no doubt that we will also be far better informed about the social and religious life of the Jews during this period.

The Late Roman Era

The political, social and, thereby, archaeological face of Israel was dramatically altered as a result of the two revolts against Rome. The first revolt (66-74) led to the destruction of Jerusalem, including the Temple, and the second (132-135) to the virtual eradication of the Jewish population from Judea. Thereafter, the Jews gradually became a minority. Evidence for these revolts has been brought to light during the last decades in dramatic fashion. Excavations at Masada and, more recently, at Gamla in the Golan region have revealed remains of the Jewish revolutionaries. These people lived frugally, in striking contrast to the lavish Herodian lifestyle of Masada, which they appear to have consciously eschewed. The living quarters, ovens, utensils and weaponry (ballast stones, arrowheads, etc.) tell us a great deal about the people who chose to defy the might of Rome.

The destructive consequences of the first revolt are manifest not only in Masada and Gamla, but in Jerusalem as well. The huge stone blocks from the Temple Mount found on Herodian streets below and the burnt house which remained as it was on the very day of destruction in the summer of 70 bear witness to the extent of the catastrophe that enveloped much of Jewish society at the time.

Remains from the time of Bar Kokhba are fewer than those from the time of the first revolt, though the consequences of the Bar Kokhba revolt were no less harsh. Fortresses with underground tunnels, caves and coins have been found, all relating to this struggle. Of particular interest are the Judean Desert caves in which

Jews (including soldiers of Bar Kokhba's army) took refuge. The papyri discovered there shed much light not only on the war effort itself, but also on many other aspects of Jewish life at the time.

Archaeological evidence from the second and third centuries is generally not as abundant. This is a period sandwiched between the extensive rebuilding of Byzantine times and the earlier Herodian construction. Consequently, relatively little remains from these centuries. However, bathhouses, aqueducts and roads became widespread, and these finds give us some understanding of the period. In several urban settings, as well, second- and third-century architecture is yet distinguishable.

Undoubtedly the most important and unusual site from this late period is Beth She'arim, located in the southwestern Galilee, east of Haifa. Beth She'arim had been excavated prior to World War II, but its uniqueness only became fully apparent after six seasons of excavations during the 1950s. The town itself was the seat of the Jewish political and religious leader, the Patriarch (Nasi), in the later second century, R. Judah the Prince. Because of his unequaled political and religious stature, R. Judah's presence made Beth She'arim an important center, both in his lifetime and after. After his burial there, Beth She'arim became a major Jewish cemetery, and deceased were brought there for burial from all over Israel and from many parts of the Diaspora. The principal finds from Beth She'arim relate to this extensive necropolis.

Altogether over 25 catacombs have been explored. Some contained places for only a few burials, others had hundreds. Some were simple shaft graves, others had numerous halls with ornate facades. Traces of at least one mausoleum were also found. The forms of burial were varied: cavities along the wall, *(arcosolia)*; cavities in the floor; *kukhim*; and sarcophagi. Most sarcophagi were stone, but lead, wood and marble ones were also found. There were two central catacombs, Number 14 and Number 20. Each had a forecourt, a triple-arched facade and a stepped area above, probably for congregating when paying homage to the deceased. Catacomb Number 14 had relatively few burial places. Inscriptions indicate that members of the patriarchal family, possibly even R. Judah himself, were buried there. The names R. Gamaliel, R. Simeon and R. Aniana (Hanina?) appear. Catacomb Number 20, on the other hand, is one of the largest catacombs, with remains of some 200 burials, including 130 sarcophagi. A number of rabbis and members of their families were interred here.

Artistic decoration found in Beth She'arim deserves particular note. Common geometric, floral and architectural decorative forms abound. Other decorations are purely Jewish in character: the menorah, Torah shrine, lulav, ethrog and shofar. Such depictions are in no way startling. Very different, however, are the animal and human representations found throughout these catacombs, even in those with rabbinic representation. All this is in marked contrast to the abstention from figural images characteristic of the earlier period. Presumably the Hellenistic social and cultural climate allowed Jews to address themselves to this dimension of artistic expression.

Another example of Greek influence as reflected in the Beth She'arim cemetery relates to the languages used by Jews. Eighty percent of the inscriptions found there are in Greek. Some are simple statements identifying those buried; others are quite sophisticated elegies. Of the remaining 20 percent, most are in Hebrew, with a few in Aramaic and Palmyrean.

The finds from Beth She'arim have provided a rich mine for scholars, and the implications of the data retrieved there range far and wide. To what degree was Jewish society Hellenized in late antiquity? Is the language pattern evident there reflective of all Jewish society, or only of the upper echelons? What was the Jewish attitude toward figural art? Did it indeed shift radically in succeeding periods? How do the burial practices at Beth She'arim compare with earlier periods? What does this material tell us of Diaspora-Israel relations, of the status of the Patriarchate, of the attitudes and beliefs of the sages? How dominant an influence were the sages within Jewish society? Was their influence felt in all sectors, or only in some? What is the relation between the rabbis mentioned in Beth She'arim and those noted so frequently in Talmudic literature?

Finally, Beth She'arim provides explicit information in an entirely different realm. Here is one site where archaeological data point to a specific date of destruction, in this case 351 C.E. Such definitive numismatic evidence is quite rare. The date itself is significant, for in the mid-fourth century the ancient world was undergoing major transformations that would lead inexorably to Christian and Moslem hegemony, the Middle Ages, and the relegation of the Jews to a secondary status, politically, socially and religiously.

Thus, with Beth She'arim we come to the end of the Greco-Roman era, a period in which archaeological finds have contributed substantially to our awareness of the past. Given the relatively abundant literary sources and the extensive archaeological remains, any synthesis of these realms will undoubtedly prove to be most fruitful. Archaeological finds have complemented, enlarged upon and, at times, even revolutionized our understanding of past eras. In short, these finds are constantly pushing the frontier of our knowledge forward, raising newer and more interesting questions about the past. The excavations at Beth She'arim have done just that.

Bibliography

Early Hellenistic Period
D. Jeselsohn, "A New Coin Type with Hebrew Inscription," *Israel Exploration Journal (IEJ)* 24 (1974), pp. 77-78.
A. Kindler, "Silver Coins Bearing the Name of Judea from the Early Hellenistic Period," *IEJ* 24 (1974), pp. 73-76.
Y.H. Landau, "Greek Inscription found Near Hefzibah," *IEJ* 16 (1966), pp. 54-70.
P. Lapp, "Soundings at Araq el-Emir (Jordan)," *Bulletin of the American Schools of Oriental Research* 165 (1962), pp. 16-34.
A. Spaer, "Some More 'Yehud' Coins," *IEJ* 27 (1977), p. 200-203.

Hasmonean Period
R. Amiran, A. Eitan, "Excavations in the Courtyard of the Citadel, Jerusalem 1968-1969 (Preliminary Report)," *IEJ* 20 (1970), pp. 9-17.
N. Avigad, "The Rock-Carved Facades of the Jerusalem Necropolis," *IEJ* 1 (1950-51), pp. 96-106.
R. de Vaux, *Archaeology and the Dead Sea Scrolls*. London, 1973.
E. Netzer, "The Hasmonean and Herodian Winter Palaces at Jericho," *IEJ* 25 (1975), pp. 89-100.

Herodian Period
B. Mazar, "Herodian Jerusalem in the Light of the Excavations South and South-West of the Temple Mount," *IEJ* 28 (1978), pp. 230-238.
B. Mazar, *The Mountain of the Lord*. New York, 1975.
Y. Yadin, *Bar Kochba*. Jerusalem, 1971.
Y. Yadin, *Masada*. New York, 1966.

Late Roman Period
B. Mazar, M. Schwabe, B. Lifshitz, N. Avigad, *Beth She'arim*, 3 vols. Jerusalem, 1973-76.
L. Levine, *Caesarea under Roman Rule*. Leiden, 1975.
L. Levine, *Roman Caesarea: An Archaeological-Topographical Study,* Qedem 2, Jerusalem, 1975.

Research on Ancient Synagogues in the Land of Israel

By Moshe Dothan

Beginning in the 13th century, Jewish and gentile travelers alike reported seeing the remains of ancient synagogues in the Land of Israel. Not until the middle of the 19th century, however, were these remains studied methodically. Four pioneering scholars deserve mention even in a brief survey—Edward Robinson, Ernest Renan, Charles Wilson and Horatio Kitchener. Between the First World War and the establishment of the State of Israel, three additional studies became landmarks: H. Kohl and C. Watzinger, *Antike Synagogen in Galilaea*, Leipzig, 1916; S.Krauss, *Synagogale Altertumer*, Berlin-Vienna, 1922; and E. L. Sukenik, *Ancient Synagogues in Palestine and Greece*, London, 1934. Since then, there has been no attempt to present a synthesis of the current state of knowledge in this field—except Goodenough's monumental study, which deals in the main, however, with synagogal symbolic art. (See E. R. Goodenough, *Jewish Symbols in the Graeco-Roman Period*, I-XII, New York, 1953-1965.)

Obviously, we need a comprehensive and in-depth study of ancient synagogues in the Land of Israel. Nor can we be content with any single work, even well produced—for instance, F. Huttenmeister et al., *Die Antiken Synagogen in Israel*, Tubingen, 1977.

Surveys and excavations conducted since 1948 have produced a great deal of material, some of which has thoroughly upset previously accepted views. Works already published cast new light on synagogal architecture and art. Inscriptions that have been discovered have clarified several specific halachic issues.

Although the remains of about 120 synagogues have been discovered in the country—including the Golan—only about 70 have been thoroughly investigated, including the 30 studied before the founding of the State. Nevertheless, much varied material has been published. I shall survey here only a limited number of the more significant contributions to our knowledge of these ancient synagogues.

Since the destruction of the Second Temple, the synagogue has been the central feature of Jewish communal life in the Land of Israel. Other institutions—for example, a Beth Midrash (House of Learning)—have often been erected next to the synagogue. The political situation, as well as the social and economic circumstances current in any given period, have had a decisive influence on synagogue architecture. Changes in the Jewish outlook on the world and the changing fashions of the day have also had a considerable effect on building styles and art.

I. Synagogues from the Second Temple Period

By far the most important discoveries of recent years have been the synagogues dating to the period before the destruction of the Second Temple. Although we had known of their existence from Mishnaic and Talmudic sources and from the writings of Josephus, the only evidence available was the Greek inscription found in the Ophel by Weill in 1913. This inscription stated that Theodotus, son of Vettenos, whose grandfather had likewise been an "archisynagogus," had built a synagogue and its adjacent installations. This synagogue has never been found, however, and only recently have archaeological excavations confirmed the fact that synagogues did, indeed, exist in the Land of Israel before the Roman destruction of the Temple. We had long been aware, though, of remains of pre-destruction synagogues overseas, particularly in the coastal region of Asia Minor.

The first pre-destruction synagogue to be definitely identified as such was at Masada. It was probably built in Herodian times. It was joined to the wall circling the site and had a basilica plan. During its first phase, it had two parts—perhaps an anteroom and a sanctuary. In its second phase, evidently during the days of the Zealots, benches were added and certain changes were made in the columns, which previously had formed a *het* ⊓ shape. The entrance to the synagogue was on the southeast, and it was oriented toward Jerusalem. Fragments from the books of Deuteronomy and Ezekiel were found in the synagogue, and this helped confirm the identification of the building as a synagogue.

A basically similar building was discovered at Herodium, where participants in the First Jewish Revolt had converted a Herodian building into a synagogue. The synagogue had a rectangular hall with four columns and benches on three sides. The entrance was on the east.

At Gamla, too, excavators unearthed a building from the Second Temple Period which almost certainly was a synagogue. This is the most splendid of all the synagogues yet excavated that date to this period. Structural alterations were made to the building during the First Jewish Revolt and the siege of Gamla. The synagogue stood near the city wall. A road from the city gate ran parallel to the synagogue. The building consists of a hall containing columns and benches. There are two doors on the southeast. This building is different from the synagogues at Masada and Herodium in that columns and benches run along all four walls. The building dates to Hasmonean times, perhaps to the reign of Hyrcanus II.

These discoveries created a new chronological period in the research on ancient synagogues. And a new category of synagogue was thereby added, which predated the Galilean synagogues. Previously, the Galilean synagogues had been considered the most ancient. However, with these new discoveries, a new scholarly dispute arose. Some scholars believe that these synagogues were the prototype for the later Galilean basilica-plan synagogues, while others suggest that they merely copy a contemporaneous Syrian plan exemplified by the religious buildings at Dura-Europos. Some confirmation of a Syrian influence is reflected in the uniform orientation, in the door on the east side—similar to the door of the Temple—and in the benches along the walls. These are all features typical of Syrian buildings. Still, we cannot ignore the basilical style of these synagogues, which is so similar to the later Galilean synagogues. Moreover, these pre-destruction synagogues were the creation principally of local builders and artisans who would naturally want to conform their plans to the needs of the community, especially with regard to the building's orientation and to the arrangement of the benches. The discovery of more synagogues dating to the first to second centuries C.E., mainly in Judea, should help us solve this question.

II. The Galilean Synagogues

The Galilean synagogues, which date to the latter part of the second century and to the third century C.E., are typically basilicas with three rows of columns each—two rows running along the length and one across the width. The exterior facades are usually decorated, and the doors face toward Jerusalem. The floors are made of stone slabs. Built of hewn stones, the buildings do not yet contain fixed places for the Torah shrine, nor do they have niches or apses. The plans and decorations are quite similar to those of Hellenistic-Roman buildings found in Syria that date to the second to third centuries C.E. Galilean synagogue remains have been preserved at a number of sites, including Kfar Nahum (Capernaum), Bar'am and Chorazim. These synagogues were either surveyed or excavated several decades ago. Recently some have been partially or wholly reexcavated.

At Kfar Nahum, the Franciscans have renewed excavations. Stratigraphical sections, principally beneath the paving in the main hall of the synagogue, led the excavators to conclude that the synagogue was built later than previously supposed, that is, during the latter part of the fourth century C.E. This conclusion is based mainly on coins and potsherds dating to the middle of the fourth century C.E. that were found beneath the paving. Scholars who contest this dating argue that the coins and sherds were discovered at precisely those places where the paving slabs had been moved and that the context in which the coins and sherds were found constitutes merely later fill. Without entering this dispute, I might point out that architectural as well as historical considerations seem to weigh against the dating suggested by the excavators. Architecturally speaking, the synagogue at Kfar Nahum and the other Galilee synagogues differ radically from those of the Byzantine Period. It is difficult to imagine, moreover, that the magnificent synagogues of the Jewish Galilee—whose external splendor must have been quite extraordinary—should have been built at the end of the fourth century, when the country was ruled by an inimical Byzantine government.

Changes in the plan of several synagogues—characterized by the addition of a fixed place for the Torah shrine and a niche in the wall to indicate the direction of Jerusalem—are attested at Arbel and in the recently discovered Golan synagogues.

Many architectural remains and some synagogue buildings themselves were discovered in the Golan, primarily between 1967 and 1973. However, only limited excavations were subsequently conducted, for example, at Katzrin. Here two rows of columns divide the longitudinal area of the synagogue into a nave and two side aisles. The building had two phases. The earlier one apparently resembled the Galilean synagogues. The entrance was in the center of the southern facade. Later, a door was cut into the northern wall, and a platform (*bimah*) was erected near the south wall. This change in orientation is also evidenced by a mosaic from the later phase. The second phase seems to have been started at the end of the third century or the beginning of the fourth century C.E. The change in orientation, the addition of the platform, the installation of a permanent Torah shrine and the mosaic floor all occurred at this time.

III. Synagogues from the Transitional Period

At the beginning of the fourth century, the first of the non-Galilean type of synagogues were built. A few were broadhouse-plan synagogues. Although their entrances were no longer oriented toward Jerusalem, the worshippers would, in fact, face the Holy City as they entered the building—and their prayers were of course always directed toward Jerusalem! A permanent place was reserved for the Torah shrine either on a platform (*bimah*) or in a niche or sometimes in a room facing Jerusalem. The principal change in these transitional synagogues, however, involved a purposeful shift in emphasis from exterior to interior decoration. Whatever splendor had been previously associated with the exterior of the Galilean synagogues was now transferred to the interior of the buildings and especially to the mosaic floors. Some scholars associate this change with a decline in the economic conditions of the Jews in the Land of Israel at the beginning of the Byzantine Period. Therefore, their only buildings had purposely dull—i.e., inexpensive—exteriors. Only a few of these transitional synagogues were discovered before 1948, but their number has grown greatly since then. I shall first discuss the Sussiya and Khirbet Shema synagogues.

The Sussiya synagogue, like its counterpart at Eshtamoa, is a synagogue type unique to Judea. Its main feature is a broad hall without columns. At Sussiya, the entrance is on the short, eastern wall. The building was transformed into a kind of broadhouse by the installation of two platforms (*bimot*). Perhaps a niche was also added. The platforms (and the niche, too, if it was there) face Jerusalem. Benches line the walls. The entire floor is paved with mosaics. The mosaic floor in front of the east platform (*bimah*) depicts an Ark of the Law and a seven-branched candela-

Inscription on mosaic floor from ninth to tenth centuries C.E.
uncovered in a synagogue at Sussiya.

*The "candlelabra" mosaic and secondary **bimah** at the Sussiya synagogue.*

brum. A Hebrew inscription reads, " . . . the year four thous[and] . . . ". This is the only known inscription that gives the date of the Creation. The Sussiya synagogue was probably built during the fourth century and was used until the eighth century. Over the years the synagogue underwent various changes; for example, a new geometric mosaic floor was laid in the middle of the prayer-hall, apparently on top of a zodiac design.

The Khirbet Shema synagogue is located in a town that might be Galilean Tekoah. In its second phase, which lasted from the fourth to sixth centuries, it was converted from a longitudinally oriented building to a broadhouse. This surely attests to the eclectic nature of the plans of these Galilean synagogues. The principal difference between the Khirbet Shema synagogue and those at Sussiya and Eshtamoa is that at Shema the entrance is on the north—on the wide side of the building. Moreover, it contains two rows of columns that divide the prayer-hall lengthwise. Both Sussiya and Eshtamoa are without columns. Even in the synagogue's earliest phase, a platform (*bimah*) and permanent place for the Torah shrine were installed on the building's wide side, which faced Jerusalem.

Before discussing synagogues that date from the fifth century onward, we must briefly consider the synagogue at Hammath Tiberias (south). Hammath Tiberias was a great Jewish center especially after the Bar Kokhba War.

A stratigraphical excavation at this synagogue revealed various alterations. The earliest structure that can positively be identified as a synagogue (stratum IIB) is a basilica-plan building. The entrance is on the north side, however, through a vestibule. This apparently was the synagogue's only entrance. Having entered, the worshippers had to turn left in order to face Jerusalem. As with other Galilean synagogues, the Hammath Tiberias synagogue did not yet have a permanent place for the Torah shrine. It did, however, have a mosaic floor—the earliest yet discovered although preserved only in fragments, which reveal that this design was probably entirely geometric. The door on the east side of the synagogue, from a later and higher stratum (stratum IIA), had been blocked up.

The vestibule was divided into separate rooms, in one of which the Torah shrine was placed. The entire floor was decorated with a magnificent mosaic. It is especially notable because of its Hellenistic-Roman motifs. Helios is in the center of the mosaic. Greek inscriptions contain the Greek names of the Jewish founders of the synagogue. All of this attests to a date toward the end of the third or the beginning of the fourth century C.E. By that time, the Jews of Tiberias had become part of the alien cultural milieu that surrounded them. When Christianity became dominant, however, we note a change in the outlook of the Jews of Tiberias, reflected in the construction of a new and large basilica-plan synagogue (stratum IB) with an apse. This plan resembles many other synagogues and churches of the fifth century. Of this synagogue, only fragments of the mosaic floor were preserved. The decoration of the mosaic is entirely different, consisting principally of animal figures.

General view of Ein Gedi synagogue, looking north.

The uppermost synagogue (stratum IA), built during the Ummayad period, contains a mosaic floor entirely void of images. The fragmentary remains of this mosaic suggest that the decoration was principally geometric, although it did include typical Jewish symbols such as a seven-branched candelabrum.

IV. The Late Synagogues

Our discussion of the later phases of the Hammath Tiberias synagogue, from the fifth to eighth centuries C.E., brings us to two late synagogues, one of which at least had earlier phases too.

At Ein Gedi, archaeologists discovered two synagogues, one built on top of the other. The upper, Byzantine synagogue is the more interesting, but the earlier synagogue, too, had some noteworthy features. The entrance to the earlier synagogue is located on the north, that is, facing Jerusalem. In this, it is consistent with the Galilean tradition in which the entrance facade faces Jerusalem. The mosaic floor of the earlier Ein Gedi synagogue contains black and white geometric designs, including a large swastika in the center. This certainly attests to the variety of synagogue architecture at the time and to the differences in design at different sites. There is thus no justification for assuming that there was only a single, clear-cut, consistent design for synagogues.

The later Ein Gedi synagogue was built in the fifth century C.E. The entrance is on the west. This synagogue had a platform (*bimah*) and a niche behind it to house

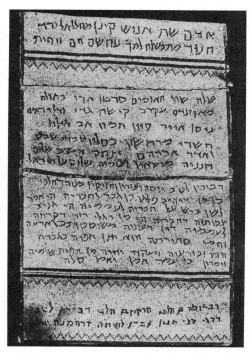

Sixth-century C.E. inscription on mosaic floor of Ein Gedi synagogue.

a Torah shrine. Fragments of scrolls were discovered in the area behind the Torah shrine. The mosaic floor contained no human images.

A most important mosaic inscription was also found here written partly in Hebrew and partly in Aramaic. One section of the inscription contains a curse on all who divide the community, slander it or reveal the location of the synagogue to non-Jews. Opinions differ as to how this curse should be interpreted and no consensus has yet been reached.

The inscription at the Ein Gedi synagogue was the longest one known until the discovery of a still larger mosaic inscription in the synagogue at Rehov—a synagogue to which we now turn and with which we shall conclude. The Rehov synagogue, south of Beth Shean, was built according to the standard basilica plan, in which two rows of columns divide the hall into a nave and two side aisles. A platform (*bimah*) was built in the southern part of the nave. A bench was placed along the eastern wall. It is interesting that this synagogue—built during the fifth century at the earliest—contained no apse. This is quite unusual, since in nearly all synagogues built at this time, and afterward also, an apse faces Jerusalem.

The Rehov synagogue became famous following the discovery of a 29-line inscription in its mosaic floor. The inscription is among the most important yet discovered in ancient synagogues in the Land of Israel. It is contained in the mosaic floor from the synagogue's later phase and may be dated to the sixth century C.E. It deals with the laws pertaining to the sabbatical year and the requirements of tithing that had to be observed in various regions of the country, especially as those laws applied to the Beth Shean district. The text differs somewhat from the parallel citation in the Jerusalem Talmud and from the partial version contained in the Tosephta. However, these were later compositions, subject to many emendations. The importance of the inscription is not limited to halachic matters. It also sheds light on historical geography, particularly as it relates to the Beth Shean and Samaria area during the Hellenistic and Roman-Byzantine Periods.

Inscriptions were also found on the walls of the Rehov synagogue. Although we had known about this kind of inscription from isolated fragments found at various synagogues, the Rehov synagogue for the first time gave us such an inscription in its full splendor. This inscription had originally been inscribed on the plaster of the walls but had fallen off. The fragments were collected and pieced together. One would have expected the decoration on the plaster walls to be geometric patterns or floral designs. However, the excavators discovered Hebrew names instead. Among the names were Isaac and Jacob, apparently donors to the synagogue. In these names, we have come full circle. Instead of such names as Theodotus, Maximus, Severus and Profuturus, found in earlier synagogues and reflecting the attempt of the Jewish community to reconcile itself, at least externally, to the Hellenistic culture that predominated in the region during the first centuries C.E., we now find purely Hebrew names in a rural synagogue of the sixth century.

It is appropriate to conclude this brief survey with a quote from the late Professor M. Avi-Yonah, who in 1973 wrote:

"The bewildering variety of plans among the two later kinds [of synagogues]—the 'transitional' and the 'late' [that is, the vast majority of synagogues that have been excavated—M.D.]—precludes any attempt to use them as a basis to determine chronology . . . It now seems that the whole question of the development of synagogal plans from the third to the sixth century [C.E.] will have to be reconsidered."*

Despite the excavation of so many synagogues and the concomitant research, we must still look forward to the kind of fundamental research called for by Avi-Yonah of blessed memory.

JERUSALEM, 1978

*M. Avi-Yonah, "Ancient Synagogues," *Ariel* 32 (1973), pp. 41-42.

Ancient Churches

By Yoram Tsafrir

When the first Christian emperor, Constantine, gained control of the eastern part of the Roman Empire in 324 C.E., a dramatic change took place in the status and condition of the Land of Israel. Although it continued to be called "Palaestina," the alien name given it by Hadrian after his suppression of the Bar-Kokhba revolt, and was to be known by this name for many years thereafter, Palaestina was no longer a province of secondary importance; it became once again the Holy Land.

While Caesarea continued to be the capital, as well as the metropolis of Christianity, Jerusalem regained its central significance in the eyes of the Christian world. Jerusalem had, after all, been the city of Jesus' death and resurrection. The leaders of the Christian church in Jerusalem prided themselves on the primacy of their congregation, which they regarded as the mother of all churches. Jerusalem boasted a bishop's throne—reputedly that of Jacob, Jesus' brother. The leaders of the church in Jerusalem carried on the fight for the precedence of their city. Ultimately, Juvenal (then Archbishop of Jerusalem) was victorious, for in the famous Council of Chalcedon in 451 C.E., Jerusalem was granted the status of a separate patriarchate—only the fifth such patriarchate to be created. Although small in size, it was nevertheless now equal in status to Constantinople, Rome, Alexandria and Antioch. At the same time, the authority of the see of Antioch over Palestine was abolished.[1]

When Christianity became the dominant religion in the Roman Empire, the pagan population of the Land of Israel converted to Christianity *en masse*. Only the Jews and Samaritans struggled to resist. The large-scale conversion to Christianity reflected in the erection of hundreds of churches throughout the land. Not a single Christian settlement was without a church, and hardly a city was without at least a few churches. The architectural style of most of these churches was the basilica. Monasteries also sprang up all over the country, even in out-of-the-way uninhabited regions such as Sinai and the Judean Wilderness. The most important churches were the "memoria" churches, most of which were not built, like congregational churches, as basilicas but were distinguished by a concentric plan, either circular, polygonal or cruciform. Such churches served to perpetuate the memory of saints or their burial places. Most important, however, they were intended to memorialize sites connected with the life and death of Jesus, with the lives of his disciples, or with events mentioned in the Bible.

No wonder that research on the Byzantine churches became one of the first focal points of archaeological investigation in modern Palestine and later in the Land of Israel. Some of these churches still stand *in situ*, like the Church of the Nativity in Bethlehem (with minor changes in the original structure) and the Church of the Holy Sepulchre in Jerusalem (with major changes in its structure).

Initially, we find only descriptions of existing monuments, surveys, and accounts of occasional discoveries. Toward the end of the 19th century, carefully planned archaeological excavations began. By the middle of the 20th century, some of the most prominent scholars in the field—researchers like Vincent, Abel, de Vaux, Saller, Madder, Schneider and Crowfoot, among others—were devoting themselves to research on churches in the Holy Land. Some of these scholars were associated with Christian research institutes, and some were academicians connected with schools of archaeology or government institutions.

Perusal of the books and journals since 1948 presents a rather spectacular picture of church research. Scores of sites were discovered and excavated, or re-excavated, including churches, monasteries, chapels and cultic caves. No less impressive is the actual number of excavators and researchers who assisted in analyzing the material—scholars from the Israel Department of Antiquities and Museums, university faculty and scholars from schools of biblical research and archaeology, as well as foreign contingents.

Although my short survey will deal with the research done during the years since the State of Israel was established, I shall include, as is proper, contributions by non-Israelis as well as Israelis, including scholars who worked under Jordanian rule, or under the Egyptian government in the Sinai.

Two points will become apparent in many instances—namely, that this scientific research is never limited by political borders and that, essentially, our work here continues that of scholars under the Jordanian or Egyptian regimes. The Six Day War in 1967 did not prove to be a crisis for archaeological projects as the war in 1948 had; in fact it marked a jumping-off point. After 1967, we see more energetic activity, a new trend toward more archaeological enterprises.

While we may rightly pride ourselves on our achievements, we should nevertheless be reminded that these accomplishments represent, in the main, new accomplishments in the compilation and collation of already existing information and in the quality of research. They do not represent either breakthroughs in unknown areas of research or the promulgation of new theories. The foundation of this scholarship was laid in the past, especially during the first half of the 20th century. Crowfoot's first book on the churches in Palestine, published in 1941 remains in many respects the best summary available.[2] Two years before the founding of the State of Israel, Grabar published his basic study on Holy Land "memoria" churches and their general relationship to the development of architecture during the Middle Ages, especially in the Byzantine period.[3] Perhaps the most important challenge facing Israeli scholars today is to synthesize the vast amount of information and material available and to use the large amount of data to understand the evolution of this architecture. We must take into account histo cal background, liturgical details, technological ability and the aesthetic notions prevalent at the time.

Admittedly, several fairly good syntheses are available. Among them are the book of the Franciscan father, B. Bagatti,[4] and A. Ovadiah's corpus of Byzantine churches in the country.[5] We should also mention A. Negev's summary article on the churches of the Negev mountains[6] and, in Hebrew, the articles published to date in the quarterly, *Qadmoniot*.[7] These publications are bound to stimulate further work in the near future.

Church research has experienced fewer major changes since 1948 than have the studies of other archaeological periods. This is plainly the result of the work of those scholars who carried the burden of research during the British Mandate and who subsequently continued their investigations under the auspices of the new State's research institutes. Foremost among these was that unforgettable mentor, Michael Avi-Yonah, who successfully combined his field experience with a broad and comprehensive knowledge of historical sources and with his remarkable erudition in the dual areas of architecture and art. He was responsible for the excavation of several churches during the 1930s and 1940s and saw to the publication of their results. During the 1950s, he headed the excavation of churches at Givat Ram in modern Jerusalem, Evron and Avdat. Professor Avi-Yonah's influence may be seen in almost every report Israeli researchers publish on ancient churches even today. Indeed, most of these scholars were his students at Hebrew University's Institute of Archaeology.

Obviously, we cannot present here a comprehensive and systematic survey of every discovery in this field of archaeological endeavor. I shall therefore mention only those finds that are typical of Israel's ancient churches, or of a particular region of the Land.

All surveys of this nature must begin with Jerusalem, since by far the greatest concentration of churches was here. There were in fact scores, but only a few have been positively identified.[8] The most important of these is the Church of the Holy Sepulchre or, as it was then called, the Church of the Resurrection (Anastasis). It was built by Constantine on the site where the Temple of Aphrodite had once stood. Its dedication (or "encaenia") occurred in the middle of September, 335 C.E. For generations afterwards, the anniversary of this date was observed as a general holiday and fair for the people. The church was destroyed and subsequently rebuilt on several occasions. Crusader rebuilding in the 12th century changed the appearance of the church completely. For many years, scholars had attempted to establish what it originally looked like but could base their ideas only minimally on archaeological finds in the area. Instead they had to depend upon Eusebius's description in his book, *Vita Constantini*.[9] Although the relevant passages in Eusebius's biography of Constantine offer a comparatively detailed account of the church, their meaning was often ambiguous. Until the 1950s, most scholars accepted Vincent's reconstruction, which stressed the tripartite division of the area; that is, the entrance ("propylaea"), the main basilica (which was known as the "martyrium"), and the rotunda (the Anastasis), at the center of which the holy sepulchre itself was located. This division, based on literary sources, is supported by the depiction of the church in the famous mosaic map from Madaba, from the second half of the sixth century C.E.

A radical change occurred when, at the beginning of the 1960s, the three principal groups governing the church—that is, the Latin, Orthodox and Armenian ecclesiastical authorities—agreed on an appropriate and comprehensive plan for its renovation. Archaeological excavations at the site were conducted as part of the renovation and reconstruction work. These were led by several archaeologists, including Father V. Corbo who excavated in the Latin section, A. Ekonomopoulos in the Greek section, and recently, M. Broshi in the Armenian section.

A provisional summary report was written by the architect in charge of the restoration, the late Father Charles Couasnon of the Ecole Biblique et Archeologique Française in Jerusalem.[10] According to Couasnon's reconstruction, the church's two principal monuments—the Rock of Golgotha and the sacred Tomb itself—were raised by hewing away at the natural rock around them. (Indeed, this area had once been a stone quarry.) These two monuments subsequently became an integral part of Constantine's building.

The entrance to the church, through the "propylaea," was on the main street, that is, on the Cardo Maximus of Aelia. When Ekonomopoulos uncovered the original apse, the basilica's orientation to the west was finally verified. A westward orientation is somewhat unusual in ancient churches, although there are some—most prominently, St. Peter's in the Vatican. (Incidentally, the apse of the present-day Greek shrine built over the ancient apse faces east.) The Golgotha Rock stood in the corner of the courtyard located between the basilica and rotunda, and a special chapel was built beside it. At a slightly later date, the Anastasis dome was built over the actual tomb monument, and an impressive entrance decorated with columns led from a courtyard on the east to the domed structure.

An illustration of a ship was found on a stone in a foundation wall in the Armenian section.[11] This drawing is apparently associated with an early period in the church's history. When the drawing was published several years ago, the Latin inscription beneath it was incorrectly deciphered. Broshi published it again recently and proposed the reading: *Domine ivimus*, "Lord, we went." Perhaps, as Pere Benoit suggests, the inscription was written by pilgrims who had come by ship from the Latin Occident and chose this way to express their joy in having fulfilled the verse in Psalms 122: "Let us go up to the House of the Lord."

Until 1959, it was thought that the "Church of the Ascension to Heaven" on top of the Mount of Olives had been an octagonal structure. This universal assumption was based on the later Crusader building, which can be seen today. In that year, however, V. Corbo's excavations proved that the original plan had been concentric, as befitted a "memoria" church, but that it was circular, not octagonal,[12] thus somewhat paralleling the Anastasis cupola above Jesus' tomb. Corbo thus confirmed a drawing by the pilgrim Arculf, who had visited Jerusalem around 680 C.E. and depicted the church as a circular building. Ironically enough, this drawing was not accepted by later researchers.

Additional churches have been discovered, particularly outside Byzantine Jerusalem, and known churches have been re-investigated. In 1954, Bagatti conducted excavations at the site of "Dominus Flevit" on the slope of the Mount of Olives. There he uncovered both a monastery and a church dating to the latter part of the Byzantine period, which may have been dedicated to St. Anne.[13] Beginning in 1949, Avi-Yonah excavated a fifth-century C.E. monastery and a church at Givat Ram. An inscription suggested that the site had been dedicated to St. George. At the Monastery of the Cross on the west side of the city, which had once been thought to date to the 10th century, Greek excavators uncovered a mosaic, as well as other remains that establish the founding of this complex sometime during the Byzantine Period.

Pinkerfeld's investigations at the Tomb of David in 1949 and Broshi's recent excavations have produced some evidence, albeit of secondary importance, concerning the plan of the Church of Zion and of the buildings around it.

In the vicinity of the Church of St. Anne (the Byzantine Probathica Church) extensive archaeological activity has produced much new data.

During B. Mazar's excavations near the southern wall of the Temple Mount, a lintel and columns belonging to a church were discovered, though obviously not *in situ*. At a nearby Byzantine building, Christian liturgical vessels were found. Some scholars have suggested that this structure was a monastery.

In the Armenian Garden area, the noted excavator of Jerusalem, Kathleen Kenyon, and the Canadian archaeologist A. D. Tushingham uncovered remains of a church and a mosaic.[14] A Greek inscription that has not yet been fully published was also discovered here. It appears to include a blessing bestowed on the memory of some of Christ's most loving benefactors. The names mentioned in the inscription are Tasilus (or Basilus) and perhaps also Bassa, a famous friend of the Empress Eudocia. These finds confirm what had already been known from various other sources—that a remarkably large number of churches and monasteries had once dotted the landscape between David's tower and the top of Mt. Zion.

After the Six Day War, Israeli scholars conducted especially intensive investigations in Jerusalem. Perhaps for this reason, some of the most important church finds have been made by Israeli archaeologists. During excavations in the Jewish quarter, N. Avigad discovered the foundations of an apse deeply concealed within a thick wall. Avigad concluded that he had come upon remains of the large and magnificent Nea Church which had been built by Justinian. Preliminary reconstruction of the huge complex was possible, based on some segments of walls and especially on a threshold and a marble floor on the west side of the complex (west of the hospice attached to the church). The threshold on the west side and the apse in the northeast are more than 100 meters (328 feet) apart. Some scholars suggest that the apse may have belonged to a secondary chapel that once stood next to the main church. M. Ben-Dov's excavation outside the Turkish city wall uncovered the southeastern extremity of this gigantic complex, while Avigad's excavation inside the city wall exposed the huge subterranean vault system that provided the foundation for the church. A monumental foundation inscription mentioning the Emperor Justinian was discovered on the southern wall of the plastered vault. This inscription is now on display in the Israel Museum. This is truly one of the most splendid of the country's epigraphic finds and it is difficult to imagine a more exciting reward for an archaeologist's efforts than the discovery of an inscription like this. It actually mentions an Emperor—Justinian—by name, as well as an Abbot—Constantine—who is familiar to us from written sources. The inscription also specifies a plausible date. Most important, it alludes to an episode—the building of the "Nea"—which is well-known from the writings of Procopius of Caesarea, Justinian's court historian.[15]

Work began on the Nea during the latter part of the fifth century C.E. Work was temporarily halted because the financial burden was too great for the people of Jerusalem to carry alone. The sainted monk, Sabbas, 92 years old, traveled to Justinian's court to secure the necessary funds. Sabbas was promised that the building would be finished, and the promise was kept. The inscription mentions the 13th year of the indiction. This could be 534/5 C.E., not long after Sabbas's visit to the emperor, which would mark the renewal of construction and perhaps even the completion of the first phase of the construction of the vaulted substructure that supported the complex. The 13th year of the indiction could also be 549/50 C.E., about seven years after the dedication of the new church.

This discussion cannot cover all of even the principal discoveries in other parts of the country, so we limit ourselves, almost arbitrarily, to those finds that are characteristic of each region. In the northeast, especially around the Sea of Galilee, Christians have conducted particularly active missionary efforts (as they did in Judea and Jerusalem), no doubt because of the associations of this area with the lives of Jesus and his disciples. However, unlike Judea and Jerusalem, where pagans readily accepted the ascendant Christian religion, the Galilee was strewn with obstacles to Christian missionary work. The Galilee then was the main center

101

of Judaism in the Land of Israel, and the Jews refused to compromise in their battle against Christianity. But although the Jews were stubborn in the struggle, Christianity did make gains; even in Jewish Tiberias a church was erected.

While Tiberias was Jewish, its rival, Sussita, was pagan. It is interesting to compare Christian gains in these two cities. While only one church has been discovered in Tiberias[16] (and even this find has not yet been definitely identified as a church), archaeologists working in Sussita in the 1950s found four churches near the main street. The churches included marble columns, mosaics and numerous inscriptions.[17]

At Capernaum (Kfar Nahum), the Franciscan excavators, Corbo and Loffreda, uncovered an octagonal structure south of the synagogue, which scholars once believed had been a baptistry or ritual bathhouse. These archaeologists now propose, however, that the building is in fact a church with a concentric plan, which was built on the site of Peter's house. The large building uncovered beneath the church's foundations appears to have been originally a private dwelling and a meeting place for Christians in the pre-Constantine period.[18] This was the period before Christianity was recognized as an official religion and before the traditional churches began to be built. If this opinion is correct, the find is certainly most significant, for we would have here the very first religious congregational meeting place ("domus ecclesiae") discovered dating to the second to third centuries C.E.

Between 1970 and 1972, on the other side of the Sea of Galilee, at Kursi (Gergasa) D. Urman and V. Tzaferis uncovered an impressively large enclosure, with a basilica church at its center. This church included chapels, a crypt[19] and beautiful mosaics. The excavators also discovered a very important Greek inscription that indicates that the "fotisterium"—that is, the baptistry—was paved in 585 C.E., during the reign of Emperor Maurice. According to Mark 5:1, it was here that Jesus exorcised the demons and the swine cast themselves into the lake.

Restrictions of space here preclude a discussion of the churches uncovered at Magdala and Beth-Yerah, in the Beth Shean area and in the Lower and Central Galilee. I will concentrate instead on the western Galilee. As early as the 1930s and '40s important churches were discovered in this region—for example, Suhmata (Hosen) and Hanita. Gradually it became apparent that the mosaics and inscriptions in these churches were typical of the region. Since the establishment of the State of Israel, additional significant finds have been made—by Avi-Yonah, Prausnitz, Edelstein and Claudine Dauphin. The western Galilee contains no sacred sites. The churches, some large and splendid, are therefore mostly of the congregational type. Important congregational churches were also discovered at Evron,[20] Shavei Zion[21] and Nahariya[22] and remains of churches at Tel Kisan, Kfar Ata, and at other sites. Claudine Dauphin uncovered an interesting building at Shelomi, which turned out to be not a church at all, but a farmhouse that had belonged to a monastery; it was decorated with an inscription, and its mosaics were similar to those usually used in churches.[23]

All the churches in the western Galilee were under the jurisdiction of the metropolis of Tyre and were subordinate to the patriarchate of Antioch. Fortunately for us, it was customary in this area to decorate buildings with magnificent mosaics and long, dated mosaic inscriptions.

In the coastal region to the south, a fusion of two opposing elements characterized the churches in particular and Christianity in general. On the one hand, several of the most pious monks in the country resided in this area: for example, Hilarion during the fourth century; Peter the Iberian, who led the Monophysites during the fifth century; and Varsanuphius, the fifth-century "Old Man." On the other hand, the local population was devoted to what they regarded as their classical Greek heritage. They continued to study and practice the classical rheto-

Mosaic floor of middle hall at church in Horvat Brachot.

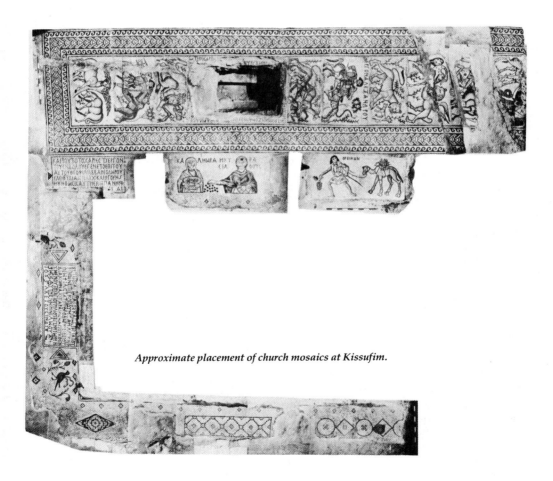

Approximate placement of church mosaics at Kissufim.

ric, philosophy and art. Gaza was especially notable for its skillful blending of the new Christian faith with its inherited classical culture. Indeed, Gaza was closer in spirit to the classical tradition than any other comparable center of scholarship and the arts in the East; it is remarkable that the church permitted this cultural deviation from pious Christian orthodoxy.

With this historical background in mind, it is easy to explain the presence of a mosaic floor dating to the second half of the sixth century recently uncovered by Rudolph Cohen near Kissufim. Cohen identifies Kissufim with the ancient town of Orda.[24] The mosaic design contains obviously classical features side by side with figures whose dress and general appearance are depicted in a purely Byzantine style. Especially surprising is a hunting scene showing Alexander the Great on his horse, with an adjacent Greek inscription: "Alexander's work." More conventional churches were found in other places on the southern coast, for example, at Ashkelon, Barnea and Magen. These, too, contained mosaic floors.

A large number of previously unexcavated churches have been unearthed in the central Negev. Reports on excavations conducted in the pre-1948 period were invariably published very late (for instance, Nitzana), and sometimes no reports were published at all (Shivta).

During the 1950s, Avi-Yonah began excavations at the two churches in Avdat. This work was completed by A. Negev,[25] who also uncovered two churches at Mamshit/Kurnub during the 1960s.[26] Renate Rosenthal published the first precise description of the north church at Shivta,[27] and the author, together with Rosenthal, excavated the north church at Rehovot in the Negev.[28] By comparing the one-apse churches with three-apse churches, Professor Negev attempted to understand the internal development of church architecture in the Negev from the fourth through sixth centuries C.E.[29] Scholars were greatly aided by the dated inscriptions, mostly burial inscriptions, found at many of these Negev churches.

The first mosaic floors in the Negev to extend over the entire nave of a church were discovered at Mamshit. Both the large east church and the small but magnificent Nilus church in the west of the city were paved with mosaics.

The large church at Rehovot in the Negev is typical of the three-apse church. It is much like the churches at Shivta. A burial inscription dating to 488 C.E. found in the large church at Rehovot in the Negev indicated quite clearly that the three-apse type of church was common in this country as early as the second half of the fifth century. A subterranean chapel (a crypt) was discovered beneath the "bema" (presbyterium) of this church. Two stairways led to and from this chapel, allowing the traffic of worshippers and pilgrims to flow smoothly. This design is typical of several churches found elsewhere in the Land of Israel that catered primarily to pilgrims. We do not yet know why this particular church at Rehovot in the Negev was regarded as sacred, with which saint it was associated nor what holy relics were kept here. These sacred relics were probably stored in the reliquary chest that stood in the apse in the crypt beneath the church's main altar on the upper level. When the residents fled during the Arab conquest of the city, they almost certainly took with them the box containing the holy remains.[30]

Excellent excavations have been conducted in the Sinai region, both in the north and in the south. At el-Felusiat (ancient Ostracine), east of Lake Bardawil, E. Oren uncovered a splendid church containing a variety of finds.[31] In the high mountains of southern Sinai, particularly near St. Catherine's Monastery, A. Goren, I. Finkelstein,[32] and U. Dahari drew and surveyed a number of chapels and the remains of monasteries about which nothing had previously been known. Similar finds were encountered near other monastic centers in the Sinai, for example, at Phiran and Raithu near et-Tur on the coast of the Bay of Suez.

The principal research in the Sinai, however, was done by the joint American-

Southern staircase leading to the crypt of northern church at Rehovot in the Negev.

Crypt of northern church at Rehovot in the Negev after reconstruction, looking east.

Apse of central church at Rehovot in the Negev.

Egyptian expedition headed by the architect G.H. Forsyth and the art historian K. Weitzmann. This team worked between 1956 and 1965,[33] and their efforts yielded both new information and new achievements in research, analysis, and classification of the ancient monuments. They also made valuable contributions in the area of conservation of ancient mosaics. One dramatic discovery connected with the magnificent church at St. Catherine's should be mentioned here. Before the work of the American-Egyptian expedition, the "Sacred Bush" chapel behind the apse of the church had been considered the earliest part of the church; monastic tradition had associated it with Constantine's mother, Queen Helena. The American-Egyptian expedition, however, proved that it clearly had been erected in medieval times and was, in fact, the most recently built section of the church.

Having gone almost full circle, I shall conclude with Judea. In the environs of Jerusalem, too, there are many sacred sites. Many have biblical connections and often New Testament associations. Others are considered holy because of their association with famous monks of the Judean wilderness who built monasteries there. Since 1948, many monastic churches have been discovered or uncovered in or on the edges of the Judean wilderness—for example, at Khirbet Mird (Hasmonean Hyrcania and the later monastic Castelium) by G.E. Wright; at Masada by Y. Yadin; at the upper levels of Herodium by V. Corbo; and at the lower levels of Herodium by E. Netzer.

J. Meimaris renewed excavations at Khan al-Ahmar, the ancient Monastery of Euthymius, previously investigated by D.J. Chitty.

East of Bethlehem, Corbo excavated the Latin Shepherds' Field and several other monasteries—for example, Khirbet Juhzum, Khirbet Abu Ghuuneim and Khirbet Bir-al-kut. To V. Tzaferis, who excavated at the Greek Shepherds' Field near Beth-Sahur,[34] belongs the most important discovery in this area: a subterranean cave church dating to the fifth century C.E. This completely preserved church sanctified the cave where, according to tradition, the shepherds were told of Jesus's birth. A structure decorated with mosaics and inscriptions was discovered above the church.

A person's own work is always dear to him, and I have therefore chosen to conclude with a description of a church Y. Hirschfeld and I unearthed in 1976 at Horvat Brachot in Gush Etzion.[35] This church, too, possessed a crypt with a double staircase and mosaics of unusually high quality. Some of the mosaic decorations are of special interest because they have very close parallels not only in contemporaneous churches but also in Judean synagogues. The decorated borders, including a guilloche pattern and circles containing bird illustrations, are remarkably similar to those found in the Khirbet Sussiya synagogue. The interior composition on the main mosaic carpet of the Brachot church has a nearly exact parallel at the Na'aran synagogue. However, the crouching lions in the Brachot mosaic have no parallel in any other mosaic in the country—unless we consider the lion and leopard on the mosaic floor of the Ma'on synagogue at Nirim as a single unit. Of course, lions do appear in various other forms in many extant mosaics.

The Horvat Brachot church eloquently testifies to the obvious ties between decorative art in early synagogues and in contemporaneous churches, as various scholars have noted. However, this most interesting subject still needs a separate profound and detailed analysis.

[1]E. Honigmann, "Juvenal of Jerusalem," *Dumbarton Oaks Papers,*V (1950), pp. 209-279.

[2]J.W. Crowfoot, *Churches in Palestine,* London: 1941.

[3]A. Grabar, *Martyrium,* I-II, Paris: 1946.

[4]B. Bagatti, *L'Eglise de la Gentilite en Palestine,*Jerusalem: 1968.

[5]A. Ovadiah, *Corpus of the Byzantine Churches in the Holy Land,* Bonn: 1970.

[6]A. Negev, "The Churches of the Central Negev—An Archaeological Survey,"*Revue Biblique,* LXXXI (1974), pp. 4-421.

[7]*Qadmoniot* 9,(1975), pp. 3-25 (in Hebrew). See also: Y. Tsafrir, *Eretz-Israel from the Destruction of the Second Temple to the Muslim Conquest,* Vol. II; *Archaeology and Art* (1982) (Hebrew).

[8]See especially, J.T. Milik, "Notes d'épigraphie et de topographie palestiniennes, IX: Sanctuaires chretiens de Jerusalem a l'epoque arabe (VII-Xᵉ)," *Revue Biblique,* LXVII (1960), pp. 354-367, 550-586.

[9]See especially, H. Vincent & F. M. Abel, "Jerusalem,"*Recherches de Topographie, d'Archeologie et d'Histoire,* II: *Jerusalem Nouvelle,* Paris: 1914, pp. 40-300.

[10]C. Couäsnon, *The Church of the Holy Sepulchre,*London: 1974.

[11]M. Broshi, "New Excavations at the Church of the Holy Sepulchre," *Qadmoniot,* 10 (1976), pp. 30-32 (in Hebrew).

[12]V. Corbo, "Scavo archaeologico a ridosso della basicila dell' Ascensione," *Liber Annuus,* X (1959-1960), pp. 205-248.

[13]B. Bagatti, "Scavo di un Monastero al 'Dominus Flevit'(Monte Oliveto—Gerusalemme)," *Liber Annuus,* VI (1955-1956), pp. 240-270.

[14]Kathleen M. Kenyon, *Digging Up Jerusalem,* London: 1974, pp. 273-274; Pls. 113-114.

[15]N. Avigad, "A Building Inscription of. the Emperor Justinian and the Nea in Jerusalem," *Israel Exploration Journal* 27 (1977), pp. 145-151.

[16]A. Druks, *Hadashot Archeologiot,* 10 (1964), p. 16; 12 (1964), p. 16 (in Hebrew).

[17]For a description and references, see: Ovadiah (Note 5 above), pp. 174-178.

[18]V. Corbo, *The House of Saint Peter at Caphernaum,* Jerusalem, 1972; "Has the House Where Jesus Stayed in Capernaum Been Found?," *Biblical Archaeology Review,* November/December 1982.

[19]V. Tzaferis and D. Urman, "The Kursi Excavations,"*Qadmoniot,* 6 (1972), pp. 62-64 (in Hebrew).

[20]For a description and references, see: Ovadiah (Note 5,above), pp. 67-69.

[21]M.W. Prausnitz et al., *Excavations at Shavei Zion—The Early Christian Church,* Rome: 1967.

[22]G. Edelstein and Claudine Dauphin, "The Byzantine Church on Katznelson's Hill in Nahariyah," *Qadmoniot,* 8 (1975), pp. 128-132 (in Hebrew).

[23]Claudine Dauphin, "A Monastery Farm of the Early Byzantine Period in Shelomi," *Qadmoniot,* 12 (1978), pp. 25-29 (in Hebrew).

[24]R. Cohen, "A Byzantine Church and Mosaic Floors Near Kissufim,"*Qadmoniot,* 12 (1978), pp. 19-24 (in Hebrew), and "The Marvelous Mosaics of Kissufim," *Biblical Archaeology Review,* January/February 1980.

[25]A. Negev, "Eboda," *Encyclopedia of Archaeological Excavations in the Holy Land,* Jerusalem: 1976, pp. 345-354.

[26]Ibid, "Kurnub," pp. 722-734.

[27]Renate Rosenthal, "Bauform und Kult in den Negevkirchen—Eine regionale Studie, I: Die Nordkirche von Sobota," *Das Heilige Land,* CVIII (1976), pp. 7-30.

[28]Y. Tsafrir, "Rehovot (Kh. Ruheibeh)—Chronique archeologique," *Revue Biblique,* LXXXIV (1977), pp. 422-426; Y. Tsafrir, "Rehovot in the Negev—Four Seasons of Excavation," *Qadmoniot,* 12 (1979), pp. 124-132 (in Hebrew).

[29]See Note 6, above.

[30]One of the crypt's vaults was beautifully restored by the antiquities restorer, Zvi Ben-Zvi, despite difficult conditions. Ben-Zvi had been killed in 1978 en route to Masada, where he was engaged in restoration work. Ben-Zvi had been responsible for numerous restorations at various ancient sites in the country, and this vault was one of his last projects.

[31]E. Oren, "A Christian Settlement at Ostracina in Northern Sinai," *Qadmoniot,* 11 (1977), pp. 81-87 (in Hebrew).

[32]I. Finkelstein, "Remnants from the Byzantine Monastic Period at Jebel Tzaftzefah near the St. Catherine Monastery," in I. Finkelstein and Z.Meshel (editors), *Sinai in Antiquity,* Tel-Aviv: 1979, pp. 385-410 (in Hebrew).

[33]The following publications are at present available: G.H.Forsyth & K. Weitzmann, with I. Sevcenko & F. Anderegg, *The Monastery of Saint Catherine at Mount Sinai—The Church and Fortress of Justinian, I: Plates,* Ann Arbor 1970, K.Weitzmann, *The Monastery of St. Catherine at Mount Sinai—The Icons, I: From The Sixth To The Tenth Century,* Princeton: 1976.

[34]V. Tzaferis, "The Archaeological Excavations at Shepherds' Field," *Liber Annuus,* XXV (1975), pp. 5-52.

[35]Y. Tsafrir and I. Hirschfeld, "A Church of the Byzantine Period at Horvat Brachot," *Qadmoniot* 11 (1978), pp. 120-128 (in Hebrew); idem, "The Church and Mosaics at Horvat Berachot, Israel," *Dumbarton Oaks Papers* 39 (1979) pp. 291- 323.

Archaeological Research on the Islamic Period

By Myriam Rosen-Ayalon

For many years, the Islamic Period did not receive the attention it deserved from scholars working in Israel. Indeed, prior to the establishment of the State, almost no excavations were conducted at sites specifically identified with this period. The two exceptions were Khirbet el-Mafjar, excavated by the Department of Antiquities of the then Mandatory Government, and Khirbet el-Minyeh, excavated by German archaeologists who had originally supposed the site to hold a Roman fort or at least some pre-Moslem building. Scholars from neighboring countries similarly showed only minimal interest in Moslem archaeology, so that from the very onset of widespread archaeological activity at the end of the 19th century until recent years, scholars have tended to concentrate their efforts at sites from more ancient periods, while the Islamic Period was rather neglected.

Since Israeli statehood, however, the archaeological investigation of this period has contributed substantially to our knowledge of Islamic culture, although it cannot as yet be said to have revolutionized this field of study.

Except for chance discoveries at more ancient sites, the most significant excavations associated with the Islamic Period have been at a few large sites—Ramla, Tiberias and Jerusalem.

I. Ramla

Soon after the founding of the State, a preliminary report was published on a subterranean complex consisting of three cisterns discovered in the courtyard of the White Mosque at Ramla;[1] these subterranean cisterns apparently dated to the Umayyad period (661-749 C.E.). Their discovery constitutes the first link in a chain of subsequent research at Ramla, which is the only city in the region to have been founded by the Moslems (approximately between 713 and 715 C.E.). These pools

Clay mold from eighth-century C.E. Ramla.

are of considerable importance because until then the only underground cisterns known at Ramla belonged to the Abbasid period (789 C.E.). It was now apparent, however, that subterranean cisterns represented the usual methodology employed by Moslem hydrological architects.

In 1965, Avraham Eitan and I led an excavation at Ramla in order to trace the Umayyad city, especially its earliest stages, for which almost no data whatever had been found in the area. The results of these excavations, concentrated in the southwestern section of the present city, exceeded all our expectations. We discovered hundreds of intact earthenware vessels as well as a unique collection of potsherds.[2] This phase of Ramla's first century was both rich and exciting—the wide variety of delicate, mostly unglazed ceramics, the varied modes of ornamentation, the decoration of ceramic molds were all quite remarkable. Moreover, several exploratory digs at nearby areas enabled us to understand ancient Ramla's topographical situation as well as its evolution as a city.

Two accidental discoveries added to the array of finds from Ramla. One is a unique mosaic floor exposed in 1973 in the courtyard of a private house located in the ancient quarter of the city. At that time very few mosaics from the Islamic

Eighth-century C.E. mosaic floor uncovered at Ramla.

110

Period had been discovered anywhere. Thus this one was especially significant, and it was the only one found in Ramla itself. The mosaic floor contained three panels, two of which were continuous. The third was cut off by a wall that had later been built on top of it. The two continuous mosaics were decorated mainly with interlocking medallions containing plant motifs, such as fruit and leaves. The third is unique: It depicts the only "mihrab" or prayer niche ever to have been depicted on a mosaic. The mihrab consists of an arch supported by two columns, between which there is an inscription composed of a verse from the Koran which summons the faithful to prayer (see p. 110).[3] The inscription too is one-of-a-kind in Islamic mosaics.

The other accidental find at Ramla was a treasure trove of nearly 400 gold coins, discovered by construction workers in 1965. Although the coins had not been minted in Ramla, they had been collected and kept at one location in the city. They date to a number of dynasties up until the 10th century C.E., and came from widely scattered regions in the Moslem world.[4]

II. Tiberias

The area around Tiberias has also contributed much information about the Islamic Period. In 1959, excavations were conducted at the Umayyad palace at Khirbet el-Minyeh near Tiberias, continuing the German excavations that had been stopped by World War II. A short season of excavation enabled us to amend certain details in the previously drawn plan of the site. In addition to a late medieval level, a mosaic floor was discovered from the Umayyad period, which, however, was not fully uncovered.[5] It would have been appropriate to complete the excavation of the site and open it to the public.

Nearly all sites in the Tiberias region, including those of ancient periods, have at least one Islamic stratum. At the Ganei Hamat excavation, conducted in the early 1960s under the direction of Moshe Dothan, a splendid Byzantine mosaic and a number of lamps from the early Islamic Period were uncovered; unfortunately, they are still unpublished.

The Hamat excavations directed by Eliezer Oren during the early 1970s yielded a great variety of vessels and sherds chiefly from the ninth century C.E. The ceramics here were notable for their polychrome glazing, thus reflecting the material culture that characterized the Islamic Period following the phase revealed at Ramla.[6] Similar artifacts, but even more varied, were found near the ancient gate of Tiberias, which has been excavated by Gideon Foerster. However, this material too has not yet been published *in toto*.[7]

III. Jerusalem

The most impressive remains of the Islamic Period come from Jerusalem. During the last 15 years, excavations at the south and southwest of the Temple Mount, directed by Benjamin Mazar, assisted by Meir Ben-Dov, have exposed an entire Islamic complex, comprising more than half a dozen magnificent buildings. Scholars were astounded at this imposing architectural achievement of the Umayyad Period; literary sources do not mention any such structures at this location during the Umayyad Period. There is, nevertheless, no doubt as to the date of the buildings.

These buildings display an outstanding homogeneity in their architectural style, their accurate planning and construction techniques, as expressed particularly in the drainage and water supply, paving, stone bonding and carving, and the frescoes that embellish the walls of various sections of the complex.

Although the exact function of each structure cannot be determined, we are reasonably confident that at least one of the buildings was the Dar al-Imara, the governor's house. During that period, the Dar al-Imara was ordinarily erected near the wall of the mosque oriented towards Mecca. This suggestion finds support not only in architectural parallels but also in historical sources. Moreover, a passageway was discovered linking this particular building to the El Aqsa Mosque. Umayyad streets, which were built on top of earlier Herodian roads, were found connecting these Umayyad buildings with the Temple Mount.

The excavations have also provided the first information from Jerusalem concerning Islamic secular architecture at the beginning of the period. Copious quantities of utilitarian items like pottery, glass, and metal provide a tangible dimension to a heretofore recondite era. The rich and diverse ceramic finds range from various types of unglazed ceramics to vividly colored, glazed varieties. Glass artifacts and bronze vessels have also been uncovered, as well as large quantities of coins dating to several Islamic periods.[8]

Discoveries at other sites in Jerusalem provide information about various phases of the Islamic Period, from its beginnings to the later Middle Ages. An excavation now in progress in the courtyard of the Citadel will be extremely important, but the finds have not yet been published. It is clear, though, that some of the discoveries associated with the first centuries after the Moslem Conquest are extraordinary.

It has often been suggested that the El Aqsa Mosque stands on the foundations of a Byzantine church built by Justinian. Recent excavations by Nahman Avigad, however, have uncovered the remains of Justinian's famous Nea Church at the edge of the Jewish Quarter. The origins of the El Aqsa Mosque are therefore traceable exclusively to Jerusalem's Moslem Period.

During the course of excavations near Zion Gate, Magen Broshi uncovered a wall that we knew, on the basis of historical sources, was reconstructed during the Ayyubid Period. According to our sources, during the first half of the 13th century, this wall was demolished by the same sultan who had built it. Broshi's excavations revealed not only a segment of the Ayyubid wall but also the remains of its gate. Broshi also found a monumental broken inscription that confirmed that the sultan had indeed destroyed the wall he had built.

Ayyubid inscription from the beginning of the 13th century C.E., discovered in Jerusalem.

Cache from Caesarea dating to the 11th to 12th centuries C.E.

To complete our kaleidoscopic picture of the Islamic Period, we shall look at the archaeological treasure trove discovered in a glazed earthenware pitcher at Caesarea. This hoard, which includes necklaces, bracelets and sundry *objets d'art*, reflects the skilled craftsmanship of Moslem silversmiths and goldsmiths, as well as their ability to cut the precious and semiprecious stones for which that period was noted. The glazed ceramics, the jewelry and an inscription all date this hoard to the end of the Fatimid dynasty, the 11-12th centuries C.E. This treasure trove was probably buried to prevent it from falling into the hands of the Crusaders.

Since Israeli statehood, the archaeological yield from the Islamic Period has been surprising and includes building complexes, mosaics and a wide variety of finds in almost every area. These finds do not yet give us an entirely balanced view of each of the respective phases of the period, but this may be because the concern of the Moslem ruler for the country during this period was similarly uneven. Although the picture is incomplete, we are at least able to sketch its outlines.

[1] I. Kaplan, "Excavations at the White Mosque in Ramla," *Atiqot*, 2 (1957-58), pp. 96-103 (in Hebrew).

[2] Myriam Rosen-Ayalon and A. Eitan, *The Ramla Excavations—Finds From the Eighth Century C.E.*, Israel Museum, Jerusalem 1969.

[3] M. Rosen-Ayalon, "The First Mosaic Discovered in Ramla," *Israel Exploration Journal*, XXVI (1976), pp. 104-119.

[4] S. Levi and H. Mitchel, "A Hoard from Ramla," *Israel Numismatic Journal*, III (1965-66), pp. 37-66.

[5] O. Grabar, J. Perrot, B. Ravani and M. Rosen, "Sondages à Khirbet el-Minyeh," *Israel Exploration Journal*, X (1960), pp. 226-243.

[6] E.D. Oren, "Early Islamic Material from Ganei-Hamat (Tiberias)," *Archaeology* XXIV (1971), pp. 274-277.

[7] This ceramic collection has been partially studied by Batiah Segel, who subsequently wrote a seminar paper on the subject.

[8] M. Ben-Dov, "The Umayyad Buildings Near the Temple Mount," in B. Mazar, *The Archaeological Excavations Near The Temple Mount*, Jerusalem, 1971, pp. 34-40 (in Hebrew).

Archaeological Research on the Crusader Period

By Joshua Prawer

The study of the Crusader period did not attract many Israeli students and scholars until this last generation. It was in the nature of things that earlier periods bearing directly on the history of the Jews in their homeland focused the attention and the interest of scholars in general and archaeologists in particular. Crusader archaeology was the domain of scholars connected with Christian institutions in Jerusalem like the École Biblique (Dominican), St. Saviour (Franciscan) and the Church of the Flagellation (Pères Blancs). At the same time, the Department of Antiquities of the British Mandate Government with scholars like Hamilton and C.N. Johns pursued Crusader studies either as a part of more general archaeological interests (Crusader parts of the al-Aqsa, of the Church of Nativity in Bethlehem, the Holy Sepulchre in Jerusalem), or specifically Crusader sites. The latter were not very numerous, but the excavations of the Pilgrim's Castle (Athlit) by C. N. Johns and the archaeological mission of the Metropolitan Museum of New York which partially excavated the castle of Montfort were outstanding.

Since 1948 Israeli scholars have pursued the field of Crusader research, and our survey relates in more detail to Israeli studies, which being often written in Hebrew, remain unknown to the larger public. The task fell to the Department of Antiquities of the State of Israel, which cooperated with such bodies as the National Park Authority and university departments. Slowly the Crusader period became acknowledged by the public at large and a new generation of Israeli scholars is now concentrating on the history of the period. At the same time much valuable work was done by foreign scholars, whether or not connected with research institutes in Israel, who continue a splendid tradition of exploration and research.

What distinguishes the Crusader period and its archaeology from the history of other, usually earlier periods, is the abundance of written material. Scores of

115

chronicles, some actually written in Palestine during the Crusader period, others written in Europe and the Near East, and thousands of acts and deeds preserved in European archives reflect this 200-year history of the country, including details of customs and material culture of everyday life. In addition, profuse geographical descriptions of the Holy Land were recorded by pious pilgrims of all three mono-theistic religions. Archaeological research profited from them all and at the same time had a major impact on our understanding of these 200 years in the history of the country. New insights were gained of religious life, warfare, agricultural tech-niques, civil architecture, urban life, reciprocal influences of East and West. All of them gained new dimensions and a process of cross-fertilization took place be-tween the richness of written sources and the archaeological findings. Conse-quently, in this period more than in any other historical period, research based on narrative and other written sources went hand in hand with archaeological explo-ration.

Ledge gargoyle shaped like the head of a young man, from the church at Kochav Hayarden.

Top part of the entrance doorpost of the church at Kochav Hayarden. Note bevel on upper section, from which the lintel's arch had originally protruded.

Let me begin our review of the Crusader period with a study tool that has become crucial in historical, topographical and archaeological research. I refer to the map of "Palestine During the Crusader Period," prepared by a team of scholars at Hebrew University and edited by Meron Benvenisti and myself. This map was published in 1960 on two colored folio sheets of the *Atlas of Israel*. It is accompanied by an index of place names (Latin, French, Arabic, Hebrew), identifi-cation indices and grid references that include almost 900 places and sites within the boundaries of the Crusader kingdom of Jerusalem.[1] The map was re-published in one sheet (without an index) in 1972 by the Survey Department of Israel.[2]

This map indicates also Crusader sites that are known to us through archaeological finds only. Our knowledge of such sites and of others for which we possess documentary sources is growing apace with the expansion of archaeological excavations.

The Archaeological Survey of Israel focuses for the time being on the coast and the map of crusader sites already appears much denser; on the other hand, a map based on narrative sources,[3] like the topographical study of the Acre region at the end of the 13th century, could provide a sound basis for further archaeological research.[4]

Meron Benvenisti, with the assistance of the Israel National Academy of Sciences, is currently (1980) investigating approximately 60 Crusader sites in Judea and Samaria. Some, but not all, of these sites are referred to in the literary sources of the period. The preliminary work has already produced a substantial list of Crusader remains. These do not belong to the monumental order of architecture, but are remains of medieval Crusader settlement, dwellings, farms, bakeries, and the like.[5] When the results of this survey are added to the map of the Holy Land under Crusader rule, they will further contribute to a field in which Benvenisti has already made substantial contributions.[6] Most of these settlements were inhabited by the native, Muslim and Oriental Christian population; only the rulers were Crusaders. Continued research should thus add a new dimension to our knowledge of the period, one beyond political and economic history.

In the meantime a major survey of all church buildings in the Holy Land is being prepared by R.D. Pringle; very often the survey comprises more than ecclesiastical buildings. The list and sketches published so far point to a major work in the field of Crusader archaeology.[7]

A different kind of survey was conducted recently by Zahavah Jacoby. Financed by Haifa University and the Israel National Academy of Sciences, its purpose was to make a comprehensive inventory of Crusader sculptural remains, whether located in museums, in private hands, or in parts of buildings that were later converted into mosques. In addition to museum collections, some of these sculptural fragments were found at Crusader sites. However, a number were discovered in other places where they had been used as building material. It is estimated that such a comprehensive survey will list almost 1,000 items. The concentration and documentation of this material will be very helpful, not only for studying Crusader art but also in other relevant areas of research.[8] Although Crusader art lies somewhat beyond our present concerns, its study does emphasize the fact that Israeli scholars, like their colleagues in this and cognate fields, are now able to examine at close quarters the remains of the Crusader Period and are engaged in this specific area of research. These remains include artifacts that were inaccessible to Israeli scholars prior to the founding of the State and, in some instances were inaccessible until the Six Day War. Examples are the Church of the Ascension of the Mount of Olives, studied by B. Kochnel; the lintels of the Church of the Holy Sepulchre, studied by N. Canaan; and Crusader paintings in the church at Bethlehem, studied by G. Kühnel. The more comprehensive work by M. Barash analyzes the remains of Crusader figural sculpture in Israel. Several studies that give a new direction to art history research were published by H. Buschhausen and by Z. Jacoby. These include a new interpretation of Crusader sculpture from Nazareth and what is entitled the "Workshop of the Temple Area."[9] These studies have in many instances radically altered our knowledge of the links between Crusader Palestine and the artistic centers of Europe during the period in Sicily, southern Italy, and central and southeastern France.[10]

M. Kesten's 1962 survey of the ancient city of Acre for the National Parks Authority has contributed greatly to topographical and archaeological studies of the Crusader period,[11] although in the northern quarter of the city a survey or excavations are still needed. Kesten's survey of Acre and M. Chehab's three volumes regarding Tyre[12] are of major importance to any future study of Crusader cities. Kesten's survey has been helped considerably by the splendid maps left to us by the Crusaders, which themselves have been the subject of a recent study.[13] Together with the Crusader maps of Jerusalem—which are now being studied[14]— the Acre maps afford a unique basis for the physical reconstruction of Crusader cities and complement the studies of urban life during the period.[15]

A turning point in the study of the old city of Acre came with the excavation and clearing of the "crypt." This was followed by the clearing of a considerable portion of the complex of buildings known as the "Crusader Halls." This is one of the most impressive Crusader complexes in the country. The Society for the Restoration of Acre, under the initial direction of Kesten, and later of G. Goldman[16] and D. Tanai, removed rubbish heaps and dismantled a reservoir near what is regarded as the "refectorium" of the Order of St. John. To appreciate how far research has come, one can compare what we know of the place today with our knowledge at the end of the Second World War (in the otherwise excellent work of Johns and Makhouly[17]).

Eastern gate of Crusader city of Caesarea.

M. Dothan's excavations at Tell Akko often spilled over to the area of the Crusader city. In these excavations an impressive array of fortifications was uncovered south of Acre's Crusader wall. Additionally, fragments of colored glass with some painted Latin letters were found in the plan.[18]

I shall not deal here with those archaeological finds that were discovered by chance and are dispersed at many locations.[19] Instead, I will concentrate on specific sites that help us understand the material culture of the Crusader rule.

Let us begin our survey with the fortified city of Baniyas, which was in Crusader hands for a short period during the second quarter of the 12th century. For the past 150 years, it was thought that Qal'at Nimrud—that is, the Nimrud Fortress—or by her earlier name Subeiba—is referred to as Castellum Paneas, or the citadel of the city of Baniyas. (Baniyas is referred to as "Fortress Dan" in the Cairo Genizah documents of the 12th century). Only after the Six Day War were scholars able to study these sites. Immediately after the war, A. Grabois began a pioneering investigation of the city,[20] and some time later the National Parks Authority cleared medieval Baniyas, discovering the citadel at a strategic location in the city. This was the fortress of Baniyas and a place of refuge in troubled times.

As to Crusader Assebébé, identified with Subeiba, it should be identified with Hasbiya in the Marj'Ayun, as already previously conjectured.[21] In any case, it seems very doubtful that there were any links during the 12th century between Qal'at Nimrud and the city of Baniyas, and this is also true for the 13th century. Mighty Qal'at Nimrud, rich in already studied Arabic inscriptions, still awaits renewed attention of scholars, to supplement the work of the late Paul Deschamps and van Berchem.[22]

In the southern part of the country, the efforts of the National Parks Authority have shed light on Crusader Ashkelon, the capital of the Crusader principality of Ascalon.[23] Only after the area near the ramparts that surround the city had been cleared was it possible to get a clearer view of the city's defenses. Many remains, walls, towers, windows, still await study. It would be desirable at least to catalogue and preserve them—even without additional excavation. One can still walk along the top of the moat, beside the remains of the giant Crusader walls and fortification of 1244, and get a fairly good picture of the Crusader city. The following description of the city's fortifications by the great historian of the Crusader Kingdom, William Bishop of Tyre, could well have been written today:

"[Ashkelon] lies upon the seacoast in the form of a semicircle, the chord or diameter of which extends along the shore, while the arc or bow lies in the land looking toward the east. The entire city rests in a basin, as it were, sloping to the sea and is surrounded on all sides by artificial mounds, upon which rise the walls with towers at frequent intervals. The whole is built of solid masonry, held together by cement which is harder than stone. The walls are wide, of goodly thickness and proportionate height."[24]

Unfortunately, we know very little about the interior of the city although we can reconstruct the fortifications, because many architectural fragments jut forth from the ground or lie quite close to the surface.

Crusader Caesarea fared far better. The National Parks Authority excavations directed by Avraham Negev[25] have contributed in an important way to our understanding of a fortified Crusader harbor city. Unfortunately, publication of the excavation report has been delayed for more than 20 years. When it becomes available, it is bound also to help solve a central problem in urban research: namely, was there an unbroken continuity in the urban history of the Holy Land? Herod's Caesarea, Byzantine Caesarea, Arab Shayzer and Crusader Cesaire are located beside, or on top of one another, and it is perhaps this fact that is the key to the problem.

The excavation and restoration of the wall, the glacis and moat—all of which are now under the care of the National Parks Authority—gives us an opportunity to see the basic components of a Crusader city's fortifications, which until now could be seen only at Crac des Chevaliers in Syria[26] and at Athlit.[27] Crusader Caesarea boasts a splendid fortified gate and a series of square towers that project from the wall above the masterfully built glacis. The gate, the glacis, and a bridge constructed of stone and beams of wood, which spanned the preserved arches built in the moat—all of this, together with three posterns hidden in the wall, the northern gate and the foundation of a bridge adjacent to it, allows us a glimpse of 13th-century Crusader fortifications in their full splendor.

Northern wall and moat of
Crusader city at Caesarea.

The gate was defended by two huge towers from which an iron grille was lowered. Marble slabs for inserting pivots served two-winged gates, and the holes in the gatepost accommodated the huge iron bolt which shut the gate from the inside. The reconstructed Z-shaped gate is in the Gothic style current c. 1250, arches and vaults resting on consoles elaborately ornamented with flower motifs. The paved section of the gate leads to the main street, part of which was excavated. It turns from the gate and heads toward the sea, having on both sides Crusader buildings, apparently a complex of shops. Herodian and Byzantine pillars with their magnificent capitals served often as the foundation for these shops.

Above the street that ran along the wall, the archaeologists discovered a series of arches over which pieces of cloth would have been stretched to shield against the sun. The archaeologists, as mentioned, discovered posterns concealed within the north and west glacis. Staircases led from the entrances inside the city to the bottom of the moat. All this added immensely to our knowledge of the Crusader city and its quaint harbor, whose northern jetty was built from Herodian columns thrown in a parallel line into the water. The citadel, or what remains of it, is built on a small promontory cut off from the city by a moat which was possibly filled by the sea in times of rain. The moat was defended by an inner wall flanked by towers in which granite and porphyry columns of ancient buildings were used.

A Crusader church discovered here is located on a hill facing the citadel. It was built in the Romanesque style with cleanly chiseled stones. Beautiful free-standing absides without a chevet are a rather unusual feature of the structure. No full report has yet been published on these excavations. Nevertheless, if we compare what we know of Crusader Caesarea today with the description of Caesarea written by the French scholar, E.G. Rey, about a hundred years ago,[28] the advance in our knowledge is remarkable.

Another Crusader city may soon come to the fore following its recent excavation. We refer to the Crusader town and fortress of Arsuf. Its Crusader name preserves some Semitic stem of Reshef and its ruins cover Roman and Byzantine Apollonia and the Crusader city. Although the plan of the city fortifications has been known since the Survey of Western Palestine, the new dig, a preliminary report of which was published recently, will certainly add to our knowledge of its Crusader remains.[29]

During the last generation it has become clear that Crusader society, its knightly and burgess classes alike, was essentially an urban society.[30] New information about the fortifications of Crusader cities has contributed to our understanding of urban planning and organization. In this connection, we should mention the excavations at the western wall of Jerusalem, from the Jaffa Gate to the corner of Mount Zion, and along the length of the southern wall, from Mount Zion to the Dung Gate. Remnants of Ayyubid construction activity, as well as an Ayyubid inscription, attest that this particular section of the wall was destroyed and then rebuilt at the beginning of the 13th century; this find confirms what had already been known from the narrative sources.[31] The excavations along the existing walls were conducted partly by Magen Broshi[32] and partly by Meir Ben-Dov and were financed by the Jerusalem Foundation; no full report on these excavations has yet been published. During these excavations, which reached bedrock, the archaeologists discovered the Ayyubid course of the wall, with its complex of towers, which extended into the interior of our city. This line of fortifications was built atop the 12th-century Crusader wall; consequently, the entire picture of Crusader fortifications has now become clearer. Further to the east, that is between the Dung Gate and the Temple Mount, scholars have followed the course of the wall. Excavations conducted by B. Mazar have shown that the salient wall connecting al-Aqsa Mosque to the city was in fact of recent origin—probably dating to the Ottoman Period—and is definitely not to be associated with the Crusader wall. The Crusader wall connecting the corner of the Temple Mount to the city wall took an entirely different course. The excavations in this area have raised a question as to when the wall in the south—irrespective of whether this was the wall of Empress Eudocia or a later wall—was shifted to follow today's line of fortifications. We cannot, as yet, answer this question with any certainty. Many scholars are inclined to believe that this significant change in the city's plan was made sometime during the 11th century.[33]

Several other Crusader sites in Jerusalem should be mentioned—for example, parts of the Church of the Holy Sepulchre, which due to restoration revealed clearly its Crusader buildings (these are unfortunately being covered) and the tomb of the Virgin in the Valley of Jehosaphat (Melissande's tomb), as well as the remains of Crusader buildings discovered in the excavations of N. Avigad.[34] The most important find within the city limits, however, is the Church of St. Mary of the Teutonic Order, uncovered when the Jewish Quarter was being restored.[35] The church and the adjoining hospice were built in the middle of the 12th century (some parts possibly in the 13th) as a German-speaking branch of the Order of St. John. It was linked to the Teutonic knights in the beginning of the 13th century—possibly during the reign of the Emperor Friederick II (after 1229).[36] It is a comparatively small structure designed in the Romanesque style. The church and adjacent buildings, which served as a hospital or hospice, have been restored by the Jerusalem Foundation. This is the only extant complex of the Crusader military orders in Jerusalem, testifying to the might of the Orders, as all other buildings were either completely or partially destroyed, or were incorporated into other buildings. This is what happened to the headquarters in the al-Aqsa Mosque, when the Eutymus market was erected in the Muristan quarter, and 'the huge

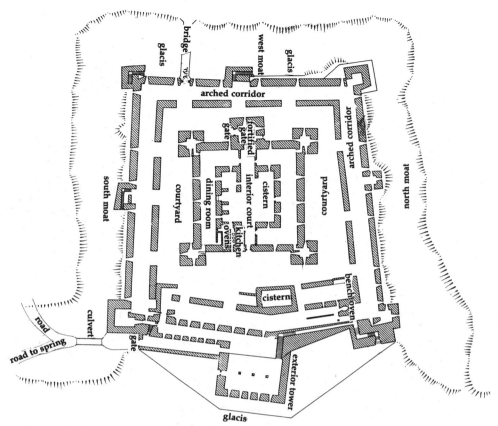

Plan of crusader fortress at Kochav Hayarden.

complex of the Order of St. John was destroyed in the early 20th century. This little church and hospice of St. Mary was the birthplace of the mighty Teutonic Order which, during the 13th century, laid the foundations for what was later to become the powerful state of Prussia.

Still in Jerusalem, let us mention the excavations of D. Bahat and M. Ben Ari near Tancred Tower[37] as well as the tentative identification by D. Bahat of the Crusader church of St. Julian.[38]

Not far from Jerusalem is a Crusader site beautifully restored by the National Parks Authority—Ein Hemed, previously known as "Aqua Bella."[39] Although the site's precise history is uncertain, there is no doubt that it was once a Benedictine monastery. The religious buildings were not preserved, but those structures above the spring and stream that did survive give us some idea about the life of recluses in the Crusader state.

I shall conclude my survey with my favorite site—Kochav Hayarden, the Crusaders Belvoir known to the Arabs as Kaukab al-Hawa (Star of the Winds). Meir Ben-Dov's excavations in the abandoned Arab village of humble houses and animal pens, folds and stables brought to light one of the handsomest Crusader fortresses ever built. Happily, we can date this fortress to within roughly a 30-year period during the 12th century (1148-1178), though some of the finds can be dated to within a few years of the 13th century when the castle was for a short period again in Crusader possession. Needless to say, such close dating is very rare.[40]

Aerial shot of Crusader fortress at Kochav Hayarden, looking southeast.

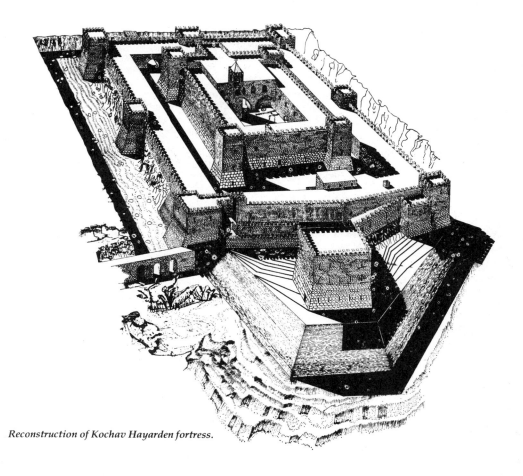

Reconstruction of Kochav Hayarden fortress.

In the fortress's general plan, its builders took advantage of the wadi to the north and the steep slope that faces the River Jordan on the east. The exterior fortifications, the covered gallery comprising the quadrangular fortifications, the interior citadel and its various installations, and the church on the second floor of the fortress have all contributed enormously to our knowledge of the Crusader Period.

It is worthwhile to end this short survey by mentioning some newly discovered tombstones of the Crusader period.[41] The most remarkable were found during the excavations of the Hospitaller complex in Acre. One is that of the Master of the Order Pierre de Vieillbride of 1244[42]; the other was assigned to the last bishop of Nazareth who resided in Acre and is dated 1290, that is one year before the loss of Crusader Acre to the Mameluks.[43]

[1]J. Prawer and M. Benvenisti, "Palestine During the Crusader Period," *Atlas of Israel* (Jerusalem, 1960), p. IX:12).

[2]Map of the Survey Department (Jerusalem, 1972).

[3]E.g. the Survey of Athlit by A. Ronan and J. Olami, *Archaeological Survey of Israel* (Jerusalem, 1978), the map of Athlit.

[4]D. Barag, "A New Source Concerning the Ultimate Borders of the Latin Kingdom of Jerusalem," *Israel Exploration Journal (IEJ)*, 29 (1979), pp. 197-217.

[5]An excellent preliminary study was already published: M. Benvenisti, "*Bovaria-babriyya*: A Frankish Residue on the Map of Palestine," *Outremer* Studies in the History of the Crusader Kingdom of Jerusalem Presented to Joshua Prawer, ed. B.Z. Kedar et al. (Jerusalem, 1982), pp. 130-152.

[6]M. Benvenisti, *The Crusaders in the Holy Land* (Jerusalem, 1970) is so far the best study of the Crusader habitat in the Holy Land. See also a shorter study by the same author, *The Crusader Fortresses in the State of Israel—Their Description and History* (Jerusalem, 1955)[in Hebrew]. Regrettably, both of these volumes were published without notes or scholarly apparatus.

[7]A. Pringle's preliminary list published in *Revue Biblique* 89 (1982) and cf. *Bulletin of the Society for the Study of the Crusades and the Latin East* 3 (1983), pp. 16-17.

[8]Mrs. Z. Jacoby lectured on the initial results of this research at Yad Yitzchak Ben-Zvi on June 2, 1980. In the meantime several studies have been published on the subject and are listed in note 10.

[9]B. Kochnal, "On the Dating of the Crusader Church of the Ascension on the Mount of Olives," *Chapters in the History of Medieval Jerusalem*, edited by B.Z. Kedar, (Jerusalem, 1979, pp. 327-337 [in Hebrew]; N. Canaan, "The Crusader Lintels of the Church of the Holy Sepulchre— Suggestions for a New Interpretation," *ibid*, pp. 313-326 [in Hebrew]; B. Kochnal, "The Crusader Sculpture of Jerusalem," (Hebrew University 1979); G. Kühnel, "Crusader Art in the Nativity Basilica of Bethlehem," Ph.D. thesis (Tel Aviv University, 1981) [both in Hebrew]; M. Barash, *Crusader Figural Sculpture in the Holy Land* (Tel Aviv, 1971). For a general survey, see J. Prawer, *The Crusaders—a Colonial Society* (Jerusalem, 1976), pp. 494-544 [in Hebrew]. We should also mention the still classical research on Crusader art: M. de Vogüé, *Les Églises de la Terre Sainte* with photographs and drawings (Paris, 1866), phot. edition with an introduction by myself and an up-to-date bibliography by Sylvia Schein (Univ. of Toronto Press, 1973). Finally there is now at our disposal *A History of the Crusades*, Vol. IV, ed. H.W. Hazard: *The Art and Architecture of the Crusader States* including studies by T.S.R. Boase and Y. Folda dealing with Palestine.

[10]B. Kochnal, *The Dating* (see above, Note 9); Barash (Note 9); Jacoby (Note 8). Z. Jacoby, "The Tomb of Baldwin V, King of Jerusalem (1185-1186) and the Workshop of the Temple Area," *Gesta*, 18/2 (1979) 3-13. *Idem*, "Le portail de l'eglise de l'Annonciation de Nazereth an XIIIe siècle," *Monuments et Memoires publ. par l'Acad. des Inscriptions et Belles Lettres*, 64 (1979) 141-194. *Idem*, "The Workshop of the Temple Area in Jerusalem in the Twelfth Century: its Origin, Evolution and Impact," *Zeitschrift für Kunstgeschichte*, 45 (1982) 325-394. Of particular interest and importance, H. Buschhausen, *Die jüditalienisch Bauplastik im Königreich Jerusalem*, Vienna 1978. B. Kühnel, "Steinmetzer aus Fontevrault in Jerusalem, Eine Bauplastik-Werkstatt der Kreuzfahrerzeit," *Wiener Jahrbuch für Kunstgeschichte*, 33 (1980) 83-97.

[11]A. Kesten, Acre, *The Old City—Survey and Planning* (Acre, 1962) [in Hebrew]. This complements and replaces N. Makhouly and C.N. Johns, Guide to Acre, Dept. of Antiquities (Jerusalem, 1946).

[12]M.H. Chehab, "Tyr à l'epoque des Croisades," *Histoire militaire et diplomatique*, I, (Paris, 1975).

[13]J. Prawer, "Historical Maps of Acre," *Eretz-Israel*, 2 (1953), pp. 175-189 [in Hebrew]. See also B. Dichter, *The Maps of Acre—A Historical Cartography* (Acre, 1973). For color reproductions see also

The *Atlas of Israel* (Jerusalem, 1960), p. I:4. Good color facsimilia: Marino Sanudo, *Liber Secretorum Fidelium Crucis,* Introduction by J. Prawer, (Toronto University Press, 1972).

[14]Milka Levy, "Jerusalem in Medieval Cartography," *History of Jerusalem in the Middle Ages,* edited by J. Prawer, I (in print) [in Hebrew].

[15]D. Jacoby, "Crusader Acre in the Thirteenth Century—Urban Layout and Topography," *Studi Medievali,* Series 3, XX (1979), pp. 1-45; *idem,* "L'expansion occidentale dans le Levant—Les Vénitiens à Acre dans la second moitié du treizième siècle," *Journal of Medieval History,* III (1977), pp. 227ff.; N. Avigad, "Excavations in the Jewish Quarter of the Old City of Jerusalem," *IEJ,* 20 (1970), pp. 137-138. J. Prawer, "The Patriarch's Lordship in Jerusalem," *Crusader Institutions* (Oxford Univ. Press, 1980), pp. 269-315; *Idem,* "The Italians in the Latin Kingdom," *ibidem,* pp. 217-250.

[16]G.Z. Goldman, "Le couvent des Hospitaliers á St. Jean d'Acre," *Bible et Terre Sainte,* 160 (1974), pp. 8-18.

[17]C.N. Johns and N. Makhouly, *Guide to Acre* (Jerusalem, 1946); see also Jacoby (above, Note 15); and compare Benvenisti (Note 6); see also B. Dichter, *The Orders and Churches of Crusader Acre* (Acre, 1979).

[18]M. Dothan, "Akko—Interim Excavation Report, First Season, 1973/4," *Bulletin of the American Schools of Oriental Research,* 224 (1976), pp. 1-48.

[19]See, for instance, J. Mayer, "Es-Samariya-Ein Kreuzfahresitz in Westgalilaa," *Jahrbuch des Römisch-Germanischen Zentralmuseums Mainz,* XI (1964), pp. 198-202.

[20]A. Grabois, "La cité de Banyas et le château de Subeibé pendant les Croisades," *Cahiers de Civilisation Médiévale,* XIII (1970), pp. 43ff.

[21]J. Richard, "Les listes des seigneuries dans le livre de Jean d'Ibelin—Recherches sur l'Assebebe et Mimars," *Revue Historique de Droit Francais et Etranger,* Series 4, XXXII (1954), pp. 567ff.

[22]P. Deschamps, *Les Châteaux des Croisés en Terre-Sainte,* I: *Le Crac des Chevaliers* (Paris, 1924); II: *La Défense du Royaume de Jérusalem* (Paris, 1939).

[23]J. Prawer, "Ashkelon and the Ashkelon Strip in the Crusader Period," *Eretz-Israel,* 4 (1967), pp. 231-248 [in Hebrew]. For a more detailed description of Crusader fortifications, see Benvenisti, *The Crusaders* (Note 6), pp. 273-338.

[24]Willemus Tyrensis, *Historia Rerum in Partibus Transmarinis Gestarum (Recueil des Historiens des Croisades, Historiens Occidenteaux)* I: 17, ch. 22.

[25]On A. Negev's excavation in Caesarea in 1960, see *IEJ,* 10 (1960), pp. 264-265 and p. 127.

[26]See Note 22 above.

[27]C.N. Johns, *Guide to Athlit* (Jerusalem, 1947).

[28]E.G. Rey, *Etude sur les Monuments de l'Architecture Militaire des Croisés in Syrie et dans l'Ile de Chypre* (Paris, 1871), pp. 221-227. Cf. Benvenisti, The Crusaders (Note 6), pp. 135ff An interesting attempt to use modern techniques was made by B.Z. Kedar, "Radio-carbon Dating of Mortar from the City-Wall of Ascalon," *IEJ,* 28 (1978) 173-176.

[29]I. Roll and E. Ayalon, "Apollonia/Arsur—A Coastal Town in the Southern Sharon Plain," *Qadmoniot* XV (1982), pp. 16-22.

[30]J. Prawer, "Crusader City," *The Medieval City,* ed. H.A. Miskimin et al. (Yale University Press, 1977), pp. 179-199; M. Chebab, *Tyr—Histoire, Tipographie, Fouilles,* 3 volumes (Beirut, 1975ff).

[31]See J. Prawer, "Chapters in the History of the Jews in the Crusader Kingdom," *Shalem,* 2 (1976), pp. 103-112 [in Hebrew].

[32]M. Broshi, "New Excavations along the Walls of Jerusalem," *Qadmoniot,* 9 (1976), pp. 75-78 [in Hebrew]; M. Broshi and Y. Tsafrir, "Excavations at the Zion Gate, Jerusalem," *IEJ,* 27 (1977), pp. 28-37. For the Crusader parts of the excavations see M. Ben-Dov, *The Dig at the Temple Mount* (Jerusalem, 1982), pp. 343-355.

[33]For a summary of the various theses proffered to date, see D. Bahat, "Physical Layout of Jerusalem During the Early Moslem Period," *History of Jerusalem* Note 14, above [in Hebrew].

[34]For the excavations at the Church of the Holy Sepulchre, see C. Coüasnon, *The Church of the Holy Sepulchre, Jerusalem (The Schweich Lectures,* 1972) (London, 1974); for Melissande's Tomb in the Church of St. Mary in the Valley of Jehosaphat, see M. Piccorillo, "L'edicola Crociata sulla Tomba della Madonna," *Liber Annuus,* XXII (1972), pp. 29ff. A. Prodromo, "La Tomba della Regina Mellisanda al Getsemanni," *ibid.,* XXIV (1974), pp. 202ff.; B. Bagatti, M. Piccorillo and A. Prodromo, *New Discoveries at the Tomb of the Virgin Mary in Gethsemane* (Jerusalem, 1975). On Avigad's excavations in this section of the Old City, see Note 15 above. The identification of these sites is still uncertain. The area was connected to the Church of Mount Zion, but the finds and other sources still need clarification. See "Chartes de l'abbaye du Mont Zion," ed. E.G. Rey, *Mémoires de la Société nationale des Antiquaires de France,* (1887), pp. 31-56.

[35]On the church of the Teutonic Order, see A. Ovadiah, "A Church from the Crusader Period in the Jewish Quarter of Jerusalem," *Eretz-Israel,* 11 (1963), pp. 208-212 [in Hebrew]; M. Ben Dov, *The Dig* (above note 32), pp. 343ff.

[36]Prawer Note 9, above, pp. 349ff. [in Hebrew]. M.L. Favreau, *Studien zur Frühgeschichte des Deutschen Ordens (Kieler Historische Studien,* XXI) (Stuttgart, 1974).

[37]"The excavations in Zahal Square," *Qadmoniot* 5 (1972), pp. 118ff.

[38]D. Bahat, "Une église Croisée recemment decouverte á Jérusalem," *Revue Biblique* 85 (1978), pp. 72-80.

[39]See Prawer (Note 9, above), p. 481 and p. 491 [in Hebrew].

[40]J. Prawer, "The History of the Kochav-Hayarden Fortress," *Yediyot,* 31 (1967), pp. 236-249 [in Hebrew]. To date, only a short outline has been published on these excavations; see M. Ben-Dov, "The Excavations in the Crusader Fortress at Kochav-Hayarden," *Qadmoniot,* 2 (1968), pp. 22-27 [in Hebrew].

[41]A very useful publication is the *Corpus Inscriptionum Crucesignatorum Terrae Sanctae,* ed. Sabino de Sandoli (Jerusalem, 1974). The original part is the paleographical introduction. The otherwise rich collection generally reproduces the original publication.

[42]J. Prawer, "Military Orders and Crusader Politics in the Second Half of the XIIIth Century," *Die geistlichen Ritterorden Europas,* ed. J. Fleckenstein and M. Hellmann, (Simaringen, 1980), pp. 217-229.

[43]*Idem,* "A Crusader Tomb of 1290 from Acre and the Last Archbishops of Nazareth," *Israel Exploration Journal,* 24 (1974), pp. 241-251.

II

"Break Forth Together Into Singing, You Waste Places of Jerusalem"

Jerusalem—"The City Full of People"

By Nahman Avigad

This short report will summarize ten years of intensive year-round excavations in the Jewish Quarter of the Old City of Jerusalem and will consider the general contribution these excavations have made to the research on Jerusalem. I shall also discuss specific finds that reflect particular aspects of the city's material culture. This survey will be limited to the First and Second Temple Periods, however, and will not include a discussion of later periods.

Our excavations, conducted in a part of the Old City never before excavated, taught us many new things, demolished old ideas, and shed light on certain ambiguous matters.

I. The First Temple Period

Any discussion of Jerusalem during the First Temple Period must of necessity deal primarily with the city's topography. Among the most difficult and important perennial topographical-historical problems has been the question of the city's boundaries during the First Temple Period. Did Jerusalem in the pre-Destruction (586 B.C.E.) period occupy just the small eastern hill, the site of the City of David, or did it extend onto the larger western ridge on the opposite side of the central valley? The question is as old as archaeological research in Jerusalem; indeed, it is only now, following our excavations, that we can say this controversy itself belongs to history!

There were two schools of thought regarding the putative ancient city boundaries; the first was that of the "maximalists," so-to-speak, and the second could be called that of the "minimalists."

The "maximalists" believed that Jerusalem gradually began to spread over both the eastern (City of David) and western ridges throughout the First Temple Period. They based their theory primarily on Josephus, who described the course of

Jerusalem's "First Wall," its earliest wall, during the Monarchy Period. Josephus wrote that this wall surrounded the western hill on its northern, western and southern sides, then joined the City of David wall. The "maximalists" took this report quite literally, and further adduced certain scriptural hints for the existence

Jerusalem in Hasmonean times. Numbers 4-7: Remnants of Hasmonean fortifications uncovered at northern wall; the circle designates area of excavations at northern wall.

130

of residential suburbs outside the City of David limits, i.e., the Mishneh and the "Machtesh."

According to the maximalist thesis, Jerusalem was a large and spacious city, as befitted the country's capital. The maximalist theory was based on nebulous historical-literary data, upon emotional considerations and upon imagination; it certainly was not founded on archaeological evidence.

The "minimalists," on the other hand, were more realistic, and would base their conclusions only on facts. It was a fact, for instance, that numerous excavations on the Ophel hill, the eastern hill or City of David, had yielded many finds dating to the Israelite period. These finds positively established that the Ophel had been occupied in that period. However, the more limited, and rather less numerous, excavations conducted on the western ridge yielded no building remains whatever from the First Temple Period. Accordingly, the minimalists concluded that the site was uninhabited during the First Temple Period and that, until Jerusalem was destroyed by the Babylonians in 586 B.C.E., it had extended over only the narrow precincts of the City of David. According to this theory, the western hill was first inhabited during the Hasmonean era.

These differences of opinion amounted, one might say, to an assessment of Jerusalem's status during the Monarchy Period. That is, was the capital of Israel and Judah just a small and limited city (10 to 15 acres), even until the Babylonian destruction, or did it in fact expand during monarchic times to become a large metropolis (about 150 acres)? The realistic argument of the "minimalists" seemed to be more persuasive, and it appeared that royal Jerusalem would be recorded for all time as having been but a small city.

Fortunately for Jerusalem, as well as for historical truth, the unanticipated occurred—extensive archaeological excavations in the Upper City became possible. These excavations in the Upper City, today's Jewish Quarter, proved conclusively that at least as early as the eighth century B.C.E., the western ridge had indeed been populated, and that it had been surrounded by a wall during the First Temple Period. Admittedly, drawing a complete picture of the city during this period is still a long way off, and the data derived from the area are somewhat fragmentary. Still, for the first time we do have a realistic point of departure for studying this long-debated aspect of Jerusalem research.

In most places where we excavated to bedrock or to virgin soil, we found that the earliest inhabited stratum dated to the Israelite Period (eighth to seventh centuries B.C.E.). Because it had been eaten away with time, or entire parts of it had been removed during the building activities of later periods, the Israelite occupation level was extremely fragmentary and yielded very few remains. Still, there were enough remnants of walls and pieces of floors and pottery to establish the existence of residential buildings at the site. Moreover, it was possible to date them. Remains of this kind were scattered throughout the Jewish Quarter.

Pottery was naturally the most common find. The vessels and sherds dated to Iron Age II and may be classified with the most common type of house and kitchenware prevalent in all Judean sites during the eighth to seventh centuries B.C.E. This period also witnessed the widespread use of another kind of ceramic product—statuettes of animals and humans. The animals are very stylized and include horses and other animals that are horse-like but difficult to identify precisely. The figurines of humans are more interesting—naked women holding their breasts. Scholars assume that young Israelite women used these figurines for magical purposes—as fertility aids, or as amulets to be worn during childbirth. This was a practice inherited from the Canaanites.

Inscriptions we found on sherds and in seal impressions on jar handles have made a very important contribution to Hebrew epigraphy. One piece of a jar contained three lines written with quill and black ink. The inscription's handsome paleo-Hebrew script is the work of an expert scribe, and the calligraphy suggests that it dates to the latter part of the eighth or the beginning of the seventh century B.C.E. The inscription is partially erased, although one can clearly make out the name "Michayahu" and the word ". . . *qoneretz,"* that is, the phrase *"el qoneh eretz"* ("Lord who has created the earth"), with the letters running together. This epithet of God appears in the blessing bestowed on Abraham by Melchizedek, King of Salem (or Jerusalem) and priest of El Elyon: "Blessed be Abram by God Most High, Maker of heaven and earth" (Genesis 14:19).

A great number of seal impressions reading "Lamelech" ("belonging to the King") were found on jar handles. These "Lamelech" handles are very common at almost all Judean sites. The word "Lamelech" is invariably accompanied by the name of one of the following cities: Hebron, Ziph, Sochoh and Mmšt. Each seal impression also includes an emblem depicting either a four-winged scarab, or a double-winged solar sphere. Scholars are still debating the purpose of these royal jars, although they do agree that the jars were most widespread during the reign of Hezekiah. Other jar handles are impressed with the seals of officials. For example, we find "Belonging to Nera/Shebna" and "Belonging to Tzafan/Avima'atz," among others.

Wall from the Period of the Monarchy, uncovered in Jerusalem's Jewish Quarter.

All of these finds clearly attest to the existence of a permanent settlement on the western hill during the Israelite Period. However, they are not sufficient to prove that this area was included within the walls of the fortified city of Jerusalem. This area could have been a suburb outside the walls.

In 1970, a discovery in the northern Jewish Quarter provided proof to settle the argument. Remains of impressive First Temple Period fortifications, including a massive wall of unhewn stones, were discovered, including a section in Area A in the northern part of the Jewish Quarter. The wall has an average width of 7 meters. Over 65 continuous meters of it were exposed. It runs from northeast to southwest, and then turns westward until it reaches today's Street of the Jews. This turn is easily explained by the topography of the area.

In the vicinity of this so-called "Broad Wall," but to the north, our team discovered another First Temple Period feature—a massive corner of a fortification, evidently a tower, preserved to a height of almost 8 meters. The tower's walls are about 4 meters thick and are made of large and roughly hewn boulders chinked with small stones; the masonry of the corner, however, is laid in headers and stretchers of smooth, finely chiseled stones. Because of its excellent state of preservation, and also because of the superior quality of its construction, the tower stands out among the impressive architectural monuments from the First Temple Period. It is, in fact, in a class by itself among Jerusalem's structural remains. Another section of the Israelite wall was found about 50 meters west of the tower.

Citadel from the Period of the Monarchy and the Hasmonean Period,
uncovered in Jerusalem's Jewish Quarter.

There is no integral connection between the "Broad Wall" and the tower; apparently they were not in use simultaneously. However, we can state that all of the remains referred to above did at one time belong to the city's northern line of fortifications. This line continued along the Transversal Valley, south of the Street of the Chain and David Street. This putative line aligns well with the ancient wall as described by Josephus. As we have noted, Josephus identified his first wall with the First Temple Period; however, this early date was not accepted by most contemporary scholars. They assumed that Josephus was mistakenly referring to a wall from the Hasmonean Period, a wall that had circumvallated the western hill. The results of our excavations, however, give credence to the relevant passages in Josephus. We can say without doubt that the view that the western ridge was surrounded by a wall as early as the Israelite Period is currently gaining favor. Moreover, Hillel Gevah, a member of our staff, has recently proposed that excavations conducted in the Citadel near the Jaffa Gate have uncovered a further section of the Israelite wall, which had not previously been identified as such because of restrictions at the site. The matter certainly requires further investigation.

Scripture offers obvious hints for the existence of residential suburbs outside the limits of the City of David. For example, it is said that Hulda the prophetess, wife of Shallum, keeper of the wardrobe, had ". . . dwelt in Jerusalem in the second quarter [*mishneh*] . . ." (2 Kings 22:14). In light of our excavations, we can assert positively that this *mishneh* was located on the western hill. It appears that the new settlement, which ultimately extended over the entire western ridge, at first comprised merely an open settlement that had no real connection with its "mother city," the City of David. Eventually, however, the *mishneh* was encircled by a wall, which in turn was joined to the City of David wall, forming one large, fortified city, truly, a "city that was full of people" (Lamentations 1:1). And the event was celebrated in the verses: "Our feet shall stand within thy gates, O Jerusalem. Jerusalem is built as a city that is compact together" (Psalms 122:2-3). We think that the city began to expand as early as the beginning of the eighth century B.C.E., but that the new section of the city was circumvallated by a wall only during the latter part of the century. This is clearly demonstrated by the archaeological evidence: The "Broad Wall" was built in part on top of the ruins of destroyed Israelite houses. It appears that when the direction of the line of fortifications was chosen, its designers paid no heed whatever to the houses that stood in the wall's path. Indeed, buildings were summarily destroyed to create space for the wall. This is clearly reflected in the Book of Isaiah, which states, "You have seen also the breaches of the City of David, that they are many, And you gathered together the waters of the lower pool. And you numbered the houses of Jerusalem, *and the houses have you broken down to fortify the walls.* You made also a ditch between the two walls for the water of the old pool" (Isaiah 22:9-11).

Although it is true that many kings fortified Jerusalem, Isaiah is apparently here referring to an episode that occurred during the reign of Hezekiah. Hezekiah is the only king who, according to scripture, fortified the walls and secured a new source of water supply for use during times of siege. Hezekiah engineered these fortifications as defensive measures against Sennacherib's invasion in 701 B.C.E. On the basis of the available data, I am inclined to ascribe the construction of the "Broad Wall" to Hezekiah. This wall also encircled the Pool of Siloam (it had been located outside the City of David), so that the pool was now also inside the defensible city. This is quite evident from scripture; moreover, it is logical. The pool was situated between the old wall of the City of David and the new wall; Isaiah is undoubtedly alluding to these structures when he declares that, ". . . you made a ditch between the two walls for the water. . . ."

A find near the Israelite citadel mentioned above has aroused great interest. A group of arrowheads was unearthed among remains left strewn over the surface at the foot of the citadel following a conflagration. We found four flat iron arrows, apparently of local origin, as well as a northern "Scythian-type" bronze arrow with a triangular fin. This type of weapon was introduced during the middle of the seventh century B.C.E., and was used principally by foreign armies fighting in the Land of Israel. This discovery is possibly the first tangible witness to the battle on the walls of Jerusalem which culminated in the Babylonian destruction of the city by fire and the laying waste of the First Temple.

II. The Second Temple Period

A. The Period of the Return to Zion

When the exiles returned to Jerusalem from Babylon, Nehemiah began to reconstruct the damaged and deteriorated city wall. But which wall was this? The "maximalists" and the "minimalists" held different opinions. In this case, our excavations enabled us to reject unequivocally the "maximalist" position, for we found no remains whatever on the western ridge dating to the period of the exiles' Return to Zion. This indicates that the site was not resettled after the Babylonian destruction of Jerusalem. Those few who returned were unable to reconstruct either the ruins on the western hill, or those on the eastern ridge. They were content merely to rehabilitate and fortify the much smaller City of David. This seems to be the burden of Nehemiah's words: "Now the city was extensive and spacious, the people in it few, and the houses not yet built" (Nehemiah 7:4). The phrase ". . . the city was extensive and spacious . . ." probably refers to the desolated large western hill, not the smaller City of David.

B. The Hasmonean Period

It is plausible to assume that during the early Hellenistic Period too (fourth to third centuries B.C.E.) people continued to settle only within the precincts of the Ophel hill. The western hill has yielded no remains dating to this period, with the exception of a few coins and solitary sherds. Only during the Hasmonean Period (middle of the second century B.C.E.) did Jerusalem once again expand its boundaries and begin to stretch across the valley to the Upper City, which was now surrounded by a new wall. When the Hasmoneans began to work on this new wall, they adopted the ancient defense lines of the Israelite Period; sections of the ruins were still visible then. The Maccabean builders proceeded to reconstruct those sections of the ancient fortifications that could still be used, and integrated them into their new defense wall. This can be demonstrated, at least so far as the northern wall is concerned, because remains of it were discovered in Area W and Area X2.

In Area W, the Hasmonean builders found the Israelite tower mentioned above, and joined their own wall to it. The new wall thus included a defense tower, 9 meters wide, which protruded from the wall to form a shape like this: ⌐⌐. A Hellenistic floor common to both towers attests that they were used at the same time. Impressive sections of Hasmonean fortifications, preserved to a height of 6 meters or more, were also discovered in Area X2. One section is joined to a section of the ancient Israelite wall. The location of these remains and the area's topography suggest that a gate was once here, perhaps Josephus's elusive "Gennath" gate. Remains of both Israelite and Hasmonean fortifications were found south of the Street of the Chain and David Street—that is, aligned with Josephus's "First Wall," which he describes as beginning on the north at Hippicus Tower near the Citadel, and continuing to the Xystus. It adjoined the Council Chamber and ended at the western portico of the Temple Mount. Josephus informs us, then,

that the western wall continued along the line followed by today's Old City wall—
that is, along the length of the Valley of Hinnom—and that it enclosed the top of
Mt. Zion on its southern side. Previous excavations and those conducted currently
by various archaeologists have uncovered many segments of this Hasmonean wall
along these precise lines. On the basis of these finds, I have proposed in this
chapter that the course followed by the Israelite wall was more or less identical
with that of the Hasmonean wall. I feel confident in taking this position despite
the fact that no remains of the First Temple wall have yet been found in the west
and south.

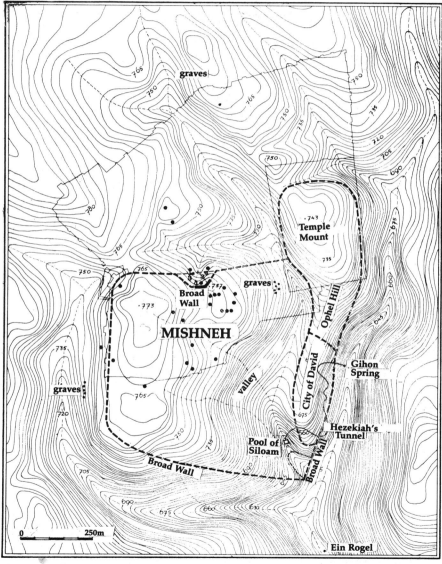

Jerusalem at the close of the Period of the Monarchy.
1-3: Remnants of Israelite fortifications uncovered at northern wall; the dots designate
excavated Israelite sites.

136

C. The Herodian Period

Finds from the Herodian Period differ essentially from those of earlier periods. We no longer find just impersonal walls, nor do we deal with the question of topography. Instead we expose the homes of real Jerusalemites and scrutinize their everyday possessions. This has allowed us a new look at a Jerusalem of which we were hardly aware. The Herodian Period, more than any other historical period, was revealed by our archaeological excavations. This was a time when Jerusalem flourished. The Herodian stratum has permitted the first sketches of a picture of urban life in ancient Jerusalem, urban life as it was lived in the Upper City, in the residential quarter opposite the Temple Mount.

We found that although they were crammed closely together, the houses themselves were very large and spacious. This was an affluent area, as the interior decoration of the houses attests. These decorations include murals and stucco and mosaic floors. In addition to well-constructed lavatory installations, we found luxury products, cosmetic aids, and other such objects. An inscription on a stone weight mentions the name of a family apparently of High Priests during the Second Temple Period (see below). The residents of this quarter fashioned their dwellings in a contemporary mode—that is, in the then-current Hellenistic-Roman style.

The buildings were remarkably well preserved, considering conditions in the Jewish Quarter. In one of them, we unearthed remains of two stories, as well as walls which were preserved to a height of 3 meters. In some instances, it was even possible to recover the entire plan of the building. Especially noteworthy in this connection is a building uncovered in the eastern fringe of the Jewish Quarter (Area P) which we nicknamed "the mansion." This house extends over an area of about 600 square meters. A series of chambers was arranged around a central courtyard paved with stone slabs. The walls of the rooms, made of dressed stones, were decorated with colorful murals consisting of plant life and architectural and geometric motifs. A large room—obviously the living room—was decorated with stucco, which had been molded into panels and imitations of drafted masonry. The decorations reflect the influence of an ornamental style encountered at Pompeii and at certain Hellenistic sites in Asia Minor. The colored mosaic floors found in this house, and at other buildings in the Jewish Quarter, are the earliest yet discovered in Herodian Jerusalem. The central motif of these mosaics usually consisted of a compass-drawn, geometric rosette pattern.

A row of steps in the mansion led from the central courtyard to the lower story, which contained storehouses, ritual baths, and water cisterns. The palatial, vaulted ritual baths with wide steps were especially noteworthy because of their double entrances—one for descending into the ritual bath (mikva) and the other for exiting after immersion and purification.

This magnificient house contained many beautiful vessels. Among them were a local kind of painted bowl, which is one of the finest of its kind yet discovered in the Holy City, and pieces of a splendid glass jug, the handiwork of the famed Sidonian glassmaker, Ennion. We also uncovered a mobile stone sundial, decorated in the then-current style—that is, with a compass-drawn, geometric rosette design. Well-crafted stone tables were the first discovered in Israel and in fact comprise the only pieces of furniture known to us from the Second Temple Period. The tables were of two types. The first consisted simply of a rectangular slab and one leg shaped like a column. The second type was a little smaller and consisted of a circular stone slab with a wooden tripod, which regrettably had long since decayed. The house must have been a splendid mansion indeed, and was surely the home of some aristocratic Jerusalem family.

Remains of a building from the Second Temple Period,
uncovered at the site of "Yeshivat Ha-Kotel" in the Jewish Quarter of Jerusalem.

Another building whose plan has been entirely recovered is a dwelling made of undressed stones, which takes up an area of almost 200 square meters (Area V). The walls are covered with smooth white plaster, and the rooms, like those of the mansion, are arranged around a central courtyard. Four ovens are set into the courtyard floor. A large stepped pool seems to have served as the ritual bath. Three niches built into the western wall must have served as cupboards for the household crockery—as the pieces of broken vessels found in these alcoves attest.

The obvious wealth of the residents is evidenced by the spacious plan of the house, as well as by the vessels discovered there. Particularly noteworthy is a series of beautiful red vessels of the Eastern "terra sigillata" type, which are distinguished for their finely molded forms. And a group of large amphorae bearing Latin inscriptions testifies that their owners must have enjoyed the Italian wine these vessels once contained. Characteristic asymmetrically shaped flasks were used to decant the wine. Interestingly enough, the house was not destroyed by the ravages of war, but instead fell victim to a now-unknown urban planner. At the end of Herod's reign, or possibly a little later, it was decided that the building obstructed a new street plan for the city, and the house was demolished. A new street, paved with large stone slabs, was then built directly on top of the ruins of this once splendid home.

The bathing rooms in these Jerusalem buildings were generally given special decorative treatment and were usually paved with colorful mosaics. Each such unit included an antechamber, a room with a bathtub, and a ritual bath. These purificatory ritual baths had obviously been an important component of every

Jerusalem home. We excavated numerous such baths—small ones as well as large vaulted ones with two entrances (similar to the one discovered in "the mansion"). The best preserved *mikva*—which, incidentally, was found to comply with all the pertinent Halachic requirements—was discovered in Area T4. It consisted of a chamber containing a bathtub, a stepped ritual bath, and what came to be known

The "Mansion" of the Second Temple Period, uncovered in the Jewish Quarter of Jerusalem (looking east).

as the *otzar,* (or "reserve"). This *otzar* was a small pool located next to the ritual bath, which contained rainwater. Ritually pure water from the *otzar*—that is, water that came from a halachically required "flowing" or "living" source or rainwater—would pour through a hole in the wall located between the two pools, and come in contact with the "drawn" water in the ritual bath. The water in the *mikva* itself would thus be rendered ritually acceptable.

Many buildings yielded obvious traces of the conflagration that followed the Roman destruction of the city. One such house was named appropriately "the burnt house"—both because it was the first burnt house unearthed and also because it contained an especially thick burnt layer. Several rooms of this house—now located on Misgav Ladach Street—were discovered. They had apparently been part of the basement level of a house whose upper story has not survived.

The burnt house is especially noteworthy because it contains a burn layer that was left entirely undisturbed by later building activity; the excavators found it in precisely the same state as it had been following its destruction by fire. The heaps of debris that filled the rooms consisted of fallen masonry scorched by the fierce fire, charred wooden beams, and layers of dust and soot that covered the many artifacts in the rooms. The artifacts included many soft stone vessels, such as

139

large, goblet-like pitchers, bowls, "measuring cups," and various lids. Mortars, pestles of basalt, grindstones and an assortment of stone weights were also discovered here. Particularly interesting were the stone tables. The preponderance of stone vessels and utensils, a phenomenon common to all of Jerusalem's residences, might be explained by the fact that stone cannot become ritually unclean. The remains of ovens sunk into the ground were also unearthed in these rooms. The finds plainly attest to pounding, measuring, weighing and cooking activity.

One of the weights in the burnt house was incised with an Aramaic inscription: *d'bar Kathros*—that is, "Of Bar Kathros." The "House of Kathros" was one of the four corrupt families of the High Priesthood whom the Talmud excoriates (Babylonian Pesahim 57a) for exploiting their lofty position, and securing offices in the Temple hierarchy for their own family members. This house may well have been the home of some members of this calumnious Kathros family. The house was destroyed in the war; an iron spear was found leaning in a corner of one of the rooms, as if ready for use; and the skeletal remains of the right arm of a young woman rested against the wall of the kitchen.

The numerous coins found scattered throughout the rooms date to the First Jewish Revolt and the war against the Romans, which indicates that the house had been in use until the end of the Revolt; it was razed in the destruction of 70 C.E.

Josephus tells us that the Upper City managed to hold out for a month after the temple was burned on the ninth of Ab. After this, however, the Romans were able to overrun it and put it to the torch. Josephus's tragic report declares simply (*The Jewish War*, Book VI: Ch. 9), ". . . and the dawn of the eighth day of the month Gorpiaeus [Elul] broke upon Jerusalem in flames . . ."

The Royal Stoa in the Southern Part of the Temple Mount

By Benjamin Mazar

T he extensive archaeological excavations conducted since 1968 near the magnificent retaining walls of the enclosed Temple area in Jerusalem enable us to arrive at certain conclusions regarding the elaborate design of the Herodian construction project, particularly since it was executed in the vicinity of "Robinson's Arch" and the southwestern corner of the Temple Mount.[1]

This was undoubtedly one of the focal points of the metropolis during the period of Herod's Temple. Here was the axis of the paved streets of Jerusalem: the main street, which ran the length of the Tyropoeon Valley and served the large markets, and the streets that branched out from it—eastward, to the gates in the southern and western walls of the enclosed Temple area, and westward, to the Upper City and Herod's palace. From this point, one ascended a flight of stairs that rested on "Robinson's Arch" and on the row of arches extending to the south of it. These arches were set at measured distances, with each arch lower than the one before it.

It is noteworthy that Flavius Josephus, in referring to the four gates of the Western Wall, pays particular attention to the fourth gate, which was the most southerly one and from which one descended, on a great number of steps, to the Tyropoeon Valley. From that point, a row of stairs led to the Upper City (*Antiquities of the Jews*, XV, 410). Near this site, beside the southwestern corner of the Temple Mount, a large hewn stone with a niche in its inner side was discovered. Bordering the niche was a Hebrew inscription: *lbythtqy hᶜlhk[rz]* "to the House of Trumpeting [to proclaim]." This stone must have fallen down from the top of the priest's chambers, where one of the priests customarily sounded a trumpet on the eve of the Sabbath and on the following evening, to announce its advent and its close (Josephus, *The Jewish War*, IV, 582).

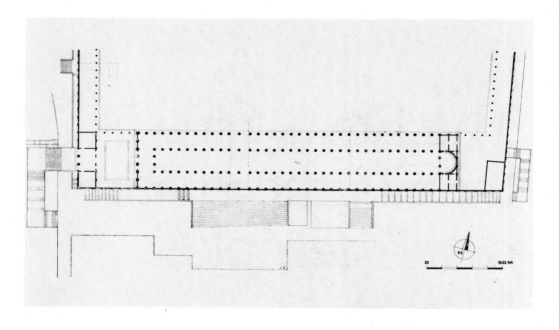

Plan of the Royal Stoa on the southern end of the Temple Mount.

In describing the enclosed area of the Temple Mount, Josephus devotes considerable attention to the Royal Stoa saying that "It is a structure more worthy to be spoken of than any other under the sun" (*Antiquities*, XV, 411-416). This magnificent stoa towered high over the southern part of the Temple court and extended from the eastern valley (the Kidron Valley), to the western valley (the Tyropoeon Valley). The main part of it was a long rectangular Hall of Columns built in the design of a basilica. The columns, 162 in number, stood facing each other in four rows the length of the hall. The first, or southern, row was set into the outer stone wall. A statement of Rabbi Judah concerning the Temple Mount is of interest: "It was called *'istonit* [stoa-like], one stoa within another" (Babylonian Talmud, Pesahim 13b). This resembles Josephus's own description of the stoas of the Temple Mount, where he refers to them as "the double stoas" (*The Jewish War*, V, 190).

According to Josephus, the columns divided the basilica hall, whose width was about 39 meters and whose outer wall was 1.5 meters thick. There were three areas of space: the middle and two lateral areas. The middle area was one and a half times as wide as the lateral ones and twice as high. Josephus is also informative in stating that it required three men, holding each other with extended arms, to reach around each column.

Generally speaking, one receives quite a clear picture regarding the character of the Royal Stoa from Josephus's descriptions; this picture is borne out with considerable accuracy by the outer measurements that have been made and by the limited investigations we have carried out at the Huldah Gates. Josephus was also correct in his descriptions of the passages leading from underneath the Royal Stoa to the interior of the enclosed Temple area, the columns (each approximately 1.45 meters in diameter), and the fragments of the Corinthian capitals. The large and decorated arch-stone, discovered along with other decorated Herodian building stones, is particularly instructive. It was found in the heap of debris piled up outside the southern wall and adjacent to it, east of the eastern Huldah Gate (the

Triple Gate), together with a fragment of a monumental Hebrew inscription, as yet unexplained. One may reasonably suppose that this arch-stone belonged to the apse, which was built adjacent to the rear, eastern wall of the Hall of Columns.

As far as the history of the Royal Stoa is concerned, one may assume that it constituted the most important part of Herod's eight-year Jerusalem construction project, which included the walls and stoas. (According to *The Jewish War*, I, 40, construction began in the 15th year of Herod's reign, i.e. 19 B.C.E., and according to *Antiquities*, XV, 380, in the 18th year.)

We must bear in mind that according to the Gospel of John (2:20), the construction work in the enclosed Temple area continued for 46 years, until the time of the Procurator Pontius Pilate (26-36 C.E.). Actually, construction work of great scope was accomplished during this period, involving the repair of the physical plant, with restoration and additions. This activity was necessitated primarily by the severe damage done to the stoas by fire and devastation caused by the soldiers of Sabinus during the time of Archelaus (*The Jewish War*, II, 49).

Presumably, the construction was executed under the supervision of Gamaliel the Elder (Paul's teacher, according to Acts 22:3). With reference to Gamaliel, it is stated, "He [Gamaliel] used to supervise the *builders*" (Yerushalmi, Shabbat, Chapter 16). According to Saul Lieberman, "from this statement, as we understand it, we learn that the Temple buildings were under the supervision of the Patriarch during the time of Gamaliel the Elder."[2]

In turn, this correlates with the received tradition that 40 years prior to the destruction of the Temple (c. 30 C.E.), the seat of the Sanhedrin was located in the "stores" (Hebrew: *hanuyyot*) within the Temple area: "The Sanhedrin moved from the bureau of hewn stone to the stores, and from the stores to Jerusalem . . ." (Talmud Bavli, *Shabbat*, 15a; *Rosh Hashanah*, 31a; *Abodah Zarah*, 8b; etc.).

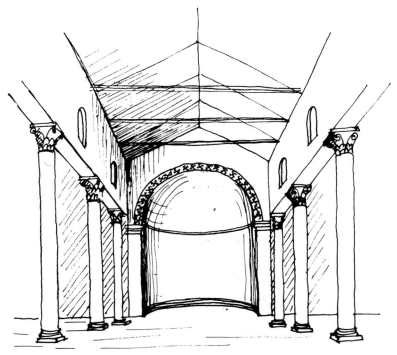

Reconstruction of the eastern corner of the Hall of Columns in the Royal Stoa.

Ornamented stone arch discovered south of the southern wall of the Temple Mount and east of the Triple Gate.

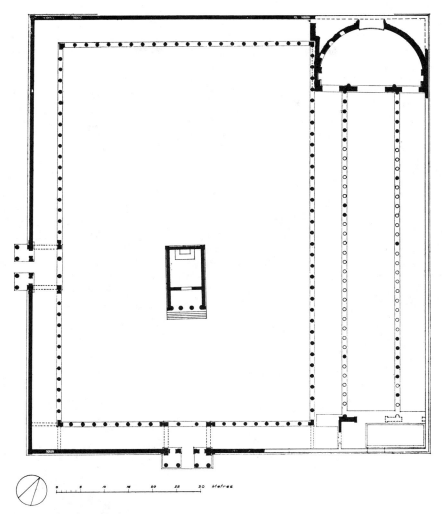

Plan of the royal stoa at Cyrene.

Although the precise sense of the term *hanuyyot* is not fully clear (in the Bible it is a *hapax legomenon* in Jeremiah 37:16), it appears to derive from Aramaic *ḥanuta* and to refer to the basilica hall in the Royal Stoa, which served communal needs, including commerce involved in sacred donations and sacrifices. It seems that for the housing of the Sanhedrin, the apse was constructed at the rear wall of the basilica, and it was also able to accommodate the sessions of the Sanhedrin. Possibly it was separated from the Hall of Columns by a partition. In any event, it is clear that Herod's architects built the Royal Stoa on the model of the Roman basilicas, which served important communal and commercial functions in relation to the Forum.

The earliest known example is the Basilica Porcia of Cato (184 B.C.E.), near the Forum Romanum in Rome. In the course of time, the basilica became common-place in the Roman Empire, and the plan was widely diffused in the eastern provinces. What distinguished the communal basilica, in general, was a hall with four rows of columns along the length of the hall, lighting in the upper portion of the hall, and a rectangular or semicircular platform adjacent to its rear wall, opposite the entrance wall. As an interesting parallel to the Temple area built by Herod, one may cite the square, enclosed temenos in Cyrene, surrounded by stoas on all four sides. One of these stoas was a basilica, with an apse adjacent to its rear wall, opposite the entrance. This type of area, enclosed with a basilica, became common in the centers of the eastern Empire, such as Antioch and Palmyra. As Sjöqvist quite reasonably supposes, the origin of this architectural style is to be found in the *Kaisareion* of Alexandria, built in the time of Julius Caesar (48 B.C.E.), which was intended to serve as an official center of the imperial cult.[3]

On this basis, we assume that the Royal Stoa in Jerusalem was erected by Herod as an integral part of the enclosed Temple area, on the model of the basilicas in the eastern provinces of the Roman Empire.

One ascended to the stoa from the markets of the city, located in the Tyropoeon Valley to the west, on a monumental staircase that led up to the Temple Mount. The stoa served primarily for commerce in cultic provisions for the Temple. It is significant, moreover, that the term *hanuyyot* was probably one of the designations for the basilica where the Sanhedrin was relocated, after Rabban Gamaliel's restoration work was finished. The Sanhedrin was probably housed in the apse, constructed on the eastern side of the Hall of Columns.

In the light of what has been discussed, one should inquire if this very place in the Temple area was the scene of the confrontation between Jesus and the purvey-

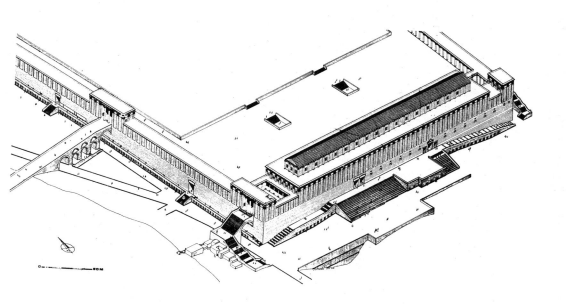

Reconstruction of the southwestern area of the Temple Mount compound in Herodian times.

146

ors of pigeons, recorded in the well-known episode from the Gospels. (Pigeons were required for sacrifices offered by women after childbirth and by those suffering from flux, according to Leviticus 12:8, 15:14.) The same would hold true for Jesus' confrontation with the moneychangers, who apparently exchanged coins bearing the image of Caesar for Jerusalemite coins. Jesus sought to expel such merchants from the Temple area.

This proposal, suggested with reservations by Dalman,[4] accords well with the previous discussion about the function of the Royal Stoa. Moreover, one should mention the fragment of a vessel, inscribed in Hebrew letters with the word *qrbn*, "offering" and showing, underneath the inscription, two inverted figures of pigeons. This fragment was found in a heap of debris on the paved Herodian street south of the Temple Mount's southern wall. It must have come originally from the Hall of Columns in the Royal Stoa.[5]

In conclusion, I should raise the possibility that those who built the great synagogues in the diaspora centers knew well the design of the Royal Stoa on the Temple Mount and constructed their communal installations to resemble it. Religious buildings were erected in the form of a basilica, with its hall of columns and a semicircular apse, which was for the elders of the community. There was also a small, anterior courtyard, apparently resembling the one that stood in the Royal Stoa, between the gate at its western end and the entrance in the narrow western wall of the Hall of Columns. An instructive example is the synagogue discovered at Sardis (Sepharad), in Anatolia.[6] Dr. Lee Levine reminded me of what is said about the great synagogue in Alexandria in the Tosefta (*Sukkah*, 4b):

"Rabbi Judah said: Whoever has not gazed at the 'double stoa' of Alexandria in Egypt has never in his entire life seen glory reflected on Israel! It was like a large basilica, a stoa within a stoa; with 71 golden seats, corresponding to the 71 elders."[7]

Therefore, many divergent and complex problems are bound up with the investigation of the Royal Stoa in the southern part of the Temple Mount in Jerusalem. One hopes that additional investigations of this area with comprehensive examination of the relevant literary materials and the numerous architectural fragments uncovered in the heaps of debris outside the southern retaining wall will provide further elucidation and new solutions with respect to the Royal Stoa.

[1]See B. Mazar, *The Mountain of the Lord* (New York, 1975), pp. 118-152; "Excavations Near the Temple Mount" in *Jerusalem Revealed* (ed. Y. Yadin) (New Haven, 1976), pp. 25-32; "Herodian Jerusalem in the Light of the Excavations South of the Temple Mount," *Israel Exploration Journal* 28 (1978), pp. 230-237.

[2]Saul Lieberman, *Tosefta Ki-fshuṭah*, Part III, Order Moʿed (New York, 1962), p. 204 [Hebrew].

[3]See E. Sjöqvist, "Kaisareion, A Study in Architectural Iconography," *Opuscula Romana* (Sweden, 1954), I, 86ff.; J. S. Ward Perkins and M. A. Ballance, "The Caesareum at Cyrene and the Basilica at Cremma," *Papers of the British School at Rome* (London, 1958), XXVI, pp. 137ff.; G. Foerster, *Art and Archaeology in Palestine, The Jewish People in the First Century* (Amsterdam, 1976), II 980.

[4]See G. Dalman, *Orte und Wege Jesu* (Gütersloh, 1919), pp. 271ff.; *Jerusalem und sein Gelände* (Gütersloh, 1936), p. 194.

[5]B. Mazar, *The Excavations in the Old City of Jerusalem*, I (1969), pp. 15-16.

[6]See Andrew R. Seager, "The Synagogue of Sardis" [Hebrew], *Qadmoniot* (Jerusalem, 1974), VII, Nos. 3-4, pp. 123ff.; Andrew R. Seager, "The Building History of the Sardis Synagogue," *American Journal of Archaeology*, 76 (1972), 425ff.

[7]See Saul Lieberman, *Tosefta Ki-fshuṭah*, Part IV, Order Moʿed (New York, 1962), pp. 273, 889-891 [Hebrew].

Past and Present in Archaeological Research on the City of David

By Yigal Shiloh

Since the second half of the 19th century, Jerusalem has been a principal focus of archaeological investigation in the Land of Israel. Despite valiant attempts to reconstruct the city's ancient history from the archaeological clues, many questions remain unanswered, especially regarding the pre-Herodian era. Ironically enough, the material available from biblical period Jerusalem is far less than that from other sites such as Megiddo, Hazor, Dan and Samaria. The paucity of material from Jerusalem results from the fact that the city has been continuously inhabited since its founding at the beginning of the third millennium B.C.E. For much of this time, beginning with the reigns of David and Solomon, Jerusalem was the capital of the country. At times the city extended over a large area; at other times, it contracted.

The city's fortifications were built, destroyed, and rebuilt as its population grew and declined with the turn of historical events. Also, a new ruler would often change the location of the city center. At first, it was the area now known as the City of David; then it changed to the Temple Mount; after that, it passed to the Upper City, then to the market area, then to the Church of the Holy Sepulchre and, finally, back to the Temple Mount area. Various sections of the city, such as Mount Zion and northern Jerusalem, were only intermittently inhabited and fortified. The southeast hill, known as the "City of David," and especially the area around the Gihon Spring, was the site of the city's initial development in the Bronze Age. In the post-Byzantine era, the City of David was outside the city walls but still maintained its identity as a sparsely populated suburb. After that, almost nothing changed in Jerusalem until the beginning of the 20th century, when new buildings were erected, particularly in the Wadi Hilwa and Silwan regions.

I. The Earliest Research—From Robinson to Weill (1838-1924)

Even at the earliest stages of modern research, investigators explored and even focused on the City of David area. From the mid-19th century until Dame Kathleen Kenyon's excavations in the 1960s, most of the surveys and excavations were conducted under the auspices of the British Palestine Exploration Fund or the British School of Archaeology in Jerusalem, or both. Edward Robinson, however, was the first researcher who, in 1838, crawled through Hezekiah's Tunnel, apparently the first person to do so in modern times. In 1865, Charles Wilson, on behalf of the Palestine Exploration Fund, carried out a detailed survey of Jerusalem's ancient remains as part of a larger, comprehensive exploration of the Land of Israel. Charles Warren joined Wilson between 1867-1870 and broadened the investigation to include the first study of buried remains. Together the two men examined remains in the northeast corner of the City of David, near the Temple Mount. They also explored the ancient water system near the Gihon Spring, which was known thereafter as "Warren's Shaft."

Between 1894 and 1897, F. J. Bliss and A. C. Dickie conducted a great number of exploratory excavations in the area south of the Old City. During these probes, Bliss and Dickie developed a more sophisticated archaeological methodology for the investigation, but they still used the shaft and tunnel systems, as had Warren. They unearthed the remains of a Byzantine church above the Pool of Siloam and, with praiseworthy persistence, attempted to trace the course of the city walls and the various buildings adjacent to them in the southern part of the city. Our own experience in excavating in the City of David has given me a certain empathy with an earlier excavator, Dame Kathleen Kenyon, who wrote (in a simultaneously laudatory and rueful vein): "With quite embarrassing regularity we found 'B and D' (Bliss and Dickie) tunnels almost everywhere we dug . . . "

Toward the end of the 19th century, additional investigations were conducted at the City of David by H. Guthe, C. Clermont-Ganneau and C. Schick. Their efforts were important principally because they located certain crucial elements that indicated the course of the city wall on the crest of the eastern slope of the City of David. These investigators also discovered various remains in the vicinity of the Pool of Siloam. All these remains were either lost or later covered by construction.

In the report he wrote of his investigations, Clermont-Ganneau encouraged a search for the "Tombs of the House of David," supposedly located in the southeastern part of the City of David. As early as 1887, he theorized that the serpentine course followed by Hezekiah's Tunnel, which makes a wide arc in the southern part of the City of David, had been purposely designed so that the Israelites who carved the tunnel out of the rock would avoid the tombs of the Kings of Judah, whose royal burial caves, Clermont-Ganneau proposed, were hewn out of the rock somewhere in this general vicinity. Bliss and Dickie excavated in part of this area, near the southern edge of the City of David, but found no tombs. Raymond Weill, who excavated in the City of David in 1913-1914 and in 1923-1924, discovered two very large, long caves that had been cut out of the rock near, but above, the large curve in Hezekiah's Tunnel. These caves came to be known as the "Tombs of the House of David," although no convincing chronological, stratigraphical or architectural evidence supported this romanticization. We should be especially grateful to Weill, however, because Baron Edmond de Rothschild purchased land in the City of David for Weill's archaeological excavation. Since this land belongs to the State of Israel, it is now available for our own excavations.

In 1909-1911 the English adventurer Montague Parker, joined the select group of those who have explored the City of David. His principal activities were confined to the area of the slope above the Gihon Spring. Father Louis Hughes Vincent, who accompanied the Parker Mission, must be credited with the publication of the expedition's most important achievement, the investigation of Warren's Shaft and the exploration of several Early Bronze I tombs.

II. Excavations Between the Two World Wars

The British School of Archaeology in Jerusalem conducted two separate archaeological expeditions in the City of David during this period. One was led by R.A.S. Macalister, who had previously excavated at Gezer. J. G. Duncan also participated in this Jerusalem excavation, which covered a wide area at the crest of the eastern slope, above the Gihon Spring. Like other excavations of the time, it was not controlled stratigraphically, but it nevertheless uncovered an important segment of wall, towers, and a stepped stone structure. The excavators ascribed all these finds to the Jebusite and Israelite cities.

The second British expedition between the two wars was led by Crowfoot and Fitzgerald. In 1927 they extensively excavated the top of the ridge in the northern part of the City of David. Compared to earlier researchers, Crowfoot and Fitzgerald were more methodologically precise in their work and thus concluded with sounder findings. They unearthed Byzantine and Moslem residential quarters in the Central Valley—The Tyropoeon—and on the western slope of the hill. Above the Tyropoeon Valley, they also discovered the "Valley Gate" that is, the City of David's western gate.

III. The First Breakthrough—Kathleen Kenyon's Excavations

Kenyon excavated in Jerusalem between 1961 and 1967 on behalf of the Palestine Exploration Fund, the British School of Archaeology in Jerusalem, and the British Academy. Her work ushered in a new era, especially in the City of David. She demanded strict stratigraphic and ceramic controls according to the methods she had developed previously at Samaria and Jericho. Her methodology was based on the excavation of rather small, narrow archaeological sections. She did, however, to her considerable credit, solve several key problems concerning the history of the City of David. However, blind adherence to a particular system of excavation, without regard to the specific context in which one is working, does have its drawbacks. It can often obscure a wider view, and inaccurate conclusions may well be the result. This happened in Kenyon's case. Her methodology resulted in a number of erroneous stratigraphical and chronological determinations, especially regarding the identification of Hellenistic-Byzantine Period remains discovered inside the Old City walls north of the City of David.

On the other hand, her work in the City of David area, and principally in her major trench—which extended from the base of the wall uncovered by Macalister down to the Gihon Spring—laid the foundation for understanding the development of the entire eastern slope of the City of David during its various periods of occupation. Buildings dating to the Israelite Period were unearthed beneath the line of fortifications originally excavated by Macalister, demonstrating that this line of fortifications must have been built during the Second Temple Period. It also became apparent that during the Canaanite and Israelite Periods the line of the city wall was lower down the slope, relatively near the Spring. The area between the ancient line of fortifications and the top of the hill was terraced with retaining walls, a construction method typical in mountainous areas. Even when later buildings were erected, these support walls remained untouched. The wall line near the top of the slope was established on the exiles' return and continued to be used during the Second Temple Period. The buildings on the terrace of the eastern slope which had been destroyed by the Babylonians in 586 B.C.E. were not resettled. Since this is the one area that permits direct access to the pre-Second Temple

Periods, we expect that in our own continuing excavations we will soon be able to investigate the vestiges of these periods, despite hundreds of years of erosion.

Kenyon was the last of the "minimalists"—those who argued that during the First Temple Period, Jerusalem covered a "minimal" area. A heated debate had long raged among scholars concerning Jerusalem's ancient boundaries. The "minimalists" claimed that the archaeological evidence clearly showed that the Canaanite and Israelite cities had been confined to the southeastern hill, now called the City of David. The "maximalists," on the other hand, argued that the ancient city had expanded to the western ridge of today's Old City—that is, up to Mount Zion and the Citadel. At first, Kenyon suggested that the boundaries of both the Israelite and Hellenistic cities were on the eastern side of the central (or Tyropoeon) valley. She further suggested that the expansion of the city in the late Iron Age occurred in the northern part of the eastern slope, near the Temple Mount. Later, in light of numerous finds from the eighth to seventh centuries B.C.E. in the Jewish Quarter excavations, she recanted. In her last publication, she changed her plans, according to these new finds.

IV. The Great Upswing—The Excavations After 1967

Archaeological research on all of ancient Jerusalem increased enormously after the Six Day War. Development projects, construction activity and restoration work in the Old City and in its environs made it necessary to embark on a large-scale survey, as well as archaeological excavations, before the final plans for the new building program could be approved. The comprehensive excavations of Benjamin Mazar in the Temple Mount area and of Nahman Avigad in the Jewish Quarter yielded a rich bounty of data. Magen Broshi continued Tushingham's excavations on Mount Zion and in the Armenian Quarter. Ruth Amiran and Avi Eitan carried on the archaeological work of C. N. Johns from the Mandate Period in the Citadel area. Ehud Netzer and Sarah Ben-Aryeh excavated north of the Old City. All of this contributed greatly to our knowledge of Jerusalem throughout the ages, especially during the Roman, Byzantine and Moslem Periods.

Professor Mazar's excavations and Professor Avigad's excavation finally put an end to the perennial controversy concerning the city limits during the Iron Age. Mazar discovered handsome rock tombs from the ninth to eighth centuries B.C.E. west of the Temple Mount. Both Tushingham and Kenyon had previously found Iron Age quarries in the Armenian Quarter, and Magen Broshi had found similar quarries nearby. All this seemed to suggest that the western hill area had been a rock quarry and burial site until the eighth century B.C.E.; at least until then, it must have been outside the city boundaries, as the "minimizers" had claimed. However, evidence from the Jewish Quarter excavations, as well as from the Armenian Quarter excavations, and from Mount Zion and the Citadel area, demonstrated that from the latter part of the eighth century this area had been inhabited. At first, only ceramic remains appeared. But later, archaeologists came across building remains as well, which indicated that the site had been quite densely settled from the end of the eighth century until the destruction of the Temple and Jerusalem in 586 B.C.E. The so-called "Broad Wall" discovered by Avigad in the middle of the Jewish Quarter was the final proof needed to confirm the "maximizers'" position. In light of this evidence, it became clear that approximately in Hezekiah's reign, the city expanded both to the north and to the west. At this time a new wall was added which effectively annexed the newly-built residential quarters on the western hill (the "Mishneh") to the city proper. Finally, remains of an apparently important public building from the late Israelite Period were discovered at the edge of the excavation area south of the Temple Mount, in the northern part of the City of David (Ophel). The connection between this structure and the

Temple Mount area is still not clear.

All these excavations have given us dramatic new pictures of the city in various periods of expansion and contraction from the Bronze Age to our own time.

Various types of Iron Age II stone weights from the City of David excavations.

V. The New Archaeological Project in the City of David

Our archaeological knowledge of Jerusalem has come a long way from the pioneering days of Warren and Wilson. There had been much initial interest in the City of David, but the focus of investigation shifted after 1967 to the Old City and to the areas adjacent to the Old City walls. The late professor E. L. Sukenik did much to advance research on Jerusalem's past by establishing the Institute of Archaeology at Hebrew University. The Institute has been the "senior partner," so to speak, in the various excavations around the Temple Mount and in the Jewish Quarter, and it was natural, therefore, that it should also participate in the recently renewed interest in the City of David.

In 1978, The City of David Society—"The Society for the Excavation, Preservation and Restoration of the City of David, Jerusalem"—was founded. Mayor Teddy Kollek is president of the Society; members include the Institute of Archaeology of the Hebrew University, the Israel Exploration Society, the Jerusalem Foundation, a group of South African sponsors headed by Mendel Kaplan, and the Ambassador Cultural International Foundation. Additional support is supplied by the Rothschild Foundation and the Municipality of Jerusalem. The author is director of the project. Its goals are to excavate on state-owned land in the City of David, principally on the eastern slope; to clean and restore the remains uncovered by earlier excavations; to preserve the remains we unearth and to incorporate all this into an "Archaeological Garden" that eventually will encompass the entire Old City. Special attention will be given to the archaeological strata from the Bronze Age to the Hellenistic Period.

Our expedition began with the excavation of five areas chosen on the basis of specific features that especially interested us and on the practical feasibility of digging in a particular location. We excavated only on State property. We also

Pottery from Iron Age II from the City of David excavations.

conducted salvage excavations in areas designated by the Municipality for development. In addition, certain safety hazards left by previous excavators were removed. The results of the first season have been published in various places, and I shall therefore present here only our principal conclusions.

A. Bronze and Iron Age Remains on the Center Terrace of the Eastern Slope of the City of David

Our first surprise came when we excavated the center terrace on the eastern slope (Area E). Natural pits in the bedrock contained sherds from the very beginning of human settlement in Jerusalem. A few of these sherds were datable to the Chalcolithic Age; most, however, were from Early Bronze Age I. The bulk of the sherds came from the late Iron Age II (eighth to sixth centuries B.C.E.). A rich assemblage of pottery from the eighth to seventh centuries B.C.E. was also discovered in a natural fault in the rock in Area D.

About 30 meters below the crest of the center terrace, we dug a series of squares covering approximately 250 square meters. Here, below seven meters of later dumps, we uncovered about 25 meters of a thick wall, which though crude, was solidly built of cyclopean stones on bedrock. We have not yet been able to determine the precise thickness of the wall, because it extends into the interior of the slope, which has not yet been excavated. This wall may have functioned as a city wall and as a retaining wall for the terrace above. The wall was therefore probably in use during the Iron Age II when the city was flourishing. The upper part of the wall is a narrower segment than the lower part and was used as a terrace wall in the Hellenistic-Roman period. Adjacent to the wall on the inside, at a narrow square that was difficult to excavate, we unearthed three phases of residential structures dating from the eighth to the sixth centuries B.C.E.

One of our most important discoveries in the first season was a large stone plaque fragment incised with a monumental Hebrew inscription in the stone collapse associated with this wall. The plaque fragment was found beneath debris that had rolled down from the top of the hill. The inscription has been dated, principally by palaeographic analysis, to either the latter part of the eighth or the

Dwelling structures and fortifications from the Period of the Monarchy in the City of David. To the left, a Hellenistic citadel.

seventh century B.C.E. The three upper lines of the fragmentary text are relatively well preserved, but a fourth is less legible. The inscription may have been affixed to a large building—perhaps a royal warehouse.

B. The Siloam Channel

Removing the debris left by Weill's excavations on the eastern slope was a major job. After thousands of cubic meters of earth had been cleared, we finally reached bedrock. Our objective was to create a sectional trench down the eastern slope, extending from the top (that is, from the line of the "First Wall" [Area D]) to the base. In the lower part of this section (Area B), we sought to uncover the openings that lead to the Siloam Channel. This tunnel, partly an open, rock-cut channel and partly a tunnel bored through the rock, extended along the length of the eastern slope from the Gihon Spring to the southern extremity of the city. We uncovered three of the tunnel's original openings and cleaned about 80 meters of it. Water from this sometimes open tunnel-channel would flow through special "windows" cut out of the tunnel's eastern wall and would thereby irrigate the agricultural plots along the wadi in the Kidron Valley—quite unlike the better-known but completely covered Hezekiah's Tunnel, whose function was merely to conduct water from the Gihon Spring to the Siloam Pool. Other openings in the Siloam Tunnel, oriented toward the upper part of the slope, were intended to collect rainwater run-off on the rocky east slope and to conduct the run-off to the pool area at the slope's southern tip. Scholars had already previously determined that the Siloam Tunnel was hewn out of the rock sometime between the tenth and eighth centuries B.C.E. and that it thus predated Hezekiah's Tunnel.

C. The Persian Period—The Fortifications of the "First Wall" at the Top of the Eastern Spur

We had hoped to uncover the Israelite residential quarters at the top of the eastern slope (Area G), where Macalister and Kathleen Kenyon had earlier excavated. We encountered instead a Persian Period stratum in a clear stratigraphical context, sandwiched between Israelite and Hellenistic levels. We cannot as yet satisfactorily explain this stratum, nor do we fully understand its position in the layout of the city following the exiles' Return to Zion. One of the difficulties arises from the fact that this stratum, which yielded an abundance of pottery, was discovered east of the supposed line of the wall that Kenyon had earlier determined was the Persian Period wall. In this layer and in the heaps of debris that covered Area E, several handles bearing the royal impression of the Persian subsatrapy, YHD (that is, Judea), in various combinations and abbreviations were found. Impressions depicting animal figures were also discovered, as well as an impression bearing the personal name of the Jewish satrap, "Ahazay," previously known from similar impressions encountered at Ramat Rahel. For the first time, we can positively identify a clear Persian Period stratum in ancient Jerusalem and need no longer rely merely on potsherds and seal impressions that invariably were found in a non-stratified context.

The main discovery of the work in Area G was a glacis about five meters thick made of beaten layers of earth ("terre pisée") and alternating pebble lenses. The facing of the glacis was composed of mud and large stones. Apparently, this glacis was the outer covering of the stepped stone glacis discovered by Macalister, which Kenyon had dated to the Second Temple Period. The ceramic finds in the glacis enabled us to date the glacis, as well as the line of the "First Wall," located in this vicinity. The glacis was built sometime toward the end of the second century B.C.E., probably as part of the Hasmonean fortification system.

During our first season we found about 70 stamped Rhodian jar handles. This unusually large quantity, as well as the hundreds of other impressions discovered earlier by Macalister and Kenyon, is evidence of the fact that, during the Hellenistic Period, settlement in Jerusalem was heavily concentrated in the City of David. A relatively small number of such jar handles have been uncovered during the last decade in all of the other excavations conducted in Jerusalem outside the City of

The city wall and buildings from the Period of the Monarchy in the City of David.

156

David. With the burgeoning of Jerusalem in the Hasmonean Age, the city center moved to the Upper City, that is, to what is today the Jewish and Armenian Quarters and Mount Zion.

We cleared an additional segment of the "First Wall," where Weill had previously excavated on the crest of the eastern slope, in Area D. This wall was used until the destruction of the Second Temple, after which it was covered with heaps of debris. It was built, in part, atop the remains of ancient quarries, a discovery that seems to refute the proposition that all the quarries found at this location date to the late Roman and Byzantine Periods. The stratigraphical postion of these quarries suggests that they were functioning, at least partially, prior to the construction of the "First Wall" and that they are to be dated at least to the Persian Period—perhaps even as early as the Iron Age. Indeed, Magen Broshi had already observed a similar phenomenon in the western part of the city, beneath the line of the Hasmonean wall.

D. The Pools and the Fortification System in the Southern Part of the City of David

The intersection of the Central Valley (Tyropoeon) and Kidron Valleys was always an especially sensitive and strategic site because the large water reservoirs were concentrated here during the Israelite era and later. The crucial importance of the reservoirs, as well as the site's vulnerable topographical position, required that additional defensive installations be erected here. Bliss and Dickie had previously found a thick "buttress wall" below the surface preserved to a height of 12 meters. While excavating in Area A, we hit the north corner of this fortification wall at the point where it meets with the rocky foundation of the City of David. North of this wall we found the remains of a building that Bliss and Dickie had incorrectly identified as a relatively "late tower." Hundreds of pottery vessels, glass artifacts, stone vessels and coins were also found here, evidence that the fortification system, including the "late tower," had been used during the Second Temple Period. Beneath this wall system we uncovered an impressive corner built of roughly dressed ashlars. Stratigraphic evidence and technical data from the site led us to conclude that this wall system belonged to the Iron Age. Few remains and walls dating to the Byzantine and Moslem Periods were found in this area.

In the course of our continuing excavations, we intend to investigate further the subjects that have been barely touched on here and, insofar as possible, to open up new areas of excavation. We hope that our ongoing archaeological project, initiated on the State of Israel's 30th anniversary, will add yet another important "layer" to our knowledge of Jerusalem's rich past. We shall thus be worthy successors to the pioneers who preceded us in exploring the history of the City of David and Jerusalem.

JERUSALEM, 1978

III

---

*Israel
Through
the Ages*

The Monarchy of David and Solomon

By Avraham Malamat

I. The United Kingdom—A Unique Political Phenomenon

The monarchy of David and Solomon, which lasted for 75 years, constituted a political phenomenon unparalleled either in the annals of Israel or in the Near East as a whole. Israel had never produced—nor did it again—rulers comparable to David and Solomon, men who possessed both the ability and the sagacity to unify all the Israelite tribes. Moreover, a monumental sovereign entity with the kind of power and dimensions displayed by the kingdom during Davidic and Solomonic times had never before existed in the Syro-Palestinian area. As an intermediate power, the Davidic and Solomonic kingdoms separated Mesopotamia and Anatolia in the north from Egypt in the south and became a principal political and economic factor in eastern Asia.

According to the accepted criteria of contemporary political science, the monarchy of David and Solomon may be included within that category of states known as "great powers," or "large states." (Incidentally, modern political science concepts may provide an extremely effective analytical tool to research ancient political systems as well as modern ones, and I shall avail myself of their terminology from time to time.) The separate kingdoms of Judah and Israel, on the other hand, must generally be classified as only "small" or "secondary" states in the international hierarchy. Even when these two states were united in an alliance and acted jointly—as occurred, for example, during the reigns of Ahab and Jehosaphat—their combined strength was probably not as great as that of the political unit which existed in Davidic and Solomonic times.

Regrettably, however, any effort to reflect upon the uniqueness of the united monarchy and its impact on the history of the ancient East inevitably encounters major methodological limitations. For instance, the large number of scriptural references to David and Solomon, as compared with the paucity of relevant, contemporaneous non-biblical documents, has restricted our ability to reach balanced conclusions and has compelled research on this period to employ a purely biblical historical approach. Nevertheless, to understand the phenomenon created by the appearance of the United Kingdom—which exceeded the narrow framework of a national state—a comprehensive historical perception is required. And this view must be based on a broader political background than the Bible reflects. The Bible's scope is limited; it probably cannot provide us with the materials necessary to assess fully the significance of the Davidic and Solomonic monarchy in a global context. Moreover, we must question the authenticity of these scriptural sources; that is, to what extent do they depict historical reality? How much are they the invention of later scribes and editors, whose purpose it was to glorify the names of David and Solomon and raise the status of their monarchy?

Despite these difficulties and obstacles, certain authentic pointers are contained in the biblical pericopes which clearly attest to the honored standing of the Davidic and Solomonic monarchy in the ancient East—for example the description of David's wide-ranging conquests, and the information concerning the contacts between both David and Solomon, on the one hand, and foreign countries, including some very distant, on the other. These allusions are scattered throughout 2 Samuel and 1 Kings and are paralleled in Chronicles. This information, particularly the account of Solomon's ramified international ties, enables us to place the history of Israel within the wider context of the contemporaneous Near East. That, in turn, permits us to assess the status of the Israelite kingdom vis-à-vis other regional powers. For the time being, let's put aside the most important "points of contact"—namely, Egypt and Syria, both of which will be discussed in greater detail below. Instead let us ask the question, "What was the pattern of Israel's external ties?" The following web of contacts provides the answer:

A. The Phoenician Coast

The Bible repeatedly mentions the strong ties between David—and, especially, Solomon—and Hiram, King of Tyre, whose kingdom was a small city-state much like medieval Venice, consisting of a kind of economic island. To Tyre's inhabitants, Israel to the south probably seemed like a backward state which had only recently attained greatness. The relationship between the two countries was based upon some kind of political and economic treaty and upon neighborly relations deriving from a shared interest in mutual aid.

B. The Coast of Asia Minor

1 Kings (10:28-29) records—albeit in an abstruse passage—that Solomon had ties with the Land of Keveh on the southern coast of Anatolia (in the vicinity of present Adnah), from which he imported horses.

C. The Red Sea Region

We find references to this region in three verses, two of which explicitly mention the Land of Ophir as the destination for Solomon's sailing ships (1 Kings 9:28; 10:11). "Ophir," incidentally, might somehow be linked to the name "Africa," minus the suffix ("ca" which was later appended to that continent's name). Various locations have been proposed for Ophir. I prefer the suggestion of the northern coast of Somalia to the notion that it was located in either southern Arabia or India. The third verse from the Bible speaks only about the ships of Tarshish, without specifying the vessels' destination (1 Kings 10:22), although this verse's later parallel in 2 Chronicles 9:21 mentions that "... the king's ships went to Tarshish." Apparently, this refers to Spain, perhaps Tartessus. The version in Chronicles, however, is undoubtedly anachronistic. Apparently when this rather unclear term (i.e. Tarshish) was used in Kings, it had no geographical connection with the Mediterranean but instead referred to a class of large ship comparable to the "Gebel" and "Knupt" vessels mentioned in Egyptian documents. These Tarshish ships carried silver ore as well as apes—probably baboons—and peacocks to the Land of Israel. They also brought raw materials from Ophir (1 Kings, 10:11, 12), including not only large quantities of silver but also ". . . sandalwood not seen unto this day . . ."—that is, not seen in the Land of Israel. (Note that the Hebrew word for sandalwood, "almug," is rendered differently in 2 Chronicles 9:10, which reads "algum" trees.)

These Biblical descriptions may appear to be merely legends, but we should recall that according to Egyptian sources, these same items—and also myrrh, frankincense and the other spices mentioned in the scriptures in connection with the Land of Sheba—were imported into Egypt from the Land of Punt beginning in the middle of the third millennium. To reach Punt—which perhaps was located near Ophir—the Egyptians, too, had to sail down the length of the Red Sea. These rare woods, exotic animals and hoards of gold (which came to symbolize Solomon's wealth and opulence) would certainly have aroused the wonder of the inhabitants of the Land of Israel. The descriptions of these imports are reminiscent of Egyptian and Assyrian rulers who displayed in their capitals hitherto unknown animals and woods from distant lands.

D. Southern Arabia

Finally, we should mention the episode involving Solomon and the Queen of Sheba (1 Kings 10:1-13). Even though this enchanting story is a late literary invention, the impressive visit to Jerusalem by a ruler (male or female) from the Land of Sheba, located in the southwest corner of the Arabian peninsula, does reflect the Red Sea region's new geo-economic reality during the Solomonic era. The opening up of *shipping* trade routes in the Red Sea by the king of Israel with the help of the Phoenicians—who were to become his partners in the enterprise—broke the southern Arabian rulers' economic monopoly, which they had held when trade routes were confined to caravans. The "riddles" with which the Queen of Sheba (if it was a she) tested Solomon—although, of course, the literal meaning of the biblical tale is quite different—most certainly dealt with vexing economic problems, the solutions of which were calculated to bring about a commercial or even possibly a political agreement between the two parties. At least according to the biblical story, the agreement was, indeed, concluded because the two rulers so impressed one another. Consistent with the rules of international etiquette, Solomon displayed great admiration for the gifts presented to him by the queen, while she, for her part, was greatly impressed by his wisdom and breadth of vision as well as by his kingdom's splendor. It is natural to wonder what reciprocal gifts Solomon could possibly have offered. Probably he exported some valuable finished products to the Land of Sheba as his gifts to the queen.

At this time Israel fulfilled an important, indeed decisive, function in the international area. While Solomon continued to develop foreign trade policy designed to obtain various goods directly from their respective countries of origin, thus eliminating an intermediary, he simultaneously sought to become a broker in the world of international commerce. To do this, he appointed a permanent economic-political envoy with responsibility for the region between Tyre (in the north) and Sheba (in the south) as well as for the area bounded by the Mediterranean on one side, and the Red Sea to Ophir on the other. If we also consider Solomon's ties with Anatolia, the Euphrates region, and Egypt, we see that Solomon's commercial interests encompassed the entire world. Solomon may be compared to a commercial octopus who extended his arms in all directions.

Certainly this elaboration tends to refute the widely held notion that the biblical description of the enormous dimensions of the United Kingdom, which is said to have reached even the River Euphrates (1 Kings 5:1,4; 2 Chronicles 9:26), lacks all substance. The celebrated historian Edward Meyer, for instance, believed the biblical account of the Davidic and Solomonic kingdom expansion to the Euphrates wholly attributable to a "later imagination." This assertion is often repeated by other scholars who contend that the kingdom at most included only the Damascus region and the Valley of Lebanon. However, these minimalists fail to explain why the supposed "legend" concerning the mighty kingdom of David and Solomon was concocted. The claim that the biblical historiographer knowingly falsified his descriptions of the kingdom of Israel's borders in order to reconcile them with the boundaries promised either to the Patriarchs or to Moses is unacceptable. The difference between the two sets of border delineations is simply too great. Futhermore, unlike the Land of Canaan promised to the Israelites (Numbers 34), the United Kingdom extended to the region in Transjordan south of the Yarmuk River (that is, Edom, Moab, Ammon). It did not include, as did the Land of Canaan, the Phoenician Coast, to which it was instead linked by various treaty arrangements.

In actual fact, the Israelite kingdom's unprecedented territorial expansion resulted naturally from the geopolitical circumstances which then prevailed. For centuries, until the latter part of the second millennium B.C.E., both Syria and the Land of Israel were subjected to unceasing pressure from Egypt in the south and the kingdom of the Mitani, and later by the kingdom of the Hittites in the north. Modern political terminology might describe this entire region as "bipolar."

With the collapse of these two great powers, a vacuum was created until Egypt regained its former strength (toward the end of Solomon's reign) and the Assyrian Empire arose in the region "Beyond the River" (beginning in the ninth century B.C.E.). During the United Kingdom the time was ripe, however, for smaller nations between the Euphrates and the River of Egypt (for example, Tyre on the Mediterranean coast, Aram in the north and Israel in the south) to assert themselves. If any one of these nations was clever enough to properly exploit this rare hiatus, it might inherit hegemony over this entire intermediate region. In other words, to use a Machiavellian idiom, this was an historic "occasione" (opportunity). But who, finally, would turn out to be the multi-talented manipulator, endowed with what Machiavelli referred to as "virtu," whose ability would permit him to take advantage of such an opportunity?

This prize ultimately fell to David—thanks to his profound sense of history, his awareness of current events, his decisiveness, and the competence with which he undertook whatever was required. These unusual qualities enabled him to overcome his adversaries in the fateful struggle against a variety of regional powers. Characteristics that usually motivate prominent statesmen—the desire for security, acquisition of power, and personal aggrandizement—certainly played a part. Because of David's efficient application of what is known nowadays as the "grand strategy" doctrine, he was able to establish an imposing imperial structure in a gradual, interconnected way.

II. Building an Empire

David's grand strategy was based on a long-range perspective; it reflects purposeful planning and the setting of well-defined objectives—administrative, military, political and diplomatic. With this outline of David's activities, we can easily find the major "signposts" in the process of establishing this empire.

The gradual growth of David's kingdom may be adumbrated schematically by five concentric circles (see plan on p. 165), each of which signifies, more or less, one phase in the historical evolution of the region: (1) tribal kingdom, (2) national

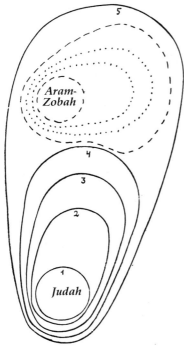

kingdom, (3) consolidated territorial state, (4) multinational state, and (5) empire.

A. Tribal Kingdom

Hebron marked the starting point in the building of David's kingdom. Here, aided by a band of supporters, and apparently also with the consent and protection of the Philistines, David was crowned king over the "House of Judah." At the beginning of his career and as was his custom during the latter stages of the empire, David founded his government upon a pre-existent organization—in this case, a union of the Caleb families and the Judean cities—whose focal point, of course, was Hebron. This early phase saw him take vigorous steps to strengthen his military position—as indicated for example by the capture of Jerusalem—and to lay diplomatic foundations—as evidenced for instance by his marriage to Maaca, the future mother of Absalom (2 Samuel 3:3) and the daughter of Talmai, King of Geshur.

Geshur was located far away, in the southern part of the Golan at the forefront of the Aramean countries. The treaty with Geshur served to neutralize that kingdom during David's later campaign against the Aramean bloc. David also cultivated ties with Ammon (as is deducible from 2 Samuel 10:2) and Moab (which, based upon 1 Samuel 22:3-4, one may conjecture). By the treaty and these ties David neutralized three states strategically located behind the northern Israelite tribes. David was thus able to outflank the northern Israelite tribes. This accelerated the second phase of the molding of David's kingdom. (Compare David's position with the situation described in 1 Samuel 14:47, in which Saul, David's predecessor, was forced to do constant battle with these same countries—Geshur, Ammon and Moab.)

B. National Kingdom

During his rule in Hebron, David's most far-reaching political act was concluding a treaty with the Israelite tribes of the north, which served to strengthen a feeling of national solidarity. After exhaustive negotiations with Abner (which ended with Abner's murder) and with Eshbaal, Saul's heir (who was assassinated), the elders of the north hurried to Hebron to crown David king of all Israel. The manner in which the northern tribes were annexed by the House of David—that is, by mutual agreement—is crucial to understanding the circumstances that brought about the division of the United Kingdom following Solomon's death 70 years later. The northern tribes regarded themselves free to set certain preconditions for the renewal of the monarchy—terms, however, that proved unacceptable to Rehoboam.

Ever since the publication of Albrecht Alt's basic research on the creation of the United Kingdom, it has been customary to see in the unification of the tribes of Israel and Judah a so-called "Personal Union" under Davidic rule. However, even though it is now well-rooted in scholarly usage, this term is fundamentally misleading in the present context. If we are to use a modern term, it would be preferable to define the relationship between Judah and Israel during Davidic and Solomonic times as a "Real Union." The essential difference between these two forms of political union is as follows: The "Real Union," unlike the "Personal Union," does not occur by chance but is the result of the common desire of two political entities to unite—as was the case with David and the representatives of the northern tribes. In the "Personal Union" two separate groups are retained in connection with both internal and external affairs, each group maintaining its status as a so-called "international legal entity." The "Real Union," on the other hand, can be said to comprise separate groups only where internal affairs are concerned, while there is a complete unity on external policy. A "Real Union" is characterized, for example, by a unified army and the joint administration of foreign affairs, which certainly well describes the situation that existed during the United Kingdom period.

C. Territorial State

The creation of a political bloc comprising all the tribes of Israel brought with it a basic change in the regional balance of power and threatened the hegemony that the Philistines had enjoyed over the western part of the Land of Israel ever since they defeated Saul on Mount Gilboa. This new situation inevitably resulted in a military confrontation between David and the Philistines. Indeed, the biblical historiographer is quite explicit on this point: "But when the Philistines heard that they had anointed David king over Israel, all the Philistines came up to seek David" (2 Samuel 5:17). In a series of battles with the Philistines, which were at first defensive but which later became offensive actions, David was able to subdue the enemy forces, although he does not appear to have conquered Philistia itself.

But what, in fact, did David gain by crushing the power of the Philistines once and for all? He could then isolate Philistia from the north Canaanite regions. He could cut off the Philistines from their sources of metal, especially iron, which seem to have been located in the area around Succot in Transjordan. Above all, David's victories led to a new political order in the country, a state of affairs to which Alt has alluded: namely, that the Philistines had considered themselves the Egyptian rulers' rightful heirs of Canaan, so that when they, in turn, were vanquished by David, that legacy, at least nominally, passed to the Israelites. Consequently, David was in effect compelled by this Philistine legacy forcibly to seize control of areas inhabited by Canaanites, just as the Philistines had done (see the list of Canaanite enclaves in Judges 1); these were principally the cities of the

Sharon and the Valley of Jezreel. This is evidenced in archaeological excavations at Tell Qasile near the estuary of the Yarkon River as well as at Megiddo, Taanach and Beth Shean.

To use the terminology of contemporary international law, we might regard the kingdom of Israel at this time as a "Successor State" to the Philistines. The latter term opens new vistas in our understanding of the international ties developed by David and Solomon, which had been developed by the previous state—that is, the league of Philistine city-states. For example, we may discern in the special ties between Israel and the kingdom of Tyre a continuation of the ties that probably existed between the Philistines and the inhabitants of the Phoenician Coast. This continuity applies, too, to commercial ties between Solomon and the Land of Keveh, which apparently were based upon the long-established contacts between the Anatolian coastland and the "Sea Peoples," including the Philistines. Further, David's army boasted Philistine mercenaries: the Cherethites, Pelethites and Git-tites (2 Samuel 15:18; 2 Samuel 1:6). If this were not the case, it would be difficult to explain David's victories over the vast Aramean charioteer force. The monopoly over the metal industry which hitherto had been in Philistine hands undoubtedly passed to the Israelites also (1 Samuel 13:19-20).

At this stage, the Israelite kingdom superseded the status of a purely "National State" and became a "Consolidated Territorial State," swallowing up large areas. The remnants of the older Canaanite population which inhabited these regions at David's death were reduced to bondservants by Solomon (1 Kings 9:20-21).

D. Multinational State

After eliminating the danger from the west (the Philistines) and thus breaching the hostile ring that surrounded the Israelite kingdom, David turned to the states on the eastern front which for generations had been Israel's foes: Edom, Moab and Ammon. (For the events that transpired in Saul's day, see 1 Samuel 14:47.) Although the precise chronological order of their conquests is uncertain, the eastern states undoubtedly fell following the "Domino Principle," one after the other, the fall of each state inevitably resulting in the downfall of its neighbor. The wars against Ammon, Moab and Edom were motivated not only by political and security considerations but also by economic goals. Moreover, the territorial annexations in Transjordan not only gave David control over the "King's Highway," the principal overland artery of communication linking Damascus to the Gulf of Eilat and thence to the Arabian Peninsula, but also provided him with access to the Red Sea.

At this point, the Israelite kingdom was even larger than the Egyptian province of Canaan in the second millennium B.C.E., which generally did not extend to eastern Transjordan south of the Yarmuk River. However, even the conquest of these eastern border states did not halt the Israelite kingdom's process of expansion.

E. Empire

The last and most decisive phase of expansion was a result of the fateful struggle against the Arameans, in which Israel's tested military machine gave her notable victories. Parallel with the growth of the Israelite kingdom—but perhaps several years earlier—a competing political bloc known as Aram-Zobah arose in Syria, under the leadership of Hadadezer. The center of this new bloc seems to have been in the Anti-Lebanon region and to its east. During Hadadezer's reign its hegemony, like Israel's, spread gradually over large areas. In the south, its rule extended to Geshur and its influence to Ammon, as is hinted by the Arameans' military alliance with the Ammonites in the latter's battle against David (2 Samuel 10:6ff.). In the northeast, the kingdom of Aram-Zobah reached the Euphrates and even ruled over regions on the other side of the great river (2 Samuel 10:16-17). In the east, Hadadezer's realm bordered the Syrian desert; in the west, it extended to the Valley of Lebanon (2 Samuel 8:8). In other words, like Israel, Hadadezer's kingdom became a super power.

According to the principle known as "competitive exclusion" (a biological science term which of late has been borrowed by political science), there was no avoiding an eventual clash between these two imperialistically inclined blocs, which consumed all of the areas that separated them. Judging by the separate strengths of David and Hadadezer on the conflict's eve, we can easily predict that the winner of the forthcoming battle would automatically become the sole ruler of the entire Syro-Palestinian region. In fact, David's complete victory over the Arameans gave him mastery over Hadadezer's entire kingdom. The Israelite kingdom's unprecedented territorial expansion to "the River"—that is, to the Euphrates—is best explained if we assume that the kingdom of Aram-Zobah was based on a complex of surrounding states, which, as a result of his victories, passed to David.

III. The Kingdom's Political Structure and Imperial Image

The kingdom of David and Solomon was not a gigantic, homogeneous block, as it has been depicted sometimes, and too simplistically. It was structurally an extremely varied and complex political entity. We might even compare it to the pre-Second World War British Empire with its settlements, protectorates and dominions, at the center of which lay the "United Kingdom" itself. The northern tribes were joined to the Israelite kingdom in a "Real Union," rather like the union of England and Scotland. Just as the Scots harbored great feelings of animosity toward the English, the northern tribes betrayed a certain hostility toward Judea.

The United Kingdom had a variegated political structure, including occupied territory like the old Canaanite enclaves such as Jebusite Jerusalem. Even the three Transjordanian kingdoms of Edom, Moab and Ammon cannot be said to have enjoyed equal political standing, or degrees of dependence, within David's kingdom. This is clear from the fragmentary chronicle in 2 Samuel 8, which informs us about Moab: "And the Moabites became servants to David, and brought presents" (2 Samuel 8:2); that is, the Moabite kingdom was turned into a vassal state, obliged to surrender a fixed annual levy. There is no scriptural allusion to the removal from office of the local Moabite royal dynasty; presumably this did not occur.

As for Edom, on the other hand, we read in 2 Samuel 8: "He put garrisons in Edom; throughout all Edom he put garrisons, and all the Edomites became servants to David" (2 Samuel 8:14). The Edomites were apparently somewhat more harshly subjugated. After the defeat of the local king, Edom became, in effect, an Israelite garrison (to which compare 1 Kings 11:15-18). The same applied to Aram of Damascus: "Then David put garrisons in Aram of Damascus . . ." (2 Samuel 8:6), while for the other Aramean countries the chronicle states simply that they ". . . became servants to David and brought presents." We see, then, that only Edom and Damascus were turned into garrisons or Israelite provinces in which a permanent Israelite military force was stationed. In this connection, we learn that sometime later a "satan" (adversary) rose up against Solomon precisely in these two places (1 Kings 11:14 and 25). Apparently, this is not coincidental. As for Ammon, here again we see some form of servitude: "And [David] took the crown of Malcam from off his head . . . and it was set on David's head" (2 Samuel 12:30); that is, David removed the Ammonite monarch from his throne and in an overt act of annexation, crowned himself with the crown of the local king.

The Israelite kingdom also contained satellite nations. It is in this context that we should perhaps view the story of Toi, king of Hamath in central Syria. Toi dispatched his son Joram, also known as Hadoram, to David ". . . to salute him and to bless him . . . and he brought with him vessels of silver and gold and brass" (2 Samuel 8:10). This account hardly bespeaks a friendly alliance between two equals, as current opinion would have us believe, but rather hints of Hamath's dependence on Israel. Solomon, incidentally, later consolidated this dependence: "And Solomon went to Hamath-Zobah and prevailed against it" (2 Chronicles 8:3). Thus both David and Solomon imposed their governance on territories beyond the Aramean domain, thereby deflecting the influence of the neo-Hittite countries.

In other words, the kingdom of Israel possessed an imperial structure *par excellence*. Consistent with one of the current definitions of the term, the kingdom ruled over a "supranational system" of peripheral territories by virtue of the political and economic control emanating from Judea, the kingdom's center.

We shall now trace the nature of the imperial image with which scripture chooses to present David and Solomon. Both kings, of course, are described quite plainly as having reigned "over Judea," "over all of Israel and Judea," "over all Israel," and "over Israel." On only two occasions is David explicitly referred to as "king of Israel" (2 Samuel 6:2 and 2 Chronicles 8:11). This title is never applied to Solomon (compare, though, 1 Kings 1:34), most certainly because of the respective characters of the sources. In comparison, the Bible waxes eloquent in its description of Solomon's imperial reign: "And Solomon ruled over all the kingdoms from the River unto the land of the Philistines, and unto the border of Egypt. . . . For he had dominion over all the region on this side of the River, from Tiphsah even to Gaza, over all the kings on this side of the River; and he had peace on all sides round about him," (1 Kings 4:21, 24). This quotation, which stresses the notion of "peace," refers to a kind of "pax Solomonica." An even more florid account appears in one of the two hymns putatively dedicated to Solomon: "May he have dominion also from sea to sea, and from the River unto the ends of the earth. . . . The kings of Tarshish and of the isles shall render tribute; the kings of Sheba and Seba shall offer gifts. Yea, all the kings shall prostrate themselves before him, and the nations shall serve him" (Psalms 72:8, 10-11).

Was the metaphor "royal majesty," with which the Chronicler described Solomon (1 Chronicles 29:25), purposefully provided by scripture to emphasize Solomon's unique royalty? It seems that the idea of political greatness and regal glory is epitomized in the Bible by the term "great king (*melekh rav*)." The term appears twice in scripture, and on both occasions the implication is that the reference is to King Solomon. One case speaks of the glory of Jerusalem: "Fair in situation, the joy of the whole earth; even Mount Zion, the uttermost parts of the north, the city of the great king" (Psalms 48:3). Even if the term actually refers to the King of Heaven and Earth—as is the normally accepted, but arguable, meaning—the metaphor *per se* derives from a human king and may here personify Solomon as the builder of Jerusalem in all its splendor. The second verse, found in an Aramaic section in the Book of Ezra, undoubtedly is a retrospective reference to the builder of the glorious Temple in Jerusalem ". . . which a great king of Israel built and finished" (Ezra 5:11).

The term "great king" (*melekh rav*) is the exact parallel of the Akkadian epithet "sarru rabu," which refers to an overlord to whom other kings are subordinate. On the other hand, scripture uses the term "great king" (*melekh gadol*) to refer only to God, or to the mortal king of Assyria. The term "King Contentious," which is still unclear, refers in Hosea only to the Assyrian King (Hosea 5:13; 10:6). Admittedly, Sihon, king of the Amorites, and Og, king of the Bashan are also described as "great" or "mighty" kings (Psalms 136:17-19; and compare Psalms 135:20-22), although here they are described sarcastically. In the present context, it may be useful to note that the term "great king" is also found in both Ugaritic and ancient Aramaic, for example in the Sefireh inscriptions. We might conjecture that when it appears in scripture, the term *melekh rav* ("great king" is wholly different linguistically from the epithet *melekh gadol* (also translated, "great king"), which undoubtedly is a direct loan word from the Akkadian "sarru rabu." We might mention here the interesting reference to a *melekh gadol* on an ivory Hebrew inscription, dating to the eighth century B.C.E., which was discovered at the Kalah excavations in Assyria.

In other words, the royal appellation by which the Bible refers to Solomon alone among the kings of Judea and Israel, even if only retrospectively, attests to a category of all-powerful ruler reigning over other, lesser kings. Such a ruler was later to be known as either "emperor" or "caesar." Another indicator of Solomon's remarkable power and his imperial standing is his marriage to the Pharaoh's daughter, which served to place the king of Israel on an equal footing with the period's greatest monarchs. We shall now, accordingly, deal with that notable event, and at the same time explore the relationship between Egypt and Israel.

IV. The Treaty Between Solomon and Egypt

The true significance of the marriage with Pharaoh's daughter seems to have been lost on the biblical historiographer, who fails even to mention either the Pharaoh's name or his daughter's. Political marriages constituted the chief instrument of Solomon's external affairs policy, a means by which he formed extensive and close diplomatic ties. Marriage replaced the military option in his strategy and brings to mind what was said of the House of Hapsburg: "Let others fight wars; you, happy Austria, marry!" Solomon's other fathers-in-law can rightly be considered the leaders of countries of low rank—Moab, Ammon and Edom (we might plausibly, however, read "Aramean wives" for "Edomite wives"), the city-states of the Phoenician coast and the neo-Hittite kingdoms. Solomon's marriage to the Pharaoh's daughter, however, was tied to a treaty with one of the traditionally great Eastern powers, Egypt. Moreover, the marriage seems to have been an unusual occurrence in Egyptian, as well as Israelite, history. Ancient Near Eastern sources, particularly letters from the 14th century B.C.E. archive at El-Amarna and the writings of Herodotus, indicate that the Pharaohs would never marry their daughters to foreign kings, with the possible exception of a few doubtful occurrences; they apparently regarded all other kings as inherently inferior, and intermarriage with them would be an insult to Egypt's dignity. From this information, which most certainly was unavailable to the biblical historiographer, we can conclude that Solomon's exceptional marriage to the Egyptian princess had an extraordinary political significance which cannot be treated lightly, as is customary in most history books.

The fact that the Book of Kings and parallel sources in Chronicles mention the Pharaoh's daughter no fewer than five times in unconnected passages which, in the main, are pre-Deuteronomic, certainly serves to confirm the historicity of the biblical account of the marriage. Despite the importance of this rare occurrence, however, the scriptural sources reflect no motives for the marriage, and since the Egyptian sources are also silent on this matter, we shall here propose a likely historical scenario reflecting the event's significance.

First, we must stress that at that time the kingdom of Israel constituted the strongest power ever to occupy the eastern borders of Egypt. Furthermore, from the end of the period of the Judges to the middle of Solomon's reign, Egypt had been divided into two political blocs. The comparatively weak Pharaohs of the 21st

Dynasty (1070 B.C.E.-945 B.C.E.) ruled only in northern Egypt, whose capital, Zoan, was situated on the eastern tributary of the Nile, near the Mediterranean. The high priests, meanwhile, ruled over the south, whose main city was Beno-Ammon. In this context, it would not overly surprise us that Solomon and one of the Pharaohs of the 21st Dynasty—almost certainly Siamun, who reigned from 978 B.C.E. to 960 B.C.E.—entered into marriage ties. The undoubtable implication is that a treaty was finalized also—the first such example of a political agreement between Israel and Egypt. Could it be that these ancient international marital arrangements, as was the case in subsequent history, constituted an affirmation of the treaty that two states had made?

The following explication of the treaty's genesis is an updated version of the thesis I previously proposed in the volume *During First Temple Times* (in Hebrew).

1. The chronological data supplied by scripture tells us, in an indirect fashion, that the marriage occurred during the first years of Solomon's reign. We can deduce that Solomon's future father-in-law, the Pharaoh, undertook the journey to Gezer, which preceded the marriage, either approximately at the time when Solomon assumed the co-regency with David or when he became sole king.

2. We can see in Pharaoh's journey to Gezer, situated in the northeastern corner of Philistia, an attempt to regain Egyptian control over the Gaza Strip and a part of the Coastal Plain—territory lost to her some 200 years before. The Pharaoh's principal aim, however, was to strengthen his rule in the Land of Israel, and certainly not, as might appear from the relevant passage, merely to hand over a fortified city to Solomon as a gesture of friendship: "Pharaoh, King of Egypt, had gone up and taken Gezer, and burnt it with fire, and slain the Canaanites that dwelt in the city, and given it for a portion unto his daughter, Solomon's wife" (1 Kings 9:16). We cannot suppose that the Egyptian king undertook such a long journey for this reason alone; such a conclusion is historically untenable.

3. The capture of Gezer, which is confirmed by archaeological excavations at the site, presented a direct threat to Israel. It is not impossible that Pharaoh's ultimate goal after his conquest of the border fortifications, which were in fact located en route to Jerusalem, was the capital of Israel itself. This was to be Shishak's aim more than 40 years later. Apparently, the capture of Gezer was an Egyptian attempt to exploit a supposed moment of Israelite weakness in the wake of David's death, to subdue the Israelite kingdom, and to regain for Egypt its mastery over the Land of Canaan.

4. It seems that Pharaoh miscalculated and that he underestimated Israel's strength. Having eliminated his foes from within, it appears that Solomon was able then to turn all his power against the Egyptians. Under these circumstances, the Egyptian invaders were forced to shelve their offensive plans and to try to evolve a rapprochement with Israel. In other words, the diplomatic option of peaceful co-existence was far preferable to an overt show of hostility.

5. As part of the peace agreement in which Solomon was at least an equal partner, Pharaoh was compelled to make certain territorial concessions to Israel. For example, Gezer, which was given to Israel disguised as a gift for Pharaoh's daughter, seems to have been just one link in a wide chain of territories in Philistia which were handed over to Israel. When Shishak ascended the throne in Egypt, however, Solomon most certainly proceeded to broaden his hold in Philistia in order to strengthen his position in anticipation of a renewed Egyptian threat.

6. The above assumptions should bring us to a deeper appreciation of Solomon's borders as they are described in scripture. Let us return to 1 Kings 5:1,4: "And Solomon ruled over all the kingdoms from the River [unto] the land of the Philistines, and unto the border of Egypt . . . for he had dominion over all the region on this side of the River, from Tiphsah even to Gaza . . ." If we accept the

traditional text in Kings precisely (in which the Hebrew reads ". . . the land of the Philistines," and not *"unto* the land . . ."") and we do not, as the commentators would have us do, emend it in view of its parallel in 2 Chronicles 9:26, we note that Philistia is depicted as a separate region under Israelite hegemony. With this extension of its borders in the southwest, the United Kingdom reached the greatest limits of its expansion by virtue of Solomon's political achievements.

Inevitably, the above prompts the following questions: Why is there no Philistine princess among Solomon's foreign wives? Is it plausible that Pharaoh's daughter, heiress of the kings who had perennially ruled the Land of Israel's southern coastal plain, would deign to exhibit herself to Solomon before Philistia had done so? What were the mutual influences that brought about the peace between Israel and Egypt, a peace that lasted for 20 years, until King Shishak of the 21st Dynasty invaded Israel in 945 B.C.E.? What tangible gains did Egypt acquire in return for peace and her territorial concessions? The answers to these questions must await another occasion.

Now, however, we should be able to evaluate Solomon's personality quite differently from the stereotypical image that has long haunted him: a ruler who conducted a static foreign policy, or only a defensive one at best. It is a mistake to see Solomon as merely the son of a dynamic conqueror who rested, so to speak on his father's laurels, which he then proceeded to lose, leaf by leaf. In Solomon's day, the accent had shifted from a strategy employing grand military actions, which had characterized the foreign policy of his predecessor, to new tactics, namely the development of international relations whose primary component was ramified economic ties.

We might say that the reigns of David and Solomon were unique not only in Israel's history: they constituted an exceptional moment in the history of the entire region. This was the only time in the Land of Israel's history that, solely through its own efforts, Israel achieved pre-eminence in the Near East.

Bibliography

S. Abramski, *The Kingdoms of Saul and David*, Jerusalem, 1977.

M. Eilat, *Economic Ties Between Biblical Lands During the First Temple Period*, Jerusalem, 1977, pp. 181-201.

J. Breslavi, "The Ships of Tarshish, Etzion-Geber and the Journeys to Ophir," in *Eilat—Proceedings of the 18th National Convention of the Israel Exploration Society*, Jerusalem, 1963, pp. 30-53.

M. Garsiel, *The Kingdom of David—Historical Researches and Studies in Historiography*, Tel Aviv, 1975.

M. Harel, "Gei Ha-Charshanim," *Studies in Scripture*, Vol. 11, 1977, pp. 91-108.

Y. Yadin, *The Art of Warfare in Bible Lands*, Ramat-Gan, 1963, pp. 236-292.

S. Yeivin, "The Wars of David," *The Military History of the Biblical Land of Israel*, Jerusalem, 1964, pp. 149-165.

B. Mazar, "The Philistines and the Establishment of the Kingdoms of Israel and Tyre," *Canaan and Israel*, Jerusalem, 1974, pp. 152-173, and "The Kingdom of Aram and Its Relationship with Israel," pp. 245-269.

A. Malamat, "Contacts between the Kingdoms of David and Solomon and Egypt and Aram-Naharaim," *Festschrift for N. H. Tur-Sinai*, Jerusalem, 1960, pp. 77-85, and "Episodes in the Foreign Policies of David and Solomon," *The First Temple Period—The Kingdoms of Israel and Judah*, Jerusalem, 1962, pp. 24-46 and "Elements of Political Decision-Making—A Parallel Sumerian-Israelite Text" (dealing with David), Jerusalem, 1964, pp. 279-290.

H. J. Katzenstein, "Hiram I and the Kingdom of Israel," *Bet Mikra* XI, 1966, pp. 28-81.

The Birth of the Hasmonean State

By Uriel Rappaport

T he birth of a state requires appropriate social, cultural and political conditions: (1) an ethnic group must be moved by a vision of some form of political independence; (2) a group of people must be prepared to strive against hostile forces to realize this goal; (3) there must be a real or assumed weakening of a previously dominant political authority; and (4) there must be a set of circumstances that transforms the ethnic group's latent strengths into action, thus giving the historical process momentum. These are some of the conditions necessary for the formation of a state.

Scholarly treatment of the revival of the sovereign Jewish state under Hasmonean dynastic rule has focused on the persecution of Antiochus IV. At the same time, the historical investigation of "The Decrees of Antiochus and Their Problems," as Avigdor Tcherikover[1] titled an article, has often included a discussion of the birth of the Hasmonean state.[2] Since, in my view, the Decrees of Antiochus cannot be taken as the sole cause of the birth of the Hasmonean state, the other conditions mentioned above most certainly merit consideration. Thus, a fresh look into the birth of the Hasmonean state is called for. Since we think that the Decrees only triggered the Maccabean revolt but were not its underlying cause, we should investigate the background and the conditions of the foundation of the Hasmonean state. How did the persecutions catalyze the historical process that finally ended with the creation of the Hasmonean state? New evidence and new scholarly publications of recent decades deserve special attention in this analysis. The discussion below is divided into the considerations listed above.

I. In the days of the Persian Empire as well as during the period of the Hellenistic Empires that followed, the Jews of the Land of Israel managed not only to preserve their organizational framework and national uniqueness but also to continue their political activities. I mention this to contradict the notion that the Jewish

173

community at the time was preoccupied only with matters relating to religion or ritual and had lost the will to establish an independent state. This view would further have us believe that the founding of the state was an entirely unanticipated event, which occurred suddenly as a result of the Decrees. Admittedly, the international political situation for much of this period prevented the Jews from attaining full sovereignty. We should not, however, conclude that the Jews therefore completely lacked national and political aspirations.

We have recently learned that during the days of the Persian and Hellenistic Empires, Jews enjoyed a considerable degree of administrative independence, which afforded them limited autonomy. Although Ephraim Stern's book[3] accurately summarizes our present knowledge of the Persian era, new evidence, including seal impressions[4] and a large variety of "Yehud" coins dating to the latter part of the Persian and the beginning of the Hellenisitc periods,[5] now supplements his information. These artifacts seem not only to attest to a succession of Jewish satraps governing Judea during the days of Persian hegemony[6] and to the perpetuation of Judea as an autonomous district under Hellenistic suzerainty but also to prove that the Jewish cultural character of Judea was not eroded; on the contrary, it apparently underwent a renewal. The change from Aramaic to Hebrew on seal impressions and coins clearly shows the influence of Jewish culture in Judea—more specifically, on the back of these coins the name of the state changes from "Yehud" (Aramaic) to "Yehuda" (Hebrew).[7]

The inhabitants of Judea apparently enjoyed an individualized organizational framework within the wider context of these foreign empires. Since the Jews were the only people who lived in this small region, they constituted a monolithic ethnic, national and religious group. We should not assume, therefore, that they had forsaken all their national aspirations, even though for the moment they were incapable of fulfilling these ambitions.[8] When the Jews came under the sway of Hellenistic culture, the experience in no way vitiated their own cultural or national distinctiveness. In fact, the opposite was true, for during this period, the Hebrew language gained considerbly in prestige. The Book of Ben Sira, composed in Hebrew at the beginning of the second century B.C.E., attests to the influence of the Hebrew language. The discovery of Hebrew fragments from this book at Masada[9] confirmed an 80-year-old hypothesis: that the Ben Sira manuscript from the Cairo Genizah does preserve the original Hebrew of Ben Sira. This book was only one of many contemporaneous Hebrew works.

It is also worth mentioning that in the Book of Daniel, which was edited and partially composed in the period of Antiochus's persecution and which is imbued with apocalyptic and eschatological ideas, the kingdom of heaven in the messianic era will be a Jewish world empire, more national than universal and, *mutatis mutandis*, similar to its four predecessors.[10]

II. The Judea that rebelled against the rule of Antiochus IV Epiphanes was certainly not, as has often been depicted, a David doing battle with Goliath. According to at least one scholarly version, the war of the Hasmoneans did not pit the few against the many.[11] Moreover, the latest research emphasizes that Judea drew its strength and indefatigable military capability to wage war aginst the Seleucids primarily from two sources: an increase in population and a cadre of professional soldiers.

A. The Judean population increased greatly during the period between the return to Zion and the Maccabean revolt. Consequently, Judea became comparatively densely settled, and many Jews chose to reside in other regions of the Land of Israel or in neighboring lands, especially Egypt. The Maccabean military effort, therefore, did not suffer from a shortage of manpower.[12]

B. Many Jews, from Judea as well as from the surrounding countries, were professional soldiers and had served in the armies of the Persian, Ptolemaic and Seleucid kings. The changing image of the Jew during the last 35 years—be that as others see him or as he now views himself—has prompted scholarly attention to this most interesting aspect of the war.[13] Because Jews served in these other armies, their numbers and experience gave the Maccabean army the force sufficient both quantitatively and qualitatively to cast off the yoke of foreign rule and to reestablish their own sovereign state.

III. At the time of the Maccabean revolt, the government of the Seleucid Empire, as well as that of its Ptolemaic neighbor to the south, was weak. Some of the most recent research, however, warns against exaggerating the enervation of the Seleucid Empire prior to this time and denies, moreover, that this could have occurred as early as the first half of the second century B.C.E.[14] Still, such caveats are not enough to cause us to dismiss the following statement by Tacitus on the international situation that contributed to the creation of the Maccabean state. He writes, "The Macedonian power was now weak, while the Parthian had not yet reached its full strength, and, as the Romans were still far off, the Jews chose kings for themselves" (*Historiae*, Book V:8).

While the Seleucid Empire was not powerless during the reign of Antiochus IV Epiphanes, it was nevertheless troubled by internal problems and difficulties. This instability aided the Jews in their struggle—although the latter's forces were in no way negligible.[15] But the relative instability of the Seleucid imperial government obviously cannot account completely for the birth of the Hasmonean state. The Jews required unswerving determination if they were to create a state of their own amidst the crumbling Seleucid Empire, especially so if that state was to be rooted in the Jewish people's historic tradition. (It might be added that the majority of contemporaneous Hellenistic dynastic states could not boast such historic roots.)[16]

IV. Antiochus's persecution was no doubt crucially important to the destiny of Judea[17] and should be regarded as one of the circumstances that accelerated its journey to independence. Foundations for research on this subject were laid in the works of Bickerman[18] and Tcherikover.[19] The topic was then analyzed anew in Hengel's comprehensive study,[20] prompting numerous articles and reviews, both for and against its thesis, and several significant critical essays and summaries.[21] To a certain degree, contributions and original approaches and insights to the theme of the Decrees may be found in the works of Efron,[22] Baer,[23] Bar-Kochva,[24] Cohen,[25] Bringmann[26] and Fischer,[27] *inter alia*.[28]

Our knowledge of these events in their broader context—including the process of Hellenization—was also enriched to some degree by new data. The influence of the Hellenistic culture on Judea, for example, is clearly demonstrated by ostraca from Khirbet el-Kom, near Hebron,[29] and by the newly revealed but as yet unpublished graffiti from Mareshah. Also, two Greek inscriptions that appear to date from the time of Antiochus's persecution were discovered in Jerusalem. One has recently been published.[30] The discoveries at 'Araq al Amir, the Transjordanian home of the Tobiads, have also aroused much interest.[31] Despite the importance of this evidence to our understanding of Judea's Hellenization and the Decrees of Antiochus, this evidence is only indirectly connected to the birth of the Hasmonean state.

A number of specialized studies have examined the principal literary sources for this period. 1 and 2 Maccabees and the Book of Daniel have been the subject of comprehensive exegetical analyses and other specialized studies. Even the publication of Abel's profound exposition,[32] however, did not discourage further scholarly commentary on these books.[33] Menahem Stern has written two books on literary sources relevant to the Hasmonean period. The first discusses documents of the era[34]; the second includes entries on several non-Jewish sources that relate these events in Judean history.[35]

As we strive to understand Antiochus's persecution, and the process of Hellenization, we should remember that these two factors did not give birth to the Hasmonean state. Rather, the inner strength—both spiritual and cultural as well as physical and military—of the Judean people[36] enabled them to regain their independence. The result of a prolonged evolution, these strengths were embodied in the Jewish national conscience and surfaced when the community was thrown into confusion, first by Hellenization and then by religious persecution. The persecution of Antiochus and the pressure to Hellenize may have precipitated the creation of the Hasmonean state, but they did not create it. The true progenitors of the new state were the Jewish nation and its Torah.

[1]A. Tcherikover, "The Decrees of Antiochus and Their Problems," *Eshkolot* 1 (1954), pp. 86-109 (in Hebrew); cf. in English: V. Tcherikover, *Hellenistic Civilization and the Jews* (Philadelphia, 1959), especially chapters 4 and 5.

[2]See, for example, Y. Baer, "The Persecution of Monotheistic Religion by Antiochus Epiphanes," *Zion* 33 (1968), pp. 101-124 (in Hebrew).

[3]E. Stern, *The Material Culture of Eretz-Israel During the Persian Period* (Jerusalem, 1973) (in Hebrew).

[4]N. Avigad, "Bullae and Seals from a Post-Exilic Judean Archive," *QEDEM* 4 (1976).

[5]A Kindler, "Silver Coins Bearing the Name of Judea from the Early Hellenistic Period," *Israel Exploration Journal* 24 (1974), pp. 73-76; D. Jeselsohn, "A New Coin Type with Hebrew Inscriptions," *Israel Exploration Journal* 24 (1974), pp. 77-78; A. Spaer, "Some More 'Yehud' Coins," *Israel Exploration Journal* 27 (1977), pp. 200-203, and Ibid. 29 (1979), p. 218; L. Mildenberg, "Yehud: A Preliminary Study of the Provincial Coinage of Judea," in "Greek Numismatics and Archaeology," *Essays in Honour of M. Thompson* (Wetteren, 1979), pp. 183-196; U. Rappaport, "The First Judean Coinage," *Journal of Jewish Studies* XXXII (1981), pp. 1-17.

[6]See Avigad, note 4 above.

[7]Idem, p. 27.

[8]Sarah Japhet, *The Ideology of the Book of Chronicles and Its Place in Biblical Thought* (Jerusalem, 1977), p. 442 (in Hebrew).

[9]Yigael Yadin, "The Ben Sira Scroll from Masada," *Eretz-Israel* 8 (1967) E. L. Sukenik Memorial Volume, pp. 1-45 (in Hebrew).

[10]L. F. Hartman and A. A. DiLella, *The Book of Daniel* (The Anchor Bible), (Garden City, 1978); A. Lacocque, *The Book of Daniel*, English edition revised by the author, translated by D. Pelaver (London, 1979). These books also contain detailed bibliographic lists.

[11]B. Bar-Kochva, *The Battles of the Hasmoneans: The Times of Judas Maccabaeus* (Jerusalem, 1980) (in Hebrew) with comprehensive bibliography.

[12]M. Stern, *Greek and Latin Authors on Jews and Judaism*, 1 (Jerusalem, 1974), p. 34; B. Bar-Kochva, *The Seleucid Army* (Cambridge, 1976); idem, "Manpower, Economics and Internal Strife in the Hasmonean State," *Colloque National du Centre National de la Recherche Scientifique* 936 (1977), pp. 167-196.

[13]A. Schalit, "The Letter of Antiochus III to Zeuxis Regarding the Establishment of Jewish Military Colonies in Phrygia and Lydia," *Jewish Quarterly Review* L (1959-1960), pp. 289-318; M. Hengel, *Judaism and Hellenism*, I-II (London, 1974); Bar-Kochva, *The Seleucid Army* (supra, note 12), p. 206; id., *The Battles of the Hasmoneans* (supra, note 11); A. Kasher, "First Jewish Military Units in Ptolemaic Egypt," *Journal for the Study of Judaism* IX (1978), pp. 57-67.

[14]Bar-Kochva, *The Seleucid Army* (supra, note 12), p. 206.

[15]For a summary, see M. Stern, "The Hasmonean Revolt and Its Place in the History of Jewish Society and Religion," *Journal of World History* XI (1968), pp. 92-106; reprinted in H. H. Ben-Sasson and S. Ettinger (eds.), *Jewish Society Through the Ages* (Jerusalem, 1971), pp. 92-106.

[16]U. Rappaport, "The Hellenistic Cities and the Judaization of Eretz-Israel During the Hasmonean Era," *Essays presented to Professor B. Z. Katz*, S. Perlman and B. Shimron (eds.), I (Tel-Aviv, 1973), pp. 219-230 (in Hebrew).

[17]See, for example, E. Bickerman, *Der Gott Der Makkabäer* (Berlin, 1937). (This important book appeared recently in English as *The God of the Maccabees* translated by H. R. Moehring, [Leiden, 1979].) See also F. Millar, "The Background of the Maccabean Revolution—Reflections on Hengel's Judaism and Hellenism," *Journal of Jewish Studies* XXIX (1978), pp. 1-21.

[18]See above, note 11.

[19]See above, note 1.

[20]See above, note 13.

[21]M. Stern, *Kiryat Sefer* 41 (1971), pp. 94-99 (in Hebrew), comprising a review of the first edition of the book, published in German in 1969; Millar (see above, note 17); M. D. Herr, "Hellenism and the Jews in Eretz-Israel," *Eshkolot* 9-10, n.s. 2-3 (1977-1978), pp. 20-27 (in Hebrew); A. Momigliano, *Journal of Theological Studies* XXI (1970), pp. 149-153; J.C.H. Lebram, *Vetus Testamentum* XX (1970), pp. 503-524; L. H. Feldman, "Hengel's *Judaism and Hellenism* in Retrospect," *Journal of Biblical Literature* XCVI (1977), pp. 371-381.

[22]Y. Efron, "The Hasmonean Revolt in Modern Historiography," in *Historians and Historical Schools—Lectures Delivered at the Seventh Convention of the Historical Society of Israel*, December 1961 (Jerusalem, 1962), pp. 117-143 (in Hebrew).

[23]See above, note 2.

[24]See above, note 11.

[25]M. A. Cohen, "The Hasmonean Revolution Politically Reconsidered," *S. W. Baron Jubilee Volume*, 1 (Jerusalem, 1974), pp. 263-285.

[26]K. Bringmann, "Die Verfolgung der Jüdischen Religion durch Antiochos IV; Ein Konflikt zwischen Judentum und Hellenismus?" *Antike und Abendland* XXVI (1980), pp. 176-190, and id., *Hellenistische Reform und Religionverfolgung in Judäa* (Göttingen/Zurich, 1983).

[27]Th. Fischer, *Seleukiden und Makkabäer* (Bochum, 1980).

[28]Cf. the collected studies edited by B. Bar-Kochva, *The Seleucid Period in Eretz-Israel* (Tel-Aviv, 1980) (in Hebrew), which included *inter alia* the studies noted above in notes 1, 16 and 22. Cf. also the "class warfare" approach of H. Kreissig, "Der Makkabäeraufstand," *Studii Clasice* IV (1962), pp. 143-175.

[29]L. T. Geraty, "The Khirbet el-Kom Bilingual Ostracon," *Bulletin of the American Schools of Oriental Research* 220 (1975), pp. 55-61; id., "Recent Suggestions on the Bilingual Ostracon from Khirbet el-Kom," *Andrews University Seminary Studies* XIX (1981), pp. 137-140.

[30]S. Applebaum, "A Fragment of a New Hellenistic Inscription from the Old City of Jerusalem," *Jerusalem in the Second Temple Period* (A. Schalit Memorial Volume) (Jerusalem, 1980), pp. 47-60 (in Hebrew).

[31]E. Will, "Le Qasr el Abd a Araq al Amir," *Comptes-Rendus de l'Academie des Inscriptions et Belles-Lettres* (1977), pp. 69-85.

[32]F. M. Abel, *Les Livres des Maccabéens* (Paris, 1949).

[33]J. A. Goldstein, *I Maccabees* (The Anchor Bible) (Garden City, 1976); C. Habicht, *2. Makkabäerbuch* (*Jüdische Schriften aus hellenistisch-römischer Zeit, I.: Historische und legendarische Erzählungen*) (Gütersloh, 1976); L. F. Hartman and A. A. Di Lella, *The Book of Daniel* (The Anchor Bible) (Garden City, 1978); see also note 10 above.

[34]M. Stern, *The Documents on the History of the Hasmonean Revolt* (Jerusalem, 1965) (in Hebrew).

[35]M. Stern, *Greek and Latin Authors on Jews and Judaism*, I-II (Jerusalem, 1974-80).

[36]Contrast A. Momigliano, *Alien Wisdom* (Cambridge, 1975) ch. 5.

The Lachish Letters—Originals or Copies and Drafts?

*By Yigael Yadin**

The Lachish Letters—almost 50 years after their discovery—still constitute one of the most important epigraphical discoveries made in Israel. They are complemented today by the Arad Ostraca which, despite their considerable significance, have done nothing to tarnish the splendid image of the Lachish Letters.

Since the discovery of the Lachish Letters, and especially since their initial, thorough publication by Professor N.H. Torczyner (Tur-Sinai),[1] and the other subsequent publications,[2] these ostraca have been considered to be original letters sent to the commander of Lachish, named Ya'ush, by a person named Hosha'yahu, located somewhere between Lachish and Jerusalem, most probably at Kiriath-Jearim.[3]

Already in the *editio princeps*, Tur-Sinai wrote: "Our Lachish Letters represent certain documents out of one correspondence, between Hosha'yahu the commander of a small outpost to the north of Lachish, probably Qiryat-Ye'arim, and Ya'ush, the military governor of Lachish, and commanders of other fortresses along the Philistine border" (*LL*, pp. 17-18). In his Hebrew edition (*TL*), published several years later, Tur-Sinai emphatically stated that the letters were originals, apparently in reaction to inner and external doubts that they might be copies: "The Lachish Letters are original letters, *not copies*, and thus no mistaken readings [sic!] are to be found in them; they comprise urgent messages, and are written in haste" (p. xxv; italics mine—Y.Y.). In his last summary paper on this subject (see *EM*), written many years later, Tur-Sinai wrote: "An examination of the content of the other letters proves that these are the remains of a single correspondence."

* It gives me great pleasure to dedicate this paper to my good friend for over 30 years, Joseph Aviram. The achievements of Israeli archaeology—excavations and publications—are intimately connected with Aviram's decisiveness, skill and, last but not least, supreme devotion.

Despite the full official publication of the Iron Age finds at Lachish, Diringer overtly doubted Tur-Sinai's readings, but even so he continued to denote the ostraca according to that publication: Letter I, Letter II, etc. (*Lachish III*, p. 67; *Text*, pp. 331ff.). Olga Tufnell, despite her hesitation lest the letters indeed be copies, also finally wrote: "... and if nothing else had been found on the site, these letters written in the time of Jeremiah would have been a rich reward" (*ibid.*, p. 48).[4] In his introduction to his translation of the Lachish Letters in *ANET* (p. 321), Albright too noted that "Most of the ostraca were letters, while others were lists of names, etc. ...." Many other scholars could be cited in this matter,[5] but we shall end by noting that actually, today, there is a scholarly consensus that these are the original letters sent to Lachish, where they were gathered together in the guard-room in which they were found.

Tur-Sinai thought that these letters were brought to this spot from an archive for some particular reason. H.L. Starkey, the excavator of Lachish, was the first to ask whether the fact that the open gate-room also served as a court of judgment had some bearing on the matter (see *TL*, p. xxxii). In his introduction to Tur-Sinai's English publication (*LL*. p. 12), Starkey expressed quite a different and interesting view on the function of the gate structure in the final phase at Lachish: "The evidence may imply that Ya'ush used the region of the bastion as his headquarters during the military preparations for the impending siege."

The aim of the present article is to challenge the conclusions and "axioms" reviewed above, concerning the nature of the ostraca from Lachish. My intention is at least to cause scholars to rethink the matter and to ask if these are not copies rather than original letters or, more precisely, if they are not drafts and copies of a limited number of letters later written out on papyrus and sent *from* Lachish, apparently to Jerusalem. In other words, the "lord" Ya'ush was a very high ranking personage ("Who is thy servant (but) a dog"), to whom Hosha'yahu, apparently the commander of Lachish itself, was subservient.

Our rejection of the generally accepted positions stems foremost from the fact that a document of principal official importance which, on the basis of its contents, should have been highly secret because it mentions a critical military movement (the journey of the commander-in-chief to Egypt) was written on an entirely overt ostracon. Moreover, on several other ostraca, which also deal with important affairs, the name of the addressee is lacking. The name of the sender, Hosha'yahu, is mentioned only in one ostracon (No. 3). This fact is especially surprising also because, in this period, papyrus was used extensively for the writing of documents. This point, well-known from the literary sources, has been confirmed dramatically by several recent discoveries.[6]

Tur-Sinai too noted this surprising fact: "There is no doubt that the most usual material for important matter at that time was papyrus ... and only as a cheap substitute for papyrus—which was scarce during wartime, when the Babylonian army hindered trade with Egypt [note, however, that at the time of the writing of the ostraca, the commander-in-chief himself was able to go to Egypt—Y.Y.]—were potsherds used as a writing material. And surely, *papyrus would have been kept especially for official state correspondence*" (*TL*, pp. xxvi-xxvii; italics mine—Y.Y.).

Another factor leading to doubts in this matter is the contents of the ostraca themselves. They are mostly fragmentary and incomplete in their texts, and there is considerable overlapping. As noted, one gains the impression that these are draft-like, variant trial versions of a particular matter. It would seem that all the various versions served, eventually, for the writing of only two or three final letters.

To summarize these introductory remarks, I wish to suggest that, in discussing the Lachish ostraca, we examine them from the following aspects:

(a) the fact that a considerable number of the ostraca are from a single pot;

(b) the fact that in all the ostraca except one, the name of the sender is not given, and on a most important one (No. 4), not even the addressee is mentioned;

(c) the fact that several of the ostraca deal with precisely the same matter, and often are written in the same style and contain numerous repetitions.[7] One of the explanations for this phenemonon—that the sender wrote duplicate letters and sent them by different means in order to assure arrival—is difficult to accept. No easier to accept is the alternative explanation that, since the particular subject was of special concern to the writer, he bombarded Ya'ush with letters on the same subject, in almost the same wording, daily;

(d) the contents of one of the ostraca (No. 4), including the phrase משאת לכש ("the beacon of Lachish"). We shall begin our discussion with this last point.

Ostracon No. 4—"The Beacon of Lachish"

This document contains one of the most famous phrases of all the Lachish Ostraca, and much to our good fortune, it is well preserved, with no doubt as to its decipherment (lines 10-13)[8] וידע כי אל משאת לכש נחנו שמרם ככל האתת אשר נתן אדני כי לא נראה את עזקה. "And let (my lord) know that we are *shomerim 'el* the beacon of Lachish, according to the signals which my lord hath given, for Azekah (or: the signal of Azekah) is not to be seen."

Assuming that the letter was written to Ya'ush, commander of Lachish, Tur-Sinai, and many others following him, interpreted this sentence as showing that the sender, Hosh'yahu—located somewhere between Lachish and Jerusalem[9]—was watching for, i.e., *looking toward*, the "beacon of Lachish," for he could not see Azekah (or its signal). From the start, this sentence appears somewhat awkward, for it could seem to prove that Tell ed-Duweir was not Lachish.[10] The assumption that this was a letter sent to Tell ed-Duweir, of course, supported such a feeling. The crux of the understanding of this sentence is the phrase אל משאת לכש נחנו שמרם. What does it mean, לשמר אל?

Based on the assumptions reviewed above, Tur-Sinai interpreted it as: "*for* the signal-stations of Lachish we are *watching (LL*, p. 79)—i.e. "to watch *for*". In *TL* (p. 117), he rendered: "שמור אל" = צפה ל..." = to watch for . . ., to watch toward." And so also Albright: "We are watching for the signals of Lachish" (*ANET*, p. 322). Biblical sanction for such a usage was found by Tur-Sinai in 2 Samuel 11: 16: ויהי בשמור יואב אל העיר, interpreting it as "while Joab was looking as if watching the besieged city" (*TL*, p. 117). But this interpretation hardly suits the plain text, and thus the commentators have held, and rightly so, that the intention is to שמר על, "watch over" (Köhler-Baumgartner); RSV—"And as Joab was besieging the city"; in any event, it is clearly *not* "looking toward."[11]

It is astonishing that neither Tur-Sinai nor the other scholars referred to the two decisive biblical verses for the meaning of this expression. They clearly show, without any doubt, that שמר אל, was identical with שמר על. Thus, in 1 Samuel 26: 15-16: ויאמר דוד אל אבנר הלוא איש אתה ומי כמוך בישראל ולמה לא שמרת אל אדניך המלך, כי בא אחד העם להשחית "את המלך אדניך. לא טוב הדבר הזה אשר עשית חי ה' . בני מות אתם אשר לא שמרתם על אדניכם על משיח ה', And David said to Abner, 'Are you not a man? Who is like you in Israel? Why then have you not kept watch over (שמרת אל) your lord the king? For one of the people came in to destroy the king your lord. This thing that you have done is not good. As the Lord lives, you deserve to die, because you have not kept watch over (שמרתם על) your lord, the Lord's annointed."Already in the first part, it is clear that שמר אל signifies שמר על, and then in the latter part, all doubt is removed, the phraseology being repeated almost verbatim but now actually using the latter form, with ועל! This interpretation was ignored, apparently, for the simple reason that it would not have tallied with the concept of letters sent *to* Lachish. Actually, in the Bible there are numerous instances of אל and על serving in identical usages.[12] Thus, we may conclude that the writer of Ostracon No. 4 states that *he is tending* the beacon of Lachish.[13]

This sentence, in the interpretation just proposed, bolsters the identification of Tell ed-Duweir as Lachish, only if we assume that the ostracon is a copy or draft of a letter which was dispatched *from* Lachish. Since the identification of this site with Lachish appears no longer to be in doubt, this is additional proof that indeed the letter was intended to be sent from Lachish and not to that city.

From the contents of this ostracon, we may conclude that the usual "battle procedure" arranged between the commander of Lachish and the personage to whom he was writing (his lord—undoubtedly in Jerusalem) was that the beacon of Lachish was to be used and tended, but only if the beacon of Azekah was not visible (whether because that city had fallen to the enemy or for some other reason). Thus, we may conclude that the most convenient signal communications with Jerusalem were via Azekah.[14]

This interpretation of the contents of Ostracon No. 4, if accepted, predicates that the ostraca are copies and drafts of letters which were subsequently written on papyrus and dispatched from Lachish. But there are further, decisive confirmations of this, as noted.

The Fact that Several Ostraca are from a Single Pot

At least five of the Lachish Ostraca (Nos. 2, 6, 7, 8 and 18) are fragments of one and the same pot. Based on the restoration of the storejar, we can assume, almost certainly, that several other of the ostraca were also from this same pot, though no direct join has survived. For our purposes, however, the five ostraca noted above suffice. The fact that they were written on sherds from the same pot proves that the ostraca were prepared within a short span of time, one being written soon after the other, and certainly all of them were written at the same place.

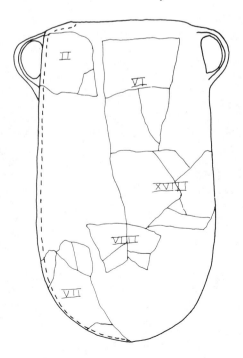

In his last summary of the subject (see *EM*, p. 520), Tur-Sinai was basically right, though exaggerating somewhat, in saying that "The very fact that several of these ostraca, on some of which the names of the writer and of the addressee are mentioned—Hosha'yahu and his lord Ya'ush—are taken from sherds of a single pot indicates that most of the letters were written by the same person, Hosha'yahu, during a period of a few days, when these selfsame potsherds were still at hand." This is a most rare instance, and the fact that the contents of the other ostraca—which cannot be proven to have originated from the same storejar—are similar to or identical with the contents of the above five, shows that a majority of the ostraca were indeed written by (or on behalf of) a single person (as concluded by Tur-Sinai).[15]

This subject therefore beckons further discussion, albeit briefly, mainly concerning the contents of the ostraca from the single pot, as well as a comparison of their contents with that of the other ostraca.

Ostracon No. 2

The text of this ostracon reads, in full: אל ארני יאוש. ישמע יהוה את ארני שמעת שלם .עת כים עת כים. מי עבדך כלב כי זכר ארני את [ע]בדה. יעבר יהוה את אמרי דבר אשר לא ידעתה. "To my lord Ya'ush. May the Lord make my lord hear tidings of peace, this very day, this very day! Who is thy servant (but) a dog, that my lord remembered his [ser]vant? May the Lord afflict the utterers of a thing of which I was not aware!"

This ostracon, like No. 6, addressed to the lord Ya'ush, links the entire group of five from the single pot with the other ostraca addressed to Ya'ush. But we must note that, despite the fact that the text is complete (that is, there is nothing missing from the text as written), there is a decided lacuna as far as the actual contents are concerned: the name of the sender has not been included (a fact typifying all the ostraca but one), and the actual subject (ignoring the conventional salutations) is contained in a single sentence, the final one. As we shall come to see, this matter—the writer's defense in the face of slander—runs like a scarlet thread through most of the ostraca.

Ostraca Nos. 6 and 18—two from the single pot—both deal with a letter (ספר) sent to the writer (No. 6 is explicit in stating that letters were sent by the king and minister[s]!), and in both texts the phraseology is almost identical: No. 6— מי עבדך כלב כי שלח ארני אות ספור המלך ואת ספרי השרם...], "Who is thy servant (but) a dog, that my lord should send the le[tt]er of the king and the letters of the minister[s ...]"; and No. 18—[...] הספר אשר שלח ארני [. . ., ". . . the letter which my lord hath sent . . . ."

The text of Ostracon No. 8 is poorly preserved, and little of relevance can be gleaned from it for our present purposes. In contrast, the text of No. 6 is quite similar in content and style to the contents of Ostracon No. 5—and this is very important for our discussion. Thus, for instance, the above-quoted sentence in No. 6 can be compared with that in No. 5: ...כלב כי [שלן חת אל עבדון] את הןספן רם "... (but) a dog, that thou hast [se]nt to [thy] servant the [let]ters." In other words, these three ostraca are almost duplicates of one another.

But actually, this topic—the letter or letters sent to the writer—recurs in various forms (often similar) in other ostraca as well. The central theme of Ostracon No. 3 is especially noteworthy; it is the most complete of the texts and the only one in which both the sender (Hosha'yahu) and the addressee (Ya'ush) are written (or are preserved). This ostracon appears to be a copy, or an almost final draft, of a letter sent to Ya'ush: ...לספר אשר שלח ארן[ני?] אל עבדך אמש... ". . . concerning the letter which [my l]ord didst send to thy servant yesterday evening . . .". The passage in Ostracon No. 5— השב עבדך הספרם אל ארני "thy servant hath returned the letters to my lord"—also relates to this matter. That is, this subject, which repeats itself in the above ostraca, appears here again, and in a fuller context.

One of the reasons suggested in explanation of this—i.e. that the letters were sent at one and the same time, or within a few days of one another,[16] in order to assure their receipt—is, of course, invalid if for no other reason than in such a case we would expect a more complete text, denoting addressee and sender, and identical contents. The assumption that at the time they were written it was already difficult to communicate with Lachish also seems untenable, for from the ostraca themselves we learn of movements to and from Lachish ("and he sent to take . . . his men from here," etc.).

A second central theme, of even greater significance for the matter at hand, is also repeated several times, almost in the same wording, on various ostraca: defense in the face of the accusation of reading a letter not addressed to the writer of the ostracon:...הספר (את| עבדך קרא ולא...כי אלהיך יהוה חי "As the Lord thy God liveth,that . . . thy servant hath no[t] read the [le]tter . . ." (No. 6); and in contrast: אם חיהוה נסה איש לקרא לי ספר לנצח ונם כל ספר אשר יבא אלי אם קראתי אתה... "As the Lord liveth, no one hath ever dared to read a letter for me; moreover, nor any letter that hath come to me, I did not read it . . ." (No. 3). These are essentially two different, albeit similar versions of one and the same matter. The same subject, it is worth noting, appears to have survived on another small ostracon, No. 12: ואתה| קור|א|תי א...א...יהוה ,וחי| "As the Lord [liveth], . . . [i]f . . . I have r[e]ad i[t]."

From the above, it can be concluded that the subject of several ostraca—some of them clearly originating from the same pot—is duplicated.[17] However, the contents of the ostraca (even in the well-preserved ones) are fragmentary and the name of the sender and often that of the addressee were not written. This fact in itself (like the meaning of the phrase שמרם נחנו לכש משאת אל) indicates that the ostraca are copies or—and I would prefer this possibility—drafts and trial versions of replies, made for the approval of the commander of Lachish, who was apparently located in the gate-bastion (as suggested by Starkey).

Using this as a point of departure, we can deduce that the ostraca represent drafts concerning several main topics, a number of which were meant to be utilized within a single final version. In other words, what we have here are nothing more than drafts for no more than two or three actual letters:

1. The accusation against Hosha'yahu by the king and the minister(s), for opening and reading a certain letter, and thus gaining the "classified" information that the commander-in-chief was going to Egypt. Hosha'yahu tried to compose a satisfactory reply (and thus the several drafts), the main argument of which was that the accusation was libelous ("May the Lord afflict the utterers of a thing of which I was not aware"— No. 2), and that he deeply regretted that the suspicions of his superiors—ministers of the highest rank—had fallen on him ("for the heart of thy servant aches [?] since you sent (the accusation) to thy servant"—No. 3). The accusation was false! Hosha'yahu had not read the letter in question ("As the Lord thy God liveth, . . . thy servant hath not read the letter"—No. 6); and neither did anyone else read it for him ("As the Lord liveth, no one hath ever dared to read a letter for me"—No. 3); and so forth. Word of the commander-in-chief's journey to Egypt came to him by other means ("And thy servant was told: 'The commander-in-chief, Coniah son of Elnathan, hath gone to Egypt; and he sent to take Hodavyahu son of Ahiyahu and his men from here"—No. 3).

2. Hosha'yahu, proclaiming his loyalty, confirms the carrying out of several instructions which he had received (No. 4): "Thy servant hath done according to all that my lord hath instructed": (1) "I have written on the 'door' (i.e. sheet of papyrus) just as my lord hath instructed me"; (2) "And that which my lord hath written concerning Beth-*hrpd*, there is no one[18] there"; (3) apparently in accord with instructions concerning "Semakhyahu, Shema'yahu hath seized him and is taking him to the city (i.e. the capital), and thy servant" will soon send him on,

upon his return (to Lachish?).[19]

3. A subject in itself (in the latter part of No. 3) concerning "the letter of Tobiah servant of the king, which came to Shallum son of Jaddua from the prophet," which contained a warning ("saying, 'Beware!' "), which Hosha'yahu states that he sent on to his lord.

4. Finally, the sender states that he is tending "the beacon of Lachish," since Azekah was not visible. This was done in accord with prior instructions. It is of interest that in this lengthy and important text, neither the name of the sender nor that of the addressee is given, and it too would seem to be a draft.

In summary:

1. These ostraca are not actual, original letters received at Lachish.

2. The ostraca, if not actual copies (though this is possible in one or two instances), are drafts prepared by a scribe (or scribes) at the gate-bastion. The actual letters would have been prepared for eventual dispatch on papyrus, and sealed with the signet of the sender.

3. Thus, the conclusion is that Ya'ush was a very high ranking personage, possibly even one of the king's sons.[20]

4. Hosha'yahu is the name of the commander of Lachish, who apparently had his headquarters at the gate-bastion.[21]

5. Acceptance of these conclusions would confirm, once and for all, the identification of Tell ed-Duweir as Lachish.[22]

---

[1]See H. Torczyner, *The Lachish Letters (Lachish* I), London, 1938 (= *LL*); idem, *Te'udot Lakhish*, Jerusalem, 1940 (= *TL*) (Hebrew); idem, in *Enṣiqlopedia Miqra'it* IV, Jerusalem, 1962, cols. 517-523, s.v. *Ḥarsei Lakhish* (= *EM*).

[2]See D. Diringer, in O. Tufnell, *Lachish III. The Iron Age*, London, 1953 (= *Lachish* III), pp. 331-339; for further bibliography up to 1950, see *ibid.*, pp. 21-23; for later material, see W.F. Albright, "The Lachish Ostraca," in *ANET*, pp. 321-322; O. Tufnell, "Lachish," in D. Winton Thomas, ed., *Archaelogy and Old Testament Study,* Oxford, 1967, pp. 296ff.; J.C.L. Gibson, *Textbook of Syrian Semitic Inscriptions* I, Oxford, 1971, pp. 32-49. Gibson accepts Tur Sinai's principal assumptions concerning the sender and recipient, and their locations; his interpretations and translations are peculiar and, in many cases, difficult to accept linguistically.

[3]Even so, it should be noted that, in the initial stages of decipherment, there were opinions within the expedition staff that the ostraca were copies, and Tur-Sinai sought to dispel such views on various occasions. Thus, for instance, in *LL*, p. 63, he wrote: "the ostraca were not, as we thought first, copies of outgoing messages (which could be written two or more on one sherd) but original incoming letters. . . ." The dilemma facing Tur-Sinai was even more pronounced in his straightforward statement, in n. 2 on the same page (which should be read very carefully in the light of matters noted by us in the continuation of our present paper): "It seemed improbable that copies of letters addressed to the same man and of the same origin should be found together at the writer's place. However, the actual fact that these sherds, originating from the same pot, reassembled at the addressee's place and remained there for 2,500 years *is not less astonishing"* (italics mine—Y.Y.). We shall return to this point below.

[4]In her article on Lachish in the D. Winton Thomas volume (*op. cit.*, above, n. 2, p. 305), which appeared in 1967, Tufnell's doubts entirely dissipated: "They were addressed by a subordinate to the Governor of the city, and they report on fulfillment of his orders. These Lachish Letters, as they are now called, are of paramount importance . . . ."

[5]A. Lemaire, *Inscriptions hébraïques*, I, Paris, 1977, pp. 85ff.

[6]For the use of papyrus in biblical times, see recently M. Haran, "Book Scrolls in Israel in Pre-Exilic Times," *JJS* 33 (1982), pp. 161-173. Besides the discoveries of bullae noted there (*ibid.*, p. 165, n. 1), note now also Y. Shiloh's dramatic discovery of several scores of bullae in the City of David.

[7]This matter is essential, and Tur-Sinai already noted it several times in his initial publication: "The fact that not only this message (No. 5), but also the other letters, are repeated in more than one ostracon is in itself very significant. These repetitions are not literal copies of one definite version, giving the same text and even the same details, but *renewed renderings of the same facts in different forms*. Therefore, they cannot be regarded as mere duplicates, sent by different messengers because their sender feared that some of them might not reach their destination—

although this may also have caused the *double message*—but rather as *repetitions* urged by the great importance of the letters, and by the writer's need to make him lord take notice of his plea" (*LL*, p. 94; italics mine—Y.Y.); or: "It is now clear that Letter VI is a recapitulation of Letter III . . . just as Letter V has its shorter counterpart in Letter IX . . . . Letter XII is another repetition of Letter VI . . . . Even Letter II, giving the main part of Letter III in one short sentence . . . and be meant as a duplicate of it, in case Letter III should get lost . . . . The fact that in the case of Letters III and VI *not less than four 'duplicates' have been preserved* . . . . They have not been copied from one another . . ." (p. 118; italics mine—Y.Y.).

[8]Prior to this sentence, it is stated: ‏כי (?) אתה שמה ישלח ארני ,ועבדך העירה ויעלהו שמעיהו לקחה וסמכיהו‏ ‏בקר בתסבתה אם‏ "And (concerning) Semakhyahu, Shema'yahu hath seized him and taketh him up to the city. And thy servant, my lord shall send him there with him, upon his return . . . ." Many scholars read: ‏הבקר בתסבת אם כי‏, i.e. "but tomorrow morning" (e.g. Albright, in *ANET*, etc. And see Y. Aharoni's comments on Arad Ostracon No. 2 *Arad Inscriptions*, Jerusalem, 1981, p. 16: ‏מחר‏ ‏ובהסבת‏"—"in the survey tour of the morning." Even so, we may note an alternate understanding of the continuation. In my own copy of *LL*, which previously belonged to my late father, E.L. Sukenik, I discovered in my father's handwriting, in the margin to line 9: ‏לו‏ ‏אשר‏ ‏יהוה‏ ‏וירע‏ ‏בקר‏"—Numbers 16:5: "In the morning the Lord will show who is His." In other words, Sukenik thought to read: ‏שמרם‏ ‏נחנו‏ ‏לכש‏ ‏משאת‏ ‏אל‏ ‏כי‏ ‏(וארני)‏ ‏וירע‏ ‏בקר‏."In the morning (my lord) may know that we are tending the beacon of Lachish." The word ‏בקר‏, here is in the sense of "tomorrow (i.e. soon) you may know that . . . ."

[9]See, e.g., *LL*, p. 15, and many other places.

[10]See especially D. Winton Thomas's rejection of Tur-Sinai's assumption that this sentence strengthens the identification of Tell ed-Duweir as Lachish (quoted in full from *PEQ* 1940, p. 148, by Tufnell, in *Lachish IV. The Bronze Age*, London, 1958, p. 39). And see now G.W. Ahlström's doubts, in *PEQ* 1980, pp 7-9, and the reply by G.I. Davies, *PEQ* 1982, pp. 25-28.

[11]Gibson, *op. cit.* (above, n. 2) also translates: "we are watching for the beacons," despite his comment (on p. 43): "The preposition ‏אל‏ is not found in the Bible with the base ŠMR in the sense here . . . ."

[12]See L. Köhler and W. Baumgartner, *Lexicon in Veteris Testamenti libros* (Leiden, 1953), p. 48: "‏אל‏ is frequently written ‏על‏ (and inversely)." (After the final typing of this paper, Professor A. Malamat drew my attention to the 3rd ed. 1967 where there is a vague reference to Lachish specifying neither ostracon nor example. If indeed it refers to our instance it can only strengthen our suggestion.) For the precise relationship between ‏אל‏ and ‏על‏, see the bibliography in E. Kautzsch, *Gesenius' Hebrew Grammar* 2nd English ed., by A.H. Cowley), Oxford, 1910, p. 378, n. 3.

[13]Tur-Sinai's comment, in *LL*, p. 83, n. 2, in defense of his interpretation, is interesting: "Unfortunately, some scholars misunderstood my Hebrew notes, thinking I had explained ‏שמר‏ ‏אל‏ as 'to keep guard over' and offered their corrections."

[14]On the subject of beacons and signals through intermediary stations between Jerusalem and Lachish, Azekah and other towns, see recently A. Mazar, "The Excavations at Khirbet Abu et-Twein and the System of Iron Age Fortresses in Judah," *EI* 15 (1981) (Aharoni Memorial Volume), pp. 229-249, esp. pp. 246-249 (Hebrew).

[15]Cf. Tur-Sinai, *loc. cit.* (above, n. 7).

[16]Ibid.

[17]As noted, Tur-Sinai himself already discussed this matter in the initial publication; cf. *ibid.*, as well as: "Further, as the potsherds II, VI, VII and XVIII are adjoining pieces of one and the same pot as II, VI [sic!] and VIII, they must also be letters of Hosha'yahu, dealing in the main with the same theme" (*ibid.*, p. 72).

[18]The word ‏ארם‏ might, however, refer to ‏ארום‏ —"Edom"; cf. ‏שמה‏ ‏ארם‏ ‏תבא‏ ‏פן‏, "lest Edom (i.e. the Edomites) should come there," in Arad Ostracon No. 24, discovered on the slope of the hill outside the fortress there; cf. Aharoni, *op. cit.* (above, n. 8), p. 46.

[19]See above, n. 8.

[20]It should be noted that the formula ‏כלב‏ ‏עבדד‏ ‏מי‏, "Who is thy servant (but) a dog," or the like, is generally to be found in various documents (El-Amarna Archive, the Bible and others) comprising correspondence between a high official and his sovereign, a vassal and his overlord, a man and his god.

[21]We have already noted Starkey's opinion that during the siege, or thereabouts, the commander of Lachish set his headquarters up in the gate-bastion (which, of course, included several chambers). In *TL*, Tur-Sinai negates this possibility (which would appear to conflict with his opinion that the gate-room served Hosha'yahu as a place of judgment). His arguments do not suit the archaeological facts, which show that the gate structure was actually a self-contained fortress (Starkey's original opinion is now also accepted by the present excavator of Lachish, Professor D. Ussishkin—oral communication).

[22]Acceptance of the main conclusions put forth here necessitates re-examination of the contents of the ostraca; this obviously lies beyond the scope of the present article.

Geographical Changes in Israel Since 1948

By David Amiran

The border between the State of Israel and Jordan was fixed at the end of the War of Independence in 1948, according to the respective armies' final positions at the front. However, this border does not, on the whole, reflect the natural boundaries of the Land of Israel's geographical regions. The border with Lebanon determined at the outset of British Mandatory rule in Palestine, as well as the straight border with Egypt demarcated prior to the First World War, are similarly inconsistent with the Land's natural boundaries. The State of Israel is thus bounded on three sides by geographically unnatural borders.

It is fascinating for the geographer to note that these arbitrary borders have nevertheless become an established fact in the region in but a relatively few years. For example, the difference between the Israeli and the Arab approach to cultivation and soil development in Judea and Samaria during the period of Jordanian rule produced a very obvious visual contrast between the areas on either side of the Jordan River.

Naturally, great changes have occurred in the State of Israel during the first 35 years of its existence. I shall deal here, however, only with geographical changes in the agricultural and urban sectors, both of which have had a crucial influence on the geographical aspects of the country's development.

I. The Agricultural Sector

At the end of the period of the Mandate (1947), the country's socio-economic base was still principally rural and relied upon an as yet undeveloped system of agriculture. In the main, cities catered to the needs of the rural population. At the same time, however, there was an incipient alternative trend in the three major cities—Jerusalem, Jaffa/Tel Aviv and Haifa—that eventually developed an urban sector that was only partially concerned with rural affairs. The country's agricultural economy was still in the first phase of its transition to modernization. In the Mediterranean climate, with its hot summers, a transition to modern agriculture inevitably requires an economy based on irrigation. Irrigated crops, however, were rare. Indeed, at the end of the Mandate, only citriculture utilized modern irrigation; this was because citrus was the only product exported. Under Israel's climatic conditions, irrigation agriculture requires a nationwide integrated water supply system. The Mandatory authorities were not, however, sufficiently organized for this purpose—and perhaps didn't want to be!

As a result, fields were watered mostly by rain and only partially by irrigation. Moreover, it soon became apparent that the burgeoning population would require much larger tracts of cultivated land to provide enough food. At the time, it was universally agreed that a "mixed agriculture" was the optimal arrangement. It is important to understand the reason for this. One consideration was to build a self-sufficient national economy which would provide the maximum possible range of agricultural products. An additional reason for diversification was to reduce the risk inherent in Mediterranean agriculture with its distinct fluctuations in rainfall. It was reasonable to assume that one could not anticipate all possible dangers concurrently—such as a sudden deterioration in market price, variations in annual precipitation, variations in the number of rainy days in the growing season, in temperature and cloudiness, and the like. Consequently, if one crop were to fail, the great variety of produce, which by definition would be available in a mixed farm economy, would nevertheless be sufficient to maintain a viable agriculture.

The mixed farm economy was originally adopted because it was well suited to the small farming units typical of a moshav (a cooperative village) or a kibbutz (a communal village). The admittedly limited scale of production would entail a labor-intensive effort on the part of the members, but only minimal capital investment would be required.

With the establishment of the State of Israel, a radical change occurred in the planning of the country's agricultural economy. With the rapid growth of the urban sector, farmers tried to keep up with the affluent standard of living typical of the cities. This, however, required more income than a mixed farm could provide. Only by specialization could farmers aspire to an urban standard of living. Eventually, the most successful and ingenious farming enterprises became highly profitable and were sustained by a much reduced labor force. On the other hand, the intensified mechanization and consequent high capital outlay required was quite beyond the means of the conventional mixed farm.

In this regard, the kibbutz had a great advantage over the cooperative moshav. The kibbutz is a large, centrally administered entity, that could train its own experts to work in a particular specialized area and could assign experienced members to manage its various operations. Moreover, unlike the individual smallholder in a cooperative settlement, the kibbutz could with comparative ease raise funds for investment in its own expansion.

Any development of the country's agriculture necessarily presupposed irrigation, which in turn required a reliable supply of water. This meant, in effect, that the farmer would no longer rely simply on the rain to water his crops. Accordingly, Israel initiated construction of the National Water Carrier in 1953, and the project was completed in 1964. This integrated water supply system, whose source is Lake Kinneret, reaches almost all regions that are within the pre-1967 boundaries of Israel and utilizes most of the Land's available water resources. It reaches as far south as Mitzpeh Ramon in the Central Negev. In recent years it even extends into the Central Jordan Valley. I shall not enumerate here the many difficulties involved in the operation of a national water network. Suffice it to recall just one example—the rise in Lake Kinneret's salinity during a year of drought, or worse, a series of drought years such as occurred around 1960. The lake's water level naturally is low during such periods, and it is precisely at this time, of course, that maximum demand is made upon the Water Carrier. The lower the water level, the lower is the hydraulic pressure the water exerts at the bottom of the lake. A number of saline springs issue at the lake bottom. The lower, therefore, the hydraulic pressure, the more saline water will issue from these springs, having a consequent negative impact on the quality of water.

One of the questions that came up during the National Water Carrier's planning stages was the diameter of the conduit's pipes. The planners had two options: (1) to lay a pipeline whose diameter would permit the flow of only a moderate quantity of water, but that would operate all year round; (2) to lay a pipeline with a large diameter, which would entail great financial outlay. The smaller pipeline could not provide the large amount of water needed when maximum demand was made on the system. The larger pipeline could cope with maximum water consumption during dry summers, but would necessitate more limited use of the Carrier during winter months. Ultimately, the planners chose the second option, and a pipeline with a diameter of more than two meters was installed. This could supply the full amount of water needed even during periods of drought. Except when maintenance work is being performed on it, the National Water Carrier functions year-round at full capacity. One advantage of the Water Carrier is that supplementary water available during the winter is used to raise the water table of the coastal plain. Since 1967, the large Arab population of the Gaza Strip has been among the principal beneficiaries of this process. Before the Six Day War, this region suffered great shortages of water because overpumping lowered the level of the water table, and this caused sea water to enter the water table.

In 1974/1975, agriculture consumed about 75 percent of Israel's water resources; in 1955/1956, the figure had been 79 percent. Agricultural water consumption almost quadrupled between 1949/1950 (332 million cubic meters) and 1974/1975 (1,208 million cubic meters). This dangerously diminished the country's water reserves. However, Israel's hydrological engineers adopted several unconventional and innovative steps to expand the country's potential sources of water:

(1) Channeling storm water to the subsoil, where it was protected from evaporation losses. It could then be drawn up in wells in the vicinity. The Shiqma Storage Dam is the principal example of this method. Similar projects have been established in most major stream courses of the coastal plain.

(2) Reclaiming treated and purified wastewater and sewage water for irrigation. This method is expected to become increasingly common.

(3) Artificially increasing rainfall by seeding clouds with a silver iodide compound during a natural rainstorm. This method, which ensures continued rainfall from the targeted cloud, differs from the conventional procedure in other countries, which attempts to induce a downpour from clouds from which rain has not begun to fall. The new Israeli method has been shown to increase precipitation by some 15 percent.

(4) Conserving water. Ironically, this will probably prove to be the single most crucial means of exploiting Israel's water resources. The agricultural community cannot increase its quota of the water supply in order to expand agricultural productivity; it must utilize what water is available more efficiently. To achieve this, a graduated program has been initiated to replace the old, wasteful system of irrigation by sprinkler with the "trickle irrigation" method. This method utilizes 90 percent of the water, as compared to only 50 percent with the sprinkler method. However, the "trickle irrigation" system does entail a large capital outlay for the purchase and installation of the necessary equipment.

A relatively new, but very significant development in irrigation has been the introduction of a single, computer-controlled irrigation system to serve an entire settlement. Specific areas are thus watered with scientifically precise quantities of water; this electronic method also allows plots to be watered during the night, when minimal evaporation occurs. The network is fitted with instruments that measure wind velocity. When a strong wind blows in a certain area, causing excessive evaporation, the computer automatically shuts off the water supply to that particular plot. Although such a system is expensive, it pays for itself in the long run, both because it affords a much more efficient use of water and also because, since it can be operated by just one person, it cuts down dependence on costly human labor.

In recent years, an even more cost-effective method has been developed, namely, the greenhouse system, in which water is recirculated for greater efficiency. This method, however, also requires a very significant capital outlay. The greenhouse system is the very opposite of traditional dry farming, where in order to increase one's yield one must cultivate ever more extensive tracts of land. With the greenhouse method, the problem is not so much the size of one's land but obviously the initial capital investment, which, according to 1976 figures, comes to almost two million Israeli lira per unit. It has been estimated, though, that even a two- to three-dunam greenhouse will soon pay for itself solely by the water that is saved. Indeed, the amount of water required to operate an average conventional farmstead could supply the needs of seven or eight greenhouse farms.

The last 30 years have seen a radical change not only in growing methods but also in the variety of plants that are cultivated and in the manner in which these are selected. The original goal of the traditional dry or mixed farm was to produce a diversified agricultural yield that could meet all the needs of the general population. Today, however, the emphasis is on the cultivation of the least labor-intensive and most profitable agricultural products, such as cotton or pond fish. This has resulted in a surplus of out-of-season items such as vegetables, fruit and flowers and has also changed the geographical distribution of agricultural settlements in the country. Consequently, regions such as the Jordan Valley, the northern Negev and the Aravah nowadays boast many settlements, while in 1948 they would have been considered entirely unsuitable for agriculture.

More than 660,000 people immigrated to Israel during the first years of the State's existence, confronting Israel with a two-fold problem: the immigrants had to be quickly absorbed into Israeli society, and agricultural productivity had to increase to cope with the new demand. An ambitious attempt was made to solve both of these problems simultaneously, by absorbing many of the new immigrants into agricultural settlements. The project was obviously not only a gigantic financial and physical undertaking but also called for the training of the newcomers in agriculture. In order to train as many neophyte agriculturists as possible by as few experts as possible, and in order to ensure the immigrants' equal benefit from Israel's educational, health and administrative services, the Lachish Region Settlement Scheme was initiated. This project became the blueprint for similar regional projects nationwide. At the outset this model project required all instructors and experts to reside in a "rural center," from which they could serve their dependent villages and settlements, utilizing available time with maximum efficiency. The principal achievement so far of this novel arrangement is the outstanding success of the new farmers at many settlements in the Lachish Region; in fact, some of these are among the most thriving settlements anywhere in the country.

The high degree of efficiency of Israeli agriculture—founded upon a complete transition to irrigation, agricultural research, all sorts of impressive agrotechnic improvements, and especially mechanization—has inevitably diminished the country's agricultural population. Although the general population increased by 131 percent between 1954 and 1981, the number of people working in agriculture dropped during this same period from 90,000 to 76,800. In other words, while the agricultural population comprised 18 percent of the general population in 1954, in 1981 it was only 6.1 percent. In 1981, farmers constituted just 5.4 percent of the Jewish working population of the country, or 62,000 persons.

The agricultural community has been noteworthy also for the instruction and training programs it has conducted in numerous developing countries.

The organizational aspects of Israel's agricultural sector are also praiseworthy. A sophisticated administrative and planning complex keeps it running smoothly, beginning with the Ministry of Agriculture, the Settlement Department of the Jewish Agency, and the Center for Agriculture, all of which are organizationally under the umbrella of the country's various settlement movements and the Agrecsco Association. The latter coordinates all agricultural exports, which in 1976 constituted 13.5 percent of the country's total export income. Moreover, if we exclude the export of diamonds, which is a unique case, the figure would be 20 percent. We should remember that this impressive contribution represents the efforts of just 6.1 percent of Israel's entire work force.

In recent years, however, the agricultural industry of Israel, including agricultural exports, has been undergoing a serious crisis as illustrated by 1981 figures. In 1981, agriculture earned only 10.6 percent of Israel's total export earnings, 14.1 percent without polished diamonds. Many cooperative village units (moshavim) are in severe economic stress, and part of the citrus orchards stay unpicked or are even uprooted. This is the result of a highly controversial policy of the present government, of exaggerated liberalization, reduction or even removal of production and export quotas beyond the capacity of export markets, and tightening loans and subsidies to agriculture.

II. The Urban Sector

Here the situation is quite different from that in the agricultural sector. The outstanding achievements of the agricultural sector do not change the fact that Israeli society is primarily urban—even though many foreigners think of the Jewish State only in terms of its kibbutzim! Eighty-five percent of the total population and 90.4 percent of the Jewish population of Israel live in cities. However, urban organization in general is not even remotely as efficient as agriculture, essentially because it possesses no comparable central planning and administrative institution. The problem, I think, originates with the early Zionist ideologists, who intentionally sought to base the Return to Zion purely on agriculture, and whose aim it was to turn the new immigrants—most of whom had been city dwellers in their former countries—into farmers and rustics. This does not excuse the present state of affairs, though, and we certainly cannot resign ourselves to the inefficiency and lack of organization that are all too apparent in many Israeli cities.

As is the case in most developed countries, the urban sector in Israel is the dominant one, and any further national development is bound up with the fate of the cities. The urban planning of Israeli cities was modeled on universally accepted mid-20th-century criteria that conferred great advantages on the larger cities and metropolises. We should not be surprised to learn, therefore, that the metropolitan areas of Tel Aviv, Jerusalem, Haifa, Beersheba and Natanya—each of which has a population of more than 80,000—are home to 70.4 percent of the State's total urban population and to 60.5 percent of the country's population in general.

The smaller towns have nevertheless made a valuable contribution toward realizing the State's declared aim of maximal population dispersal, although their role has been quantitatively modest and is not always significant qualitatively or economically either. Dispersing a population is relatively simple; establishing a viable industrial base in outlying regions is a much more difficult task.

I shall discuss below two aspects of the urban sector—the large cities and the new "development towns."

A. The Large Cities

The perceived advantages of city life, as well as the natural inclination of the immigrants—most of whom, as we have noted, had come from an urban environment—resulted in the burgeoning of the larger cities. Sixty and one-half percent of the general population (67.6 percent of the Jewish population) is concentrated in these urban centers. It was inevitable, therefore, that the cities would begin to expand and take over cultivated lands. This was true especially in Tel Aviv and Natanya and, to a certain extent, around Haifa. Every large city has older quarters in its central sections that eventually must undergo some form of renovation or development. However, renovation of the Jerusalem, Tel Aviv and even Haifa city centers has only just begun. Many 50-year-old (or even earlier) one- to three-story houses have been neglected, and sometimes even abandoned. In addition, Israel's major cities continue to expand to the suburbs. In Tel Aviv, for example, the movement is toward Afekah and Ramat Hasharon, and in Haifa it is in the direction of Kiryat Tiveon and Ahuza on Mount Carmel. This process militates against the preservation of a decent quality of life in the older city centers and often results in the deterioration or decline of these once-fashionable sections of the city. Such urban expansion also lengthens commuting time and exacerbates the already dense flow of traffic. This, of course, is a universal phenomenon of our times. (For figures cf. p. 193 below.)

Let us hope that another 35 years will not pass before we are able to cope with these problems, and an energetic program of rehabilitation is initiated in these city centers. Let us hope as well that irreplaceable agricultural lands will cease to be swallowed up by these sprawling cities.

B. Development Towns

The need for a massive absorption of immigrants and the proclaimed principle of population dispersal brought about the establishment of more than 20 "development towns," which are home to over 350,000 people. These towns comprise 13 percent of the nation's Jewish urban population. After 25 to 35 years, we can point to a number of outstanding successes, but several towns have been beset by sociological and economic problems, as well as by difficulties that sometimes arise because of the town's geographical location. Some of these problems occasionally reach the newspapers. However, former kibbutz members—the kibbutz is the most venerable institution in Israeli society—have helped many of these towns by filling managerial positions and running various services.

In many respects, the "development towns" enjoy a preferred status in Israel's economy. Enterprises set up in these towns—especially in the most successful regional developments—are usually provided with subsidies and loans amounting to almost all of the required capital investment. Nevertheless, a number of these towns are constantly troubled by economic problems, most of which are attributable to two causes: (1) too many industrial plants that, although providing an adequate volume of work for the local labor force, cannot successfully market their products. As in many other developing countries, these plants are usually a branch of the textile industry, which in Israel is perennially liable to financial crises; (2) a dependence on just one or two types of industry. If these fall on bad times, the effect on the entire community is tragic.

We have already noted that the main consideration in the choice of a town's geographical location was the principle of population dispersal, but not the utilization of regional resources which could have ensured the prosperity of the town. In certain cases regional resources are a solid foundation for a town's development, for example, the resort industry of Eilat. In other cases, the early forecasts proved over-optimistic or conditions changed, such as the relocation of the road to Eilat through the Aravah, which left Mitzpeh Ramon "high and dry." Many a development town has no specific regional resource base to rely upon; its economy, therefore, depends on neutral or footloose industries.

III. Life Outside the Cities

While people employed in agriculture make up just 6.1 percent of the country's total labor force, 88 percent of Israel's settlements can be classified as rural. That is, most people who live in provincial settlements are not employed in agriculture. Most residents, in fact, travel to work in the cities each day. As the quality of life in the inner cities has declined, moving to rural areas has become increasingly popular. This trend is encouraged, moreover, by improvements in communications— telephone, radio and television—as well as by other factors, all of which have attenuated the differences between rural and city life. These new developments have also eliminated the feelings of loneliness and separation from society that in the past were the lot of rural dwellers. Roads have been improved and the number of privately owned vehicles has skyrocketed—these developments, too, have contributed to the flight from the cities. In 1951, there were just 9,600 privately owned vehicles and only 24,000 in 1960, but by the end of 1981, 453,634 private vehicles were registered. In other words, in 1951 there was one vehicle for every 164 persons; in 1960, one for every 90 people. In 1981, there was approximately one vehicle for every 9 Israelis.

The above developments, and the fact that this kind of rural orientation is nowadays common to all Western countries, perhaps justify my attempting to forecast what things will be like for the next generation. I expect, first of all, that the cities' rate of growth will slow down considerably and that the people's urge to reside in a rural environment will continue to gather momentum. This will be achieved either by the migration to rural settlements of an increasingly non-agricultural section of the population or by the transformation of previously agricultural settlements into non-agricultural communities to an ever-increasing degree. We shall probably also see the establishment of new settlements with non-agricultural inhabitants alongside the older agricultural settlements. I surmise, too, that agriculture will continue to play roughly the same role that it does in contemporary Israeli society.

Recent years have witnessed an additional development in settlement policy involving ideological motivation and economic expediency. The present Likud government, for ideological and political reasons, is initiating settlements in Judea and Samaria, the areas which had been annexed by Jordan between 1949 and 1967. All possible facilities are extended to new settlements there, including a well-developed road network and regional infrastructure, and no less important, most favorable incentives for individual settlers, such as low prices for housing and favorable mortgages at attractive rates of interest. The proclaimed aim of the government is to bring about an intertwined net of Arab and Jewish villages in this area which will make it impossible to separate the "West Bank" once more from the rest of Israel.

The great majority of the area allotted to the new settlements is "rocky ground" and not agricultural land, making building and infrastructure there rather expensive. Most of these places are within 25-50 minutes' commuting distance from the Tel Aviv metropolitan area or from Jerusalem (a similar development, though on a smaller scale, has occurred in Galilee, i.e., Israel proper, in part related to Haifa).

The economic attractions of these places and the lure of a "rural environment" bring to them many people from the core area of Israel, including young couples, who can afford very adequate housing here that in Tel Aviv or Jerusalem would be beyond their means. All this, apparently, is going to increase the number of non-agricultural settlements in rural mountain areas, in part "dormitory settlements," in part performing semi-urban functions. Quite apart from this, the political consequences of this development will be far-reaching, focusing on the main and irreconcilable controversy in Israeli politics today: Israel including the entire "Land of Israel," the whole of mandatory Palestine, with a large Arab minority which for reasons of population dynamics will increase with time, *versus* a Jewish State in Israel on territory less than the whole "Promised Land," but the vast majority of its population being Jews, which is the homeland of the Jewish people, and of Jewish culture, without the permanent threat of conflict between two antagonistic peoples.

If these predictions are accurate, then planners must be ready to cope with a more mobile and increasing rural population. A speedy development of the regional infrastructure in the rural areas will be required, as well as an extension of the present road network. Furthermore, if we are to avoid turning the Land's streams into stagnant mires, a proper national sewage system has to be installed.

Israeli society is one of the most urbanized in the world, but its congested cities regrettably do not boast a large number of parks or open spaces. The need is great, therefore, for nature parks and recreation areas. Forests, woodlands, beaches and other areas suitable for recreation are indispensable to an urban population. Indeed, even parts of the desert with their fascinating environment could be utilized for leisure and recreation, as some are already being used.

Urban expansion and its concomitant pollution present a challenge to preservation of the natural landscape. And this is just one of the problems facing the planner who must decide on a sensible usage of lands in rural regions. The planner should not mix the various uses to which the land is to be put and must clearly distinguish, for instance, between agricultural and residential areas, and between industrial and recreation areas. Also significant is the cultural heritage, such as Israel's numerous archaeological and historical sites, as well as nature preserves. Proper environmental management demands a clean spatial division of these different types of land use. The environmental nuisances and attrition that beset the residential quarters located near the Reading power station in Tel Aviv, or the residential quarters near the chemical and petrochemical works in Haifa Bay and in Beersheba, may be cited as consequences of bad planning. Naturally, a superior plan is in itself not sufficient if the appropriate authorities do not see to its strict implementation.

The caliber of planning and implementation achieved by the government will, to a great extent, determine whether the State of Israel will experience the same nuisances and travails, and commit the same oversights that now characterize many highly industrialized countries: namely, crowded housing conditions, defective spatial organization, pollution of the environment and the landscape and too few recreation areas for the use of a highly urbanized population. The sort of reasonable planning described above and the enforcement of strict environmental standards will certainly contribute to an improvement in the quality of life for Israel's future citizens. This surely is an ideal to which the Jewish nation in its homeland must aspire.